Patchwork Kid:
A Boy's Transplant Journey of Hope through the Midst of Tragedy

ROGER R. ZIEGLER

Dedicated to the families that fight tirelessly in their efforts to save their children from the clutches of sickness — all forms. Mothers and fathers who carry the burden with their children; sisters and brothers who do the same with their siblings. And to other family members and friends who come alongside with helping hands.

Finally, to the children who face the harshness of chronic illness and step up to the plate every day, fighting in the trenches, holding on tightly to hope, and being the bravest you can be. This book is dedicated to you because you help the rest of us experience the fantastic purpose of loving you through the toughest parts of your life. You make us proud.

CONTENTS

INTRODUCTION

A distance runner trains for the entire length of a race. Not for a portion or only half, but for the miles that separate the start from the finish. Forget about the sprint and never mind the 100-meter. Sorry Mr. Usain Bolt, we're talking about miles upon miles – a long distance race. Where grueling battles ensue between exhausted muscle tissue and a mind focused on the goal: to cross the finish line. This is where distance runners persevere. In a race for time they win, minute by minute.

These runners understand the road ahead and the task at hand. They suppress weakness under duress in order to reach their goal. Perspiration is their award for their discipline. Exhaustion is their prize for maintaining their efforts. Pain is a trophy they wear upon their tired frames. And yet they continue, one foot in front of another. Each step seems so hopeless to take, but the ground gained is precious even though it consists of only a small group of inches. Setbacks occur and still, they press on. They press on toward an achievement not many have experienced. They finish the race.

Noah can identify with these athlete's strict course of perseverance. No, he is not a long distance runner. Nor an athlete that trains day and night to obtain greatness. He's not even a popular figure that some would cheer for. No, he is merely a boy – our son and considered by those who know him to be a regular everyday person. But, he is fully engaged in a race that he must run. Not a race for time, distance, or money. Actually, it's a race for his life. Sometimes day by day. Many times minute by minute.

You see, Noah is a kid who faced amazing odds that opposed his survival. He chose to remain disciplined in his strict regimen of care with specific medicines that help to sustain his life. He chose to follow narrow guidelines set before him by some of the most gifted and brilliant surgeons on this planet – all for his survival. Noah is a three-organ transplant recipient. He has suffered through many afflictions and has held on through life and death situations. Through the darkest times in his life, he held onto hope and pushed forward with an intense will to survive.

This is his story. Now the world can partake in these amazing and miraculous moments, the tearful and joyous occasions, and in the display of love distributed graciously to the brokenhearted. Recipients of such love have acquired a fresh perspective and a newness of breath exhaled delicately and with assurance. I invite you into this wonderful assortment of memories gathered to illustrate how precious life really is.

I see him through the eyes of a father as my dear son. I also regard him as my hero and an incredible inspiration. Noah is a courageous boy with a powerful identity. With the delicate fabric of two lives stitched together into one, he became...our Patchwork Kid.

1
ONCE UPON HIS TIME

4020:35:15

BELIEVE. IT'S SUCH A STRONG WORD and, when applied to a set of circumstances that are overwhelming, becomes a strength, a passionate vision, and the path to true hope. Strength for when we are weak, passionate vision for when we have eyes, but perhaps no sight, and the way that leads us to true hope – there's really only one kind.

I know things happen for a reason. In life, events occur that shapes the path we travel – sometimes without notice or forewarning. On August 19, 1993, one of those radical events took place in our lives. Was it without advanced notice? Yes. Did it occur without any warning? You bet. And looking back I can understand how these important details of tragedy would forever shape our lives and our destiny. Yes, they definitely happened for a reason.

My beautiful wife, Paula, was pregnant (and glowing) with our second child. Our first child, Shelby (princess in the making), was our center of attention and she was born a year and a half earlier. Paula and I were very excited. No, we were thrilled at the idea of having another baby. It seemed like she was good at the birthing process and I was good at being a labor and delivery semi-coach/part-cheerleader, and a little crazy dad-to-be. Needless to say, we looked forward to the day our second baby was to be born and become the next addition to the Ziegler family.

Paula's pregnancy went very well, mostly. There were no complications other than the standard upset stomach, tremendous mood swings, vitamin imbalances, and such. In fact, with her two sonograms performed over the course of several months during this time, no problems were detected in the "womb factory." I often played tag with the unborn baby (me on the outside of mommy's stomach and the little one from the inside). The movement from within her belly was acting as if there were armies of hands and feet inside rearranging the furniture. I sensed that our baby was healthy and there were no indications of inhibited development to be concerned with. We also made sure we did the right things to support the health of Paula and our baby.

Now, we were very curious to know if the baby would be a boy or a girl. Did we have the means to check with our physician? Yeah. Did we learn of this during her pregnancy? No way. Listen, the sheer excitement of learning this incredible fact at the time of birth is reason alone to bear the anticipation for about nine months. The sonogram technician was politely informed not to disclose the baby's sex during those two occasions when the tests were performed. And yes, we waited.

**

"Baby day" had arrived. I drove Paula to the hospital in Santa Ana – our designated labor and delivery facility. Her contractions had become intense and I was behind the wheel navigating the mild traffic with every "hee-hee-blow" cheer I could proclaim. It was irritating to my sweet wife, but coaching is coaching, right? I parked our car in the emergency parking lot and helped her to a wheelchair waiting at the entrance to the hospital. *Here we go again,* I thought calmly.

So, after many hours of hard labor, it was time. She had entered the hour of the most intense pain and suffering. Paula was in position and the medical team was ready for our little baby to enter its new world. The scene was set. The tension was thick. She began to bear down and push through each wave of labor pain. She was very tired and her face showed signs of exhaustion. Finally, at that most wonderful moment, the baby's head crowned and I switched positions. Now, from looking into Paula's eyes to a quick shift down to her waist area, I was eagerly anticipating the first glance.

Then, in a matter of a few seconds, our baby boy was delivered completely. I stood there…shocked…amazed. I must have had the most puzzled and worried look on my face as Paula asked with concern,

"Honey, what's wrong?"

Our newborn son was immediately wrapped and rushed across the room by nurses at a smooth but frantic pace. You see, he was born with gastroschisis, a condition where the small and large intestines are formed outside of the body and the stomach is enclosed, leaving them exposed. I saw strange glossy, purple-colored intestines that appeared to be a layering of tubes gathered on his body. Needless to say, I was not expecting that at all. Were my eyes deceiving me?

I turned to Paula and assured her that our son was alright. She was in disbelief as the doctor approached us and explained the baby's condition. It was like a sock to the stomach with an oversized sledgehammer. I couldn't understand how this was undetected throughout her pregnancy. There was just no way this could have been missed. No excuse. No reason. I held my wife tenderly as she wept bitterly.

We always hear the familiar comments made by expecting parents. The words are basically the same and are genuine: *As long as the baby is healthy*, said with a warm smile. That's wonderful…in a perfect world or in the game of Candyland. But, when the harsh reality explodes onto your life's canvas and is displayed in shocking colors and tones that don't fit inside of your cute little box – then what? What if the baby is not healthy? Does this mean they will love him or her any less? Of course not, but I suggest we tweak our mindset a shade and not allow the room for any disappointment to invade.

"Is he going to be okay, doctor?" my sweet wife asked.

"He will be fine," the doctor assured us. She explained that he needed to be prepared for transport to Children's Hospital, located just a few miles away, for immediate surgery.

My mind raced through so many things at once. It was a nightmare. Our little Noah, the name we chose for a boy, had to endure so much in the next several hours of his new life. It was not fair. I looked at the group of medical specialists working on Noah. He was crying like infants normally do. His wailing touched my heart even more so than usual, knowing his medical situation.

They quickly and carefully placed special coverings over his exposed intestines. What now? What would happen next? I mean, this kind of thing doesn't happen every day.

"It's time to transport him," the doctor said. Paula looked at me with an amazing expression of love in her eyes. It was love for her little Noah; love for me. These were the greatest gifts she could bless me with – our precious baby boy and our sweet little girl, Shelby. I kissed her and held her for a moment. Just enough time to caress her and take in this incredible moment together. But, I had to leave very soon and meet Noah at Children's Hospital. Time was critical.

I left the hospital with disappointment and grief in my heart. The drive was short to where they had taken Noah. I rushed into the softly lit NICU (Neonatal Intensive Care Unit) room and found the surgical team being briefed by the transport team. I watched helplessly as the nurses prepped Noah for surgery. He was placed inside of a bed that was also a crib. It was made with a stainless steel frame and was open on both sides for easy access. No, it didn't have the colorful patterns of a new baby's room or the plush bed guards typically seen. It was purely functional.

He was positioned on his back and safely asleep (with medication). His tiny arms were outstretched and opened wide like he was waiting for a hug. I wanted to hold him and tell him that I was right there waiting for him. I wanted to be sure he understood, that no matter what would happen to him he would be fine. He was in God's hands and mistakes never happen as long as God is on His throne.

The surgeon who would perform the surgery met with me and explained the procedure. The goal was to place his large and small intestines back into the abdominal cavity and close his opening without any problems. He asked me to wait in the patient waiting room until the surgery was completed. I thanked him and left the NICU area.

The team wheeled little Noah away to the operating room. I felt empty. I felt helpless and crushed. My stomach turned. Paula and I didn't have a chance to prepare for this. Now c'mon, it was never detected during her full-term pregnancy? It was like a slap in the face by reality. Now what?

I found a pay phone and called my mother to explain the day's events as well as the details of the procedure. After the phone call, I waited in a cold, poorly lit waiting room – alone. I couldn't process what had occurred during those last few hours because it happened so suddenly. As I sat there for hours, the playback began. Image after image. Conversation after conversation. But why?

I wondered how Paula was feeling as she recovered and rested. I'm certain that her heart bled for little Noah and she longed to be closer to him. It was a very long evening for me, but probably an eternity for her.

Finally, hours later a doctor walked into the room. Finally, some sort of news.

"Mr. Ziegler? Your son is alright," his words were calming as it soothed my troubled heart. "We were able to safely place his intestines into his cavity all at once. His large chest and abdomen area certainly helped." I thanked the doctor with relief in my voice.

"You can come and see him very soon," he added. He kindly smiled, paused, and then walked away.

I was relieved and concerned at the same time. How long will Noah take to heal? How long will he spend in the hospital? These were not situations one trains for or one can be ready to deal with easily. But I had peace in my heart for Noah, my baby boy. A peace only God could provide.

As I was taken back to see him in the NICU by a nurse, I noticed the stainless-steel crib walls that surrounded his small body. It looked like a tiny jail cell. He laid in the center of the mattress with enough room for five other babies his size, easily. I was amazed at the IV in his arm, the nasal cannula taped to his face, and a large amount of dressing that covered his stomach. He was on his back sound asleep from the anesthetics with his arms above his little head. It was a position of surrender. He lived just a few hours in this cruel world and he was already on his back – geez. I stood in awe of this tremendous procedure and the amazing success the doctors achieved. I also felt sorry for little Noah. What a way to start living this life.

Paula and I only had Shelby at the time. She was twenty months old and was blessed with no health problems. I already pictured her holding her little brother gently as if he were a dolly.

I asked God to heal him and raise him up to be strong. Little did I know that God would bring Noah through incredible circumstances years down the road. This was his initiation so to speak; his introduction into a world that many do not experience. It was also our training ground for what storms lay ahead.

**

The weather was beautiful in this hot September month. Blue skies and warm rays embraced Southern California at the end of summer. All schools were in full force. Vacations were over. It was a perfect time for a walk down the beach. Instead, Paula and I were at Children's Hospital of Orange County with Noah. It was a month after his eventful birthday and he was ready to be discharged from the hospital.

A month in the hospital was plenty for us to endure. Our visits with him in the NICU were so different than our previous hospital visits over the years to see other loved ones. The setting was new to us and so were the procedures. I mean, we had to walk into a prep room just before entering Noah's area. We would spend several minutes scrubbing our hands thoroughly with special small brushes to reach deep into every small crevice in our hands. Once our hands and arms were sterile clean, we helped each other put on gowns – the kind that ties in the rear. It felt like dress up as we placed mouth covers on our faces. This was all so important to see our little Noah and keep him away from our germs. He was our special "tiny package" with superstar treatment and he was so deserving.

We were anxious to have him home with us. After his surgery, Noah spent the next thirty days or so recovering in the hospital. Since his intestines and digestive system were traumatized, he was not able to have any milk initially. Shortly after surgery, he was able to have very small increments from mini-sized bottles designed to hold only four ounces only (Paula pumped breast milk and froze it for hospital use). We knew that breast milk had all of the nutrients necessary and immunities important for Noah's health. We started with one ounce a day and over time gradually increased the feeds to four ounces a day. Otherwise, he was being fed through an IV to give him what his body required for growth. Needless to say, he didn't gain any weight. In fact, it looked like he was going backward in this area. He was so thin and small compared to his birth weight that he looked like a little old man. But that didn't matter, because he was precious in our sight. In time he would gain back those precious pounds he had lost.

At home, he did quite well. He healed nicely and had no issues at all. He pooped like he was supposed to and ate like he was supposed to. As Noah grew, he drank more milk and tolerated it just fine. We had to feed him a soy-based formula as he was allergic to other types. To him, it was just delicious milk. Mmmm.

Noah's belly was very unique and required a second glance to comprehend the obvious difference – he had no belly button. Okay, this is definitely kind of weird. The scar from surgery was several inches long and ran straight across his belly; from his lower abdomen up to just below his rib cage. And the best part was how the surgeon had created a faux belly button for him. Now, this creation was not your usual "innie" or "outie" variety, but a small area of scar tissue fashioned in a circular pattern right where his umbilical cord once was. A make-believe belly button. Clever.

Of course, Paula and I spent hours discussing the complexities of teenage youth, related to boy and girl relationships. You know, attraction and all that stuff. Paula's face showed some concern as she pictured her striking young Noah right smack in the middle of his sixteenth year walking along the Huntington Beach shore showing off his pecs – and his imitation belly button. In her mind, it probably went sort of like this...

All of the young ladies stood nearby the lifeguard tower lowering their sunglasses slightly as if to check out Noah's blistering guns. His smile made them melt and his charm danced around in their heads. They were impressed and giggling uncontrollably, until...

"Is that his belly button?" one brunette shouted. The girls became puzzled and immediately began to study this young man's deformity. The curiosity turned to shock. Shock turned to fright. Fright to panic as they ran off like a herd of gazelle avoiding a predator.

"I can't stand little, immature girls," Paula exclaimed. "So catty and ridiculous." It took a few moments to understand what she was thinking because, in my mind, I viewed a similar scene.

"You're so cute when you get angry, Paula," I said. I couldn't resist. "You've got the biggest mother's heart on this planet and I love you for that."

We realized how important Noah's journey would be physically and emotionally. At this point, we believed the doctors when they said Noah would grow up to be as normal as the next kid. The gastroschisis would become a distant memory, as the years fade away. There really was no reason for us to think he would have any issues in growth or development. The thought of a scar on his belly was a small price to pay for the ability to enjoy life – even at the beach. No, he would do just fine.

Noah was behind schedule according to the growth charts. You know, the kind of details you hear about from the pediatrician. By his first birthday, he still had that "little old man" appearance (thin and lean) and he was under his weight class. By comparison, Shelby was an amazon by her first birthday. There was definitely a noticeable difference between the two.

He was so cute. His hair was slightly reddish in color (my mother, Grandma Velma, called him "Red") and his skin was fair just like Paula's. Yeah, he was a cute little guy, no doubt. Sort of calm and quiet, but he loved to smile. Like Shelby, he was a late walker. Fourteen months and Noah was cruisin' around the apartment. From the sofa to the coffee table. From the coffee table to the television. He was coordinated and had good balance.

I noticed that his hands were pretty big for his size. I guess my hands are large, with long fingers. Yup, he has my hands. We would laugh and say what big paws Noah had. I was proud that he had at least one attribute from his pops. Paula would often declare how many similarities there were in Noah – that came from her. Yeah, he did look like her as far as facial features are concerned and skin color too. She did have reddish hair (normally a dark brown color but she wore a nice strawberry blonde tint that made her eyes sparkle). Alright, she won. My hands versus her hair, features, and skin. Rats.

As Noah began to enter his toddler years we made sure his doctor check-ups were regular. We did notice that one of his testicles was higher than the other. We showed our pediatrician and he told us to have him checked by a urologist to be safe. So we did and there was no cause for alarm. We kept our eye on him and sure enough, the "little guy" eventually dropped into position just like his "big brother."

Another medical issue arose with Noah, he developed asthma. I guess he has me to thank in this department. Well, let's see, my hands and now my asthma. I'm gaining on Paula. I was practically born with serious asthma and fought through all of the symptoms for about fourteen years. I remembered all of those horrible memories and hoped that Noah would not have to endure the life of an asthmatic. Little did I know it would just be a speck on his health, compared to a future medical condition that would rock his world – and ours as well.

2
SWEET AND SIMPLE

"GET THE CAMERA," I SAID to Paula. We did a pretty good job of capturing all of those great childhood memories our children were experiencing. Today was no different. It was April 5, 2000, and our fourth child, Luke, became a big boy by hitting his first-year mark. We were all gathered around the birthday cake: Shelby, Noah, Brooke (Noah's other younger sister), Paula, and Luke. The grandparents hovered nearby smiling down at their little grandson. The candle was lit and we gathered in for a picture.

"Ok, say cheese everyone," I said as I snapped a precious shot with our camera. It was amazing to see how our little Luke grew up so fast. Not to mention that Brooke was already approaching five later that month and Shelby was practically a grown up at eight-and-a-half.

And then there was Noah. Our walking miracle boy at almost seven years old. He made your day with his enormous grin and silly charm. He wore his eyeglasses proudly to help his football-shaped corneas see properly. Again, he has me to thank for this one too (I think that makes three). He was as healthy as can be; as youthful and vibrant as any other child his age. He thoroughly enjoyed playing with his siblings. In fact, you could already see his bond with Brooke develop as they were the middle children.

I stood there for a moment and gazed at them all. I was proud too. Even more so than the grandparents. Paula and I raised these wonderful kids with so much love and care. I imagined how they would interact as teenagers. I realized that time would somehow race up to that point very soon and I would look back at these days and embrace these great memories. True, I would see them grow up so very quickly. As if time would be folding huge chunks upon another and surge ahead. But, I cherished every day we spent as a family. I guess it was all we had – our family. We had each other.

I was trying for years to become a police officer. It was no easy task. At least not in Southern California where it seems like thousands of others were trying to compete for the same job opportunities. I wanted to experience the thrill, the honor, the pride, and most of all the reward of helping and protecting people. Yeah, it was in my blood. I could nearly taste it as I drove down busy streets and would pass by a car stop or a police cruiser running code-three at blistering speeds. Yeah. I would have to wake myself up from daydreaming and keep pushing forward.

My ultimate goal was to provide for my family and I wanted something more than just living paycheck to paycheck. I wanted to enjoy a home we could call our own instead of just renting. To afford the things in life like baseball for the boys, without having to delay a bill or two, would be great. Maybe even have the girls enjoy a dance class or maybe a painting class. I don't know, maybe an instrument or something. How about a nice dress for Paula and some earrings to complement the outfit without having to wait for a tax return? Sometimes those things are nice to have.

I was working at an office full-time and a night job a few nights as well every week. We did our best to stick with our agreement early in our marriage: Paula would remain a stay-at-home mom and be a blessing to our children as they grew. Let me tell you, it was a significant joy to experience, or shall I say, for our children to experience this every day. It was worth every sacrifice and every bit of inconvenience. I think the icing on the cake would be to have that financially rewarding career that would eliminate the need for me to miss so much extra time from home. It would help us get to a place where we could stabilize our finances and have some of those extras in life. A career to grow in and promote through the ranks. Yeah, and even retire from after twenty or thirty years. Hmm. That sure sounded nice.

But, we had each other and nothing could separate us. That was something of huge value; it was priceless. The financial struggles or the stress of circumstances we faced early in our marriage could not separate our bond. I loved Paula so dearly and would lay down my life for her. My children were my wonderful blessings and I loved them with my whole heart. I guess you could say that I had it all in life. Yup, I really did. Thank you, Jesus.

Noah started his first year in baseball at eight years old. I was thrilled! I'm sure you've seen those emphatic and overjoyed parents on the sidelines cheering for their kids. Well, that was me. I was jumping for joy. Oh, of course, he was going to become the next Ron Cey or Steve Yeager (yeah we were Dodger fans). Noah was primed for a great career in the major leagues. Why not? He had a swell arm and hand-eye coordination that would make you sick with envy...if you were a kid.

"Keep your eye on the ball son," I always shouted across the field. "Stay ready and hustle!"

He looked back at me and nodded his head from the outfield. He wanted to make me proud of his performance. But, I was already proud of him since the day he was born.

He played with the Reds. His bold red jersey looked like the one I wore in high school; cardinal red and white. He was in a tee ball league and I thought he was ready to make the little league. I worked with him often at the local park where I pitched many baseballs for him to hone his batting skills. A tee? Are you kidding me? Let my kid show you how the Babe did it and whack it out of the park, buddy.

Well, instead I cheered for Noah as he stood in the batter's box while he swung hard at the ball only to have it barely make it to second base. In my head, that ball was screaming across the springtime air. It punched a hole in the sky as it ripped through the atmosphere; it was a rocket bursting through the sound barrier – boom!

"Did you see that rocket, honey?" I asked Paula with such conviction.

"Rog, it rolled across the grass just past the pitcher. What game are you watching?"

Her reply was quick and sure. She had no baseball sense. I forgave her inadequacies in this area. Still, she was very pretty though.

"Go get 'em, Noah!" I exclaimed. He was disappointed when he didn't hit it over the outfield wall. Hey, no kid ever did that. After all, it was Tee-ball and not the minor leagues. It didn't matter. He loved being part of his team and they were his new friends. After the games, the parents took turns and provided snacks for the Reds. Noah sucked down his Capri-Sun punch along with his pals.

"Good game son. Did you have fun?" I said with a big grin on my face.

"Yeah, dad. It was great. Maybe next time I'll hit it farther." He said.

I didn't understand what he was saying. I saw a rocket blast explode from his bat and it shot straight into the deep blue sky. He sprinted across the edges of the infield from base to base and drove through the home plate with his hands raised up high. I knew it was him. Or maybe he was at a different game too.

He was a social kid. He enjoyed playing with other kids his age. He definitely got along with his siblings. Often times they would be playing something together; huddled around an area of toys designed to be something like a busy kitchen at a fast-food restaurant. Noah didn't really mind that he had two sisters for playmates in the house because Luke was just a little guy. They pretty much were interested in the same things: Disney videos like The Little Mermaid, toy water guns, and ice cream.

Paula and I really loved to see the children in how they would interact together. I was an only child until I was a freshman in high school, so observing the dynamics of our large, young family was wonderful. Paula was one of four children herself, so she poured into our children with her experiences. Yes, those years were so amazing in many ways.

You could say that Noah had what all little boys his age wanted in life:

playing baseball with his buddies, an exciting life filled with learning and playing with close friends, a fantastic mother who stayed home to be with him and his siblings when they returned from school, and finally candy and ice cream all year round. You've got to love it! The simple things in life were all around him and he appreciated them.

I could see those great blessings too and I appreciated them. You know, the way you feel inside your chest when you're at the dinner table with your wife and kids; an overwhelming sense of warmth, love, and peace that is real. Or the early morning calmness in the home just before the sun rises and all are asleep, except for you and your hot cup of coffee. How about those moments when you hold your wife's hand and there's no other place in the world you would rather be? Yeah, those sweet blessings.

The simple things were not necessarily triumphant achievements in life, but merely those blessings every human being can take for granted so easily. If we are so consumed with living the rat race in the fast lane of life, how can we experience those moments at all? They can be ignored or overlooked without even thinking about it.

3
19 ½ HOURS

"Sometimes life doesn't send you a warning shot."
-Inky Johnson

663:17:25

October 28, 2002

THE DAY WAS PRETTY STANDARD AND TYPICAL as they come. The most pressing news was that Noah had woke up with flu-like symptoms and felt crummy throughout the day. Paula called me and happened to reach me during my down time while on patrol. I was a policeman for the City of Cypress and it was the last day of my work week. My day at the office began at 5:30 AM and my shift ended at 6:00 PM – a majority of it spent inside of a patrol car.

Paula's phone calls throughout the day kept me updated on Noah's condition.

"He has a fever, but it's only low grade," Paula reported.

We had four children and experienced common colds, influenza bugs, parasites, stomach pains, and many other illness symptoms. This was nothing new.

As my shift grew to a close, I looked forward to watching game seven of the World Series. Our home team, the Anaheim Angels, were playing the San Francisco Giants. It was sure to be a fantastic ending to an exciting series. October 28, 2002, would mark a day in baseball history for one of those teams who would become world champions. It would not only mark an important day for a baseball franchise, but it would also mark the beginning of a tough journey for a 9-year-old boy named Noah Paul Ziegler.

I arrived at our townhome around 7:00 PM.

"I'm home Paula. How's Noah feeling?" I asked as I walked through the garage door and into the hallway.

"He's looking pretty sick," she replied from the kitchen area, "I think we should take him to urgent care."

I walked around the hallway corner and into our small living room. I found Noah laying face up on the sofa. He looked bad. No, really bad. His face was pale and his eyes were closed, but he was not sleeping. His breathing was irregular like he was running a sprint but in very short and shallow breaths. I had not seen any of our kids look like this before. For as bright and cheery as Noah was, it was hard to see him in this way.

"Noah," I asked quietly, "How do you feel?"

"I feel sick," he replied in a soft voice. He opened his eyes and turned to me. His eyes were strange looking for a small boy. His pupils were dilated and very dark overall. *Oh no*, I thought, *this boy is in bad shape*.

"Paula, I need to get some pants on him right now and take him into the ER," I called out as I looked at him closely.

"No. I'll just call 911," she said firmly.

"I'll drive him there faster," I argued.

She sped upstairs to his room and returned with some pants.

"Noah, I'm going to put your pants on and take you in, okay?" I said as my hands slipped each pant leg over his feet.

He didn't answer. His breathing was still very rapid and shallow. I slipped his jeans up to his waist and asked him to stand up if he could. He didn't move much at all; he moaned a little as he tried to sit up on the sofa. We took our time and paused continuously. After a couple of minutes, he stood for a few seconds then he collapsed onto the sofa like a bag of potatoes.

"Noah! Hey, talk to me!" I raised my voice in my concern as he passed out briefly. I tried to reach my arms under his back and Paula hovered over him as well.

"Honey, what's wrong?" She said with deep concern in her words.

He looked up at us with just a blank stare and we helped him get back to his feet. As he stood, he began to vomit. We were just a few feet away from the restroom, so we both helped him get to the toilet as he just let everything out onto the floor and into the bowl. Except, this was not just any vomit. It was dark red with tiny specs of what appeared to be coffee grounds.

"Roger, that looks like blood," Paula said in a shocked tone. We were trying to keep him up over the toilet and trying to wipe his face at the same time. I picked up Noah and held him close as I rushed to the garage.

"I'm taking him to the ER now," I said. I moved quickly but kept calm. Paula rushed ahead of me, opened the garage door and opened the passenger side door to our mini-van.

"Lower the seat back so he can lay flat," I asked Paula. She positioned the seat as far back as she could and laid the upright portion back down so

Noah could be comfortable. I gently placed him in the passenger seat and helped secure him with the seat belt.

It never occurred to me that I probably should have called an ambulance or paramedic. Although, Paula sure did. Maybe it was a sense of denial that my boy was extremely ill and in grave danger. Sure, anyone could Monday morning quarterback the situation in retrospect. After all, I was a police officer who dealt with crazy and intense situations, especially in busy Southern California – I simply reacted.

"Hold on Noah," I said as I turned to him, "You're going to be alright."

He didn't say anything. He just laid there with a blank stare in his eyes, then he would close them for a while. I didn't know what I was dealing with.

I pulled out of the garage and rolled out onto the street. *Here we go,* I thought. My mind raced for my quickest route to the ER (emergency room). I hopped onto the freeway just a short distance from our home. Before no time, we were heading south on the 405 Freeway towards Huntington Beach. I remembered driving Brooke, my baby girl who was seven at that time, to a nearby hospital for stitches. I kept an eye on Noah every couple of minutes or so. I asked him how he was doing several times along the way. He mostly moaned under his breath.

"We're almost there Noah," I said as we exited the freeway at Beach Blvd and drove southbound. We pulled into the driveway of Huntington Beach Medical Center's ER. I stopped abruptly into the closest parking space I found near the entrance. After turning off the van, I jumped out and raced to his side. As I carefully peeled him off of the seat and gently picked him up, his eyes looked gaunt and lifeless, but he was conscious. I kept talking to him.

I carried him through the entrance and approached the front desk area. It was a small counter with a receptionist sitting behind a desk and a computer. I held Noah and looked at her with piercing eyes.

"My son is very sick and needs medical attention now! He has shallow breathing and dilated pupils," I said quickly.

"You'll have to wait until we have a bed available sir," the receptionist said in a rather cold tone.

"Wait for a bed? Are you kidding me?" I replied. I was disgusted with her answer. She walked away from the counter to find someone.

I sat in a chair in a rather empty waiting room with Noah leaning on me. I felt so bad for him. He needed to be seen immediately. My mind raced for a new plan. I pulled out my cell phone and dialed the dispatcher service we use at our police station. They were a tri-city police department service and the neighboring city to ours had a hospital. I had answered a call for service once where the victim was transported there, so I was familiar with the facility. I dialed the number and one of our dispatcher's answered.

"Police department. How can I help you?" she said.

"Hi, this is Ziegler (we always used our last names when we called) and I'm off duty," I told her.

"Hi, Ziegler. What can I do for you?" she said.

"Can you please connect me with Los Alamitos Hospital, specifically the ER department? I need to get my son seen immediately."

She replied, "No problem. Give me a second to connect you. Good luck."

I was connected to the ER across town. It was a backup plan and I could run him down there in about twenty minutes flat.

"Emergency room. How can I help you?" A calm voice answered. I explained to her what my situation was and asked if there were any available beds. They had some available and she asked me to call them back if I chose to do so.

"Thank you," I replied.

Noah remained in critical condition – not worse. Thank God! His skin was pale and I needed to get him well, somehow. I walked back to the front desk, but the attendant was not there. I called out for help and another healthcare worker suddenly appeared. I gave him a quick report of my sick son.

"You have to get him back there now," I was very persistent. He walked through the main doors from the patient care area and into the waiting room. When he approached us and saw Noah's condition he knew that he had to be seen right away. He rushed back through the doors and returned with a gurney. We lifted Noah gently onto the bed and we wheeled him back.

A doctor and a nurse came over to us; I began to explain Noah's symptoms and condition. The team checked his vitals and prepared to give him an IV access line. As they continued to work on getting him stable and diagnosed, I prayed in my head for God's peace to come upon Noah. He must have felt so scared.

I waited until the doctor finished a quick assessment and then he said that Noah could possibly have pancreatitis.

"What? Are you sure?" I said to him. "He had no previous symptoms before this weekend and he has been very healthy overall. Can't it be something else?"

The doctor said he would run some tests, starting with an x-ray of his abdomen area. Noah's fever was still low grade and he seemed somewhat stable. They wheeled Noah away to the x-ray room and I stepped outside to call Paula. She was completely in the dark since we left.

I walked outside and called our home.

"Hi, honey. We're at the Huntington Beach ER, just off of Beach Blvd. They sent Noah back for an x-ray. They think he may have pancreatitis," I said with concern.

"What? That sounds bad Rog. Yvette is almost here now and I will get there as soon as I can," Paula replied.

We ended the call and I looked around the parking lot almost in a daze. The sky was deep blue with shades of lavender and orange towards the horizon. A mild breeze passed over me. It was about eight o'clock or so in the early evening. My brain continued to replay the events that led up to this moment. I tried to mentally digest how sick Noah was and hoped for a quick recovery. I still had no clue what was about to take place.

"We have to transport him to a larger facility that can care for him," the doctor told us a couple of hours later after the x-ray was taken. "We have an ambulance on their way to pick him up and take him to Kaiser Hospital in Anaheim Hills. Your son is very sick and we can't treat him here."

Noah's x-rays were negative for anything that could identify his condition. He was coherent and seemed like there was a slight improvement in contrast to when we had arrived a few hours earlier. Paula gently rubbed his head as she leaned over him.

"You're going to be alright," she spoke softly to Noah. I sat in a chair next to his bed looking intently at his reaction to her voice. I wondered what was troubling him on the inside that we could not see. He stared back at her expressionless; the concern behind his eyes was all he revealed.

The ambulance team arrived and wheeled a transport gurney to his bedside. The nurses began to relay important medical data to the team. One member approached us and introduced himself.

"We will be driving code-3 on our way to Kaiser in Anaheim Hills. Do either of you want to ride with Noah?" He asked us.

I turned to Paula and she answered without hesitation, "I will." I told her I would meet her there once I got directions from the staff.

Noah was prepped and secured for his trip. I leaned over and reassured him, "I'm driving separately and will meet you there. I love you." He just nodded and turned toward the exit as they began to wheel him to the ambulance. Paula was nervous and wore a worrisome look as she walked with the team behind Noah.

With directions in hand, I walked outside to the parking lot. I stood there and watched Noah inside the emergency vehicle. The interior was illuminated brightly so the paramedic could continue to monitor him while en route to their destination.

"Lord, please watch over them and get them there safely," I prayed.

The ambulance began to pull out of the parking lot as the piercing sirens and the light bar was activated. They sped off northbound onto the main road and disappeared. I could hear the horns and sirens alternating, becoming softer and softer with every few seconds as they rushed our son to safety.

**

"Hello. I am Dr. Dodt and I have read Noah's information," said a kind doctor with a sweet smile. She was the pediatrician in charge at the ER Noah was taken to. "We will do everything we can to support your son and also continue to run tests. We don't know exactly what he's suffering from."

Paula and I thanked her and she said a few words to Noah as he lay there on his bed. Her bedside manner was fantastic.

His eyes were closed and he seemed uncomfortable. He began to moan softly and held his tummy. He leaned over to his right side and began to vomit more of what looked like coffee grounds. Paula and I reached over to him as we called for the nurse. We cleaned his mouth and tried to comfort him as best we could. The nurse arrived and tended to him. She also called for an attendant to clean up the mess.

"What's wrong with him, Roger?" Paula said. "I can't stand seeing him like this."

Dr. Dodt rushed over to Noah's bed and began to ask him for specific feelings and symptoms. She was trying to get to the bottom of his unknown illness and I could see the determination on her face. Yet, you could sense her frustration in the lack of a diagnosis.

"Mom, dad, can I speak with you over here please?" Dr. Dodt pointed away from Noah's bed.

"Sure," we both answered. We walked over to the nurse's station several feet away from Noah's bed. The doctor began to address her concerns. After all, Noah's condition still continued to decline slowly and there was just no way for them to treat him adequately.

"I'm afraid of keeping your son here at this facility any longer," the doctor said with concern in her voice. "His vitals are holding, but he continues to vomit dry blood. Are you sure he had no trauma to his abdomen area at all today or yesterday?" Dr. Dodt asked.

"None at all," we said.

She continued, "His lab work shows elevated pancreas numbers consistent with someone who is a severe alcoholic and his white blood count is rising." Paula and I glanced at each other in amazement and in disbelief.

The doctor continued, "I am calling for a Life Flight medical transport to have Noah taken to our largest facility in the area – Kaiser Sunset (Hollywood). If he becomes worse, I don't have the equipment or the facility capable of caring for him. I must get him to a much larger facility soon."

Her words were healing because she made a decision. She would not sit still and do nothing or let Noah slip through her fingers. No, she developed a plan that made sense and would ensure our son's safety. We asked her how long it would take for the helicopter to arrive. She said a couple of hours or so. It was a busy night for them.

We walked back to Noah's bedside and sat down. He was resting quietly, but clearly, he was not well. I stared at him with so much concern in my heart. I could not believe what was transpiring this day. I remembered back to the morning when I dove to work and started a somewhat normal day. Huh, this was far from normal.

My days at work were filled with excitement and sometimes with calls for medical aid. But when it happens to your family, it means a whole lot more in terms of how you feel. This is your son, not a stranger. This is not some routine call for service where I was just a player in a cast of characters, involved in a short part of the scene. Then I had the privilege to say goodbye and drive away. No, this hit home. And it was like a shock to the system. I sat there somewhat numb. I was very tired, but how tormented did Noah feel?

Hours passed and it was now four o'clock in the morning – Monday. The Life Flight crew arrived and walked in the unit like some Special Forces team who owned the room with their confidence. There were three of them; all wearing royal blue jumpsuits with name patches and moved with a purpose. They stood near the nurse's station and began to unravel tubes, open bags of equipment, and sorted out special medical gear. It was all very impressive. I knew Noah was in great hands.

Again, we were informed that one of us would be able to ride with Noah. It seemed like a good idea that Paula went for the trip. I knew she was exhausted and the car ride to Hollywood was at least an hour. I didn't want anything to happen to her and I still wanted one of us to be with Noah. She agreed.

"Mr. and Mrs. Ziegler?" a Life Flight member asked. "There are precautions we have to take in order to get your son to his destination safely. We keep an IV line for access during flight. Even though the time in flight will be relatively short, the elevation is always a concern. Our team consists of one doctor and one nurse who will remain at his side throughout the trip." He went on to describe the movement of the aircraft and unexpected turbulent shifts. It was like we were being prepped for our first trip to the moon.

By the time Noah was ready to be transported, it was near four-thirty in the morning. We were utterly exhausted both physically and emotionally. The helicopter landed as close as possible to the facility – a baseball field located just behind the hospital. Paula and I followed the team closely as they pushed Noah through the maze of empty hospital hallways in quick fashion. Like I said before, they moved with purpose. Dr. Dodt joined us for the march to the aircraft.

We exited the building to the rear of the campus and negotiated through the walkways lit by a soft, yellow glow of light. The sky was heavy like a dark blanket; it felt like perfect conditions for deep sleep – but not us. No, not now. We could hear the deep humming of the engine and propellers as we approached the large field of grass. The morning was very cold and a misty layer covered the ground. The chill pierced my lightweight sweater and cut into my skin. I was nervous too, which didn't help. As we walked through the baseball field towards the large helicopter, we stopped several feet away and I embraced Paula quickly.

"See you at the hospital," I said loudly over the wail of the propellers.

"Alright baby," her reply was delivered with loving eyes.

She turned and followed Noah who was already placed in the belly of the aircraft. I stood there with Dr. Dodt holding our collective breaths as we watched Life Flight transport slowly raise up into the night sky. It lifted above the thick tree line around the field and headed off into the distance. It was tough not flying with Noah and Paula, but I knew it was the best option.

I turned to Dr. Dodt and thanked her as we walked back to the hospital building.

"Are you going to be alright, dad?" her words were filled with concern.

"Yeah, I'll be fine. I just need to get to the hospital right away," I replied.

"They will take very good care of him," she added.

"Yeah, I know," I said.

I believed my words, but I only knew part of the information. My concern was what I didn't know about the circumstances. Why was he so sick? Nothing made sense. Could Kaiser Sunset diagnose him and care for him before he became worse? I had to get there as soon as possible to find out these answers.

**

The ride was turbulent. The helicopter shook and struggled to get through the early morning, unstable autumn climate. Paula wore a helmet and was strapped securely into her seat. Noah's special transport gurney/medical bed was merely inches away from her legs; the cabin was densely occupied. His eyes were closed and he was strapped in with restraints for safety. Two team members sat strapped into their seats next to Noah. They watched the monitor closely and kept checking his vitals.

Suddenly, red lights flashed and a warning alarm sounded. The crew acted swiftly and began grabbing syringes pre-filled with clear fluids. Noah began to code. His blood pressure fell rapidly and the situation became grave immediately. Paula sat there in shock – front seat to this ongoing nightmare. The aircraft shook in the black sky on its way to the hospital. Paula now in tears as she witnessed one of the team members unfasten his seat belt, stood to his feet and rendered medical aid to our son.

"Sit down!" The other flight nurse shouted to his partner above the roar of the engine. "It's too dangerous!"

Instead, he stood hunched over Noah trying to maintain his balance among the unstable ride. He began to use a large syringe that he connected to Noah's IV line and manually pushed fluid into his body to keep his pressure from lowering any more. He was in a fight to keep Noah alive and would not give up. The moment was surreal.

Noah did not respond to the voices or commands given by the angel dressed in a blue jumpsuit. He only had a faint pulse and his blood pressure was dangerously low. The minutes seemed like hours. They were nearly at their destination. More fluid was pushed into Noah's blood system in a frantic effort to keep him alive. It seemed like chaos with the roar of the engine, the erratic course of the flight, and Noah's medical equipment alarms in a frightening continuous chorus.

Paula could only pray through her tears. Her crying was covered by the hysteria of sounds and motion. Our son strapped into the gurney, he laid there helplessly only to be the recipient of masterful care administered by the most gifted air ambulance technician this world has ever seen. He was simply brilliant and unfazed. Like I said, an angel.

She could now see the hospital building below as they began to slow their flight and descend. The cabin shook as they lowered onto the landing area. The only person standing continued to infuse fluids into Noah right up until they touched down. He was alive and his vitals were low but stable. Still, he was nowhere near safety – not yet.

Noah was quickly transferred from the aircraft and into a waiting ambulance. He now had to be driven to Kaiser Sunset's ER. You see, the Life Flight landed three blocks away at Children's Hospital of Los Angeles; there was no landing pad at Kaiser. Now, the urgent race for time continued almost like the baton was handed to the frantically waiting ground team.

The code-3 lights and sirens that were all too familiar during these last several hours still filled the air. Noah, along for the ride of his life, was not coherent. Paula felt the insides of her body twist and, with each passing moment, her mental anguish increased. Seconds passed and the possibility that Noah would not make it through this became more real. The short ride across three city blocks was eternal. It was torturous for a mother.

The ambulance swiftly pulled into the parking lot entrance of the emergency room – finally. The doors opened to the outside chilled air and the medical responders pulled Noah from their vehicle to deliver him to his new home. Paula carefully stepped out and briskly walked alongside Noah and his escort. They rushed him through the entrance doors and into an elevator, then up to the pediatric intensive care unit where a new team had eagerly waited to receive him.

When the transport team arrived with our son, they helped Noah transition onto a new bed. The information exchange took place and all of Noah's vital medical data was delivered to the new personnel. There were new pumps, monitors, and other new surroundings to absorb. It was his third medical facility within ten hours and still, no one knew what plagued him.

**

I drove through the empty Los Angeles freeway system with ease, although the early Monday morning traffic began to appear. I fought back droopy eyes and feelings of drowsiness. After all, I had now been up for twenty-four hours straight. I glanced at the clock on the dashboard: 5:45. What a day this was. I tried my best to think clearly and sort through the last few hours. It started to hit me a little bit; Noah was in a very serious situation that was not looking very well at this point. Unless someone could identify his medical condition, he would likely continue on this tailspin. But, to crash and burn was not an option.

I arrived at Kaiser Sunset, entered the PICU and was directed to Noah's bed by the hospital staff. I approached the foot of his bed and saw Paula sitting there at his side, almost lifeless.

"Hey baby," I softly said to her. She looked up at me with fatigue and disappointment.

"He's been like this since we got here Roger," she said motioning to Noah. He laid there connected to plastic tubes feeding life into his arm. Medical lines attached to his body in various places were monitoring his heart rate, blood pressure, oxygen levels – you name it. He was unconscious. I could only hope he was not in any pain. He was finally in a state of peace, somewhat.

I sat down in a cold chair next to Paula. We both felt like we had been through a war, in all phases of our being. She began to explain what had occurred to Noah while in flight. She described the situation and I was speechless. Until the words, "I'm sorry," crept out from my mouth.

How could a mother go through what she did? To witness such horror. To see our precious Noah face such horror and be so helpless to it all. I felt responsible for allowing her to escort the Life Flight team. If I was there in her place, she would not have been there to see him in that terrible state. Her scars would run deep from this traumatic episode during the transport, but they would only be shallow scratches when compared to those that would develop in the years to come.

"I called my mom already Roger. You better call your parents," Paula said.

I made those two calls shortly after. The first to my mother and stepfather who lived in the Inland Empire; maybe an hour and a half away with no traffic. I told her what happened to Noah earlier that day. She was shocked to hear the incredible details and said they would be at the hospital as soon as they could.

The next call I made was to my father and stepmother. They lived in San Diego. This was about a two and a half hour drive. He couldn't believe it either. He said he would begin to pray and would arrive as soon as possible.

I could see sunlight peering through the windows from the nurse's station where I made the phone calls. Cell phones were not permitted and I didn't want to leave Noah's side. I had been away from him for too long.

Hours had passed and family members began to arrive throughout the late morning and early afternoon. They occupied the waiting room and came in groups of two to visit the PICU.

By noon, our youth pastor had arrived, Pastor Robert. He worked with the teenagers at our church and was also a police chaplain. He met us with his Bible in hand and embraced us both with tenderness. We described the turn of events concerning Noah and he stood there in amazement, shaking his head in disbelief. He prayed with us there in the hallway and God's comfort fell upon us. I knew that God was with us that day, no matter what the circumstances. He was with Noah too in that PICU room. And He was with all of the other children who were sick in the same hospital.

Noah remained in a state of unconsciousness. With all of the tests performed by these specialists we still had no diagnosis, no treatment, and no way to make him better. Talk about helpless.

It was now three o'clock in the afternoon – nineteen and a half hours from the time Noah and I entered the Huntington Beach Medical Center's ER. Unbelievable. The PICU's leading physician met with us for a moment. It was a conversation he did not want to have, but he had no choice.

"Your son is suffering from the inside out. We have no way to know what is going on unless we perform exploratory surgery," his voice was filled with deep concern. "The surgery might be too much for his body right now and he might not make it. If you choose to say your goodbyes, we can provide you with a private room." Our hearts sunk to the deepest parts of the earth when we heard him speak.

"If you decide to allow us to perform the surgery, we need to act now or it will be too late. If so, we need to have you sign a consent," he said with compassion. We agreed. We now understood that our son was close to death and the only chance he had was to allow the surgeons to do their best and save him.

I turned to Paula. She was dazed. It was yet another blow we had endured that day. We had waited hours and hours for someone to come in and rescue our son; to deliver him from his sudden and curious illness. We had questions, but there were no answers. Now we must wait for surgeons to open him and find something to repair. But what will they find? I signed my name on their release and consent form to treat my son. By doing so, I delivered him into the hands of these brilliant medical physicians that saved countless lives before we ever arrived with our son. Noah was next.

Family members, two at a time, walked in to see Noah. But, he could not see them. He could not greet them with a hug or with a kiss. There were no gifts handed out or pleasantries exchanged. There were no jokes or pats on the head given today. No, it was very melancholy and quiet.

I observed each relative say a few words to Noah as he laid there motionless. They reached over and touched his hand and bent over to kiss his forehead. It was touching. As some walked away from his bed, they were crying or trying to hold back their tears. They wiped their eyes and came over to us and embraced Paula and me. I felt like we were at a funeral or something. It was a tough moment to endure. I was trying to stay positive amidst the grief. *He's not gone yet,* I thought.

The medical staff prepped Noah for transport to the operating room. Minutes seemed like hours. I stared at his closed eyes hoping for a chance for him to see us by his side. Just a glimpse into his happy, brown eyes. Maybe a chance to tell him we loved him. I hoped he could reflect back upon this moment and know that his mom and dad were at his side through this situation. Instead, we had a corpse-like son who lay in a bed waiting for his life to be saved.

When the staff was done preparing Noah, they wheeled him out of the intensive care unit and we followed them down the hallway. Could this be the last time we saw our son alive? Is this how the day was going to end for us? Really? The team stopped as we approached the double doors that entered the operating area. We took our turn to hold Noah briefly and kiss him too. I experienced a moment of Deja vu; nine years ago he was a newborn and now a nine-year-old boy soon to be placed in the hands of surgeons. Similar circumstances, but this time it was to save his life.

The doctors didn't reveal their suspicions and how they felt he had little chance of survival. He was critically ill, but their display of hope reassured our hearts. No, they didn't tell us how low his chances really were before they escorted our son away into the operating room. Didn't they understand that our hope was in God who is bigger than the universe and absolutely larger than this circumstance? Noah was God's precious son and nothing could have prevented Him from performing His will in Noah's life – including surviving this exploratory surgery.

You see, in God's perspective, this was as minuscule as me tying my shoes or licking a postage stamp. It was a cinch for the very one who breathed life into my son nine years earlier.

We bent down to Noah's ear and told him we loved him and that he would be alright. Our lips gently kissed his brown hair just above his forehead. We knew he was unconscious, but maybe, just maybe he could hear us. As we stood there in that brightly lit hallway with blank stares, the nurses wheeled him through the large double-doors and out of our sight. We physically felt so helpless and sort of numb. It was a shock to our system. *This couldn't be happening,* I thought.

Now faced with an uncertain amount of wait time, we found some comfort knowing we had family here with us. I walked Paula to a small private room offered to her by the staff. It was a dimly-lit waiting room with two sofas and a small table. It was quiet and a perfect place for her to get some rest. We were so fatigued and I urged her to get some sleep in this peaceful room. She would sleep there while I waited for the surgeons in the large waiting room along with our family.

As we waited, my father stood and approached a hospital staff member behind a desk. After a brief conversation, she led him to a closed door nearby and unlocked it to allow our group access to a more private seating room. It was a secluded area with many chairs reserved for grieving families. We thanked her and gathered inside, then closed the door.

My father brought his bible with him. He began to read from it in a calm tone, just loud enough so we all could hear. His voice soothed my troubled heart. I tried to focus on the words, but my mind wandered back to Noah.

Time moved at a snail's pace; the minutes crawled slowly. I looked down at my watch – it was four-thirty. I hoped for an update soon. Why did the surgeons take so long to update the situation? Maybe this was a longer surgery than expected. I was desperate and longed to hear something.

At least three hours had passed. I waited for a word from someone, from anyone. Finally, words broke the silence of the waiting room as someone opened the door.

"Mr. Ziegler? They are done now and the surgeons would like to speak with you," the friendly staff member said. I quickly stood and followed her out to the main lobby area. I met two men in scrubs and I eagerly anticipated their first words.

"Mr. Ziegler?" one doctor asked and I nodded. "Your son is alright. I'm doctor Appelbaum who performed the surgery." He went on to explain that Noah had a twist in his gut. It was called a midgut volvulus. I tried to process this new information and my jaw dropped as I stood there in disbelief. Somehow Noah had experienced this twist exactly where the intestine received its main blood supply. As a result, blood flow was cut off and starved the organ of its nutrients and life.

"Did he experience any trauma to the stomach area?" the doctor asked.

"No," I said. "We went to my cousin's house Saturday to celebrate his son's birthday party. He was fine and didn't seem sick at all, but he jumped around in the inflatable bouncer with the other kids." I continued, "He banged around pretty good, slamming against the other boys. He was just having fun and he didn't get hurt."

Doctor Appelbaum explained further that since ninety-five percent of his intestines were removed as a result of necrosis (dead tissue from lack of blood supply) and the toxins in his bloodstream had nearly killed him. My son survived by the grace of God. It was a miracle procedure.

Noah's recovery would require IV nutrition called TPN, administered through a central line placed inside of his upper chest. Without an intestine to absorb nutrients from meals, the liquid nutrition was absolutely vital to feed his organs, tissues, and everything else we can't see beneath our skin.

Food, eaten orally as we know, would be unnecessary because there was nothing to process and extract nutrients; it was now merely something only the tongue would enjoy and it would require a slow introduction back into his body as well.

Noah also had a jejunostomy on his lower abdomen, just above his waistline. The doctors only had a few centimeters to work with beyond his stomach and as difficult of a procedure it was, they were able to create the jejunum's exit right at his upper belly.

Here's a brief lesson on the order of the digestive organs: After the food is carried down the esophagus and into the stomach, it exits the stomach and lowers into the duodenum, then into the jejunum – the largest part of the digestive tract at approximately twenty-two feet in length. Once through the jejunum maze, food continues into the ascending colon followed by the descending colon and sigmoid colon – approximately six feet of the large intestine. Then food exits into the rectum and the rest is history.

To get a sense of scope, the doctors had to remove from just below his duodenum and down to his rectum – basically, twenty-seven feet and so many inches of total digestive system lost. This left a nub at the top (his jejunostomy) and a non-working bum, if you will, clamped down below. I was completely blown away and knew there were volumes of questions, but I couldn't form the words. I was shocked.

"When can I see him?" my words were thin and I sounded exhausted.

"You will be able to see your son in the surgery recovery room in a couple of hours," the doctor said with softness and with as much comfort as he could offer. "He will make it through this," he added.

"Thank you so much, doctor. I really appreciate your help," was all I could offer in return.

My uncle Robert looked at me and said that Noah was going to pull through. My family reassured me that Noah would be fine. Their words were comforting and their presence was even more appreciated. I could not imagine going through this amazing day without them near.

I walked back over to the elevator all alone and pushed the button to the sixth floor. I returned to the small private room where Paula was resting.

"Honey," I gently touched her arm as she lay asleep on her side. "Noah is fine."

She opened her eyes and looked at me with tired confusion.

"What?" She was trying to get her bearing. "Noah is okay?"

"Yeah. The doctors just met us in the waiting room and told us they had to remove his intestines." I went on to explain, as best as I could, the details conveyed to me by the life-saving doctor. She was just as amazed and stunned as I was in what she had just learned. We still had a hard time understanding and processing it all. This sort of incident just doesn't happen all of the time. In fact, I don't ever remember hearing about it before.

We sat there for several minutes trying to absorb this entire nightmare, minute by minute. We were exhausted and worn out, to say the least. I tried to replay the events in my mind that took place over the last twelve hours.

"What's going to happen with Noah now?" I asked Paula. "I mean how does someone live without their intestines? How long will he have to stay here in recovery?"

We both had so many unanswered questions. Now was the waiting game. Hopefully, we would learn about our son's condition and be able to make any adjustments at home, with our lifestyle, and to care for Noah's new medical situation sufficiently.

We wanted this nightmare to end. I waited for someone to walk into my bedroom and turn on the lights. This would be fantastic as we would suddenly awake from this torturous dream-like situation. But, not one soul walked into our room to save us from this moment of reality. It stung. Like crushed salt forcefully pushed into a fresh wound, it stung.

4
ADJUSTING TO CHAOS

Life's as easy as juggling elephants.

661:04:30

THE BLINKING LIGHTS ON THE MONITORS were enough to drive someone crazy. The beeps and other alarms didn't help either. It was now Wednesday and we were staying blocks away from the hospital, but pretty much remained at Noah's bedside daily. Paula and I called the Ronald McDonald House home for at least through the next few weeks. It was a huge blessing having a place to sleep that was walking distance from the hospital. Shelby, Brooke, and Luke were being cared for by our relatives. During these past few days, all we could think of was Noah's recovery. It consumed us. The trauma of this experience just began to settle in.

Noah had pulled through the terrible ordeal of having his entire intestines removed just two days ago. Entire bowel…now gone. It was hard to comprehend. Here was a mother and father of a wonderful nine-year-old boy who loved life tremendously, now sat helplessly at his bedside; we hoped and prayed for positive news. The sobering memory of his horrible birth came rushing back into my mind, and I'm sure into Paula's as well. I thought we went through a very difficult time then. Well, the situation became even more overwhelming and it would be that way for days, weeks, and months to come.

"Would you like some Halloween candy for your son?" two nurses asked as they walked into our room holding a basket of all sorts of sweet candy.

"No thanks," we both replied. "He can't eat candy."

I turned to Noah who was asleep and I felt helpless as he lay there in silence. I wanted him to be able to eat some of that awesome candy. This was going to take some getting used to – big time.

Up to this point, we have not had a conversation with Noah for over four days. After his surgery, he was placed in a medical coma to help keep him stabilized and continue to recover. His body was pushed through the limits of fighting for survival. Survival. This word held a new meaning in my life and defined the moments that took place just days before. The toxins in his system from decaying bowel tissue should have killed him. Yet by the grace of God, he was alive.

This coma was such an eerie state of being. He laid there under a cover of sheets so still. His eyes were closed as if he was merely asleep, but the monitor and other medical equipment that was perched above his bed was a constant reminder of his reality. The nurses told us to speak to our son just as if he was awake and alert. It took some getting used to, but we were both pros in no time.

Not only was he not able to communicate with us, but he was intubated – he had a breathing machine controlling his rate of breath. The large plastic hose taped across his mouth was secured so that it was not easily pulled from his throat, had he somehow woke up startled. The machine at his bedside had so many dials and setting displays. Each number represented something crucial to Noah's breathing. It was amazing to see how well the staff was familiarized with this very important equipment.

The doctors kept us very informed soon after Noah's surgery was performed. The road would be long for us as he would remain hospitalized until he could eventually eat food again in small amounts. He was now on daily IV infusions of TPN (total parental nutrition) and lipids, or fats. I could not imagine what he would be going through once discharged and back to normal daily routines. After all, this was a boy who enjoyed the likes of delicious pizza, toppling hamburgers, sloppy ice cream sundaes, and candy straight out of Wonka's factory. He required these IV feeds every day. They would run on such a slow rate over twelve hours – TPN for twelve hours and lipids over eight hours, at the same time.

The doctors had also explained that his small intestine was surgically separated (the healthy portion from his decayed tissue) at his jejunum. This made it interesting because he had to use an ostomy bag for waste. The jejunostomy was about two inches long and looked like it was poking through his skin. Just imagine a mini volcano made from the skin on the inside of our mouths – pink and moist. We joked that it was angry at times and that it could erupt at any moment.

The ostomy bag consisted of a two-part system: a base that adhered to his skin and surrounded his stoma and the bag that fastened to the base via a plastic ring. It was a necessary nuisance and would take some getting used to.

There was also a new diet for Noah because of his missing bowel. Food became difficult to process and would create problems if he were to eat something. Although he would be able to eat certain things, it would be extremely limited to complex carbs, certain proteins, and water. Basically, it was a very bland diet without the luxuries of any sugars, chocolate, any milk products, baked goods, caffeinated drinks, and anything else kids enjoy eating. The results would be harmful if he were to eat the wrong foods, including dehydration from a huge loss of fluid through his ostomy.

Are you kidding me? How is Noah going to cope with this new way of life? I couldn't wrap my head around this and I felt so bad for him. But, if there was someone on this planet that could possess the right attitude, it was Noah. Absolutely. We knew this would be a long journey, but we had no idea it would be an intense battle for his health, for years to come.

Nurse Betty was precious in her demeanor and in her care for Noah. She treated him just as if he were her child. She helped us understand that Noah was unconscious, but needed our loving touch and conversation. She showed us how to massage his hands, arms, legs, and feet with lotion. The massage kept tissues replenished with nutrients from blood flow into those areas. It was awesome to see such dedication from complete strangers. I hoped she would be the one to care for Noah often.

The days went by slowly during this first week. We had a typical routine we had followed. At the end of the day, somewhere around eight o'clock, we met the night shift nurse after shift change. The nurses typically worked in a ten or twelve-hour shift. We made sure Noah was doing well before we left each evening to the Ronald McDonald House. After a gentle kiss and a softly spoken "goodnight" to our little boy, we made our way out of the pediatric intensive care unit.

As we made it back to our room just a couple of miles away, we discussed Noah's progress. We kept our communication open because only the two of us knew exactly how intense this was. We helped each other get through one day at a time. This overwhelming situation would take its toll, but we were very present for each other.

**

"Hi Noah," We both said as his eyes opened for the first time in a while. His face looked like he had been asleep for months. His expressions were slow to react to our words and to his surroundings. He was puzzled and confused. The last thing he remembered was from the night before I took him to the hospital on that fateful Sunday. It was like he blacked out for a week.

It took days for Noah to regain some strength in his body. He made improvements in his healing too. The nurses took great care in changing his very large dressing that covered his long scar. It ran across his belly from one side to the other. They looked very deep and would take a while to completely heal. The most important strides were yet to come: eating.

It was in the weeks that followed that our little champion began to sip on very small amounts of broth. I mean we're talking an ounce here and there if that.

"How is it, Noah?" I asked him thinking how foolish my question was, as though he never tasted food before.

"It's fine dad," his words were believable and he wore a smile as he delivered his response.

"I'm sorry my sweet pea," Paula said offering her condolences to his situation. She rubbed his hair tenderly as she sat in his bed next to his side. You could see a strength in her when she was near Noah, but when she was out of the hospital the strain was visible. We both wanted to be positive for him and try to encourage him through the last phase of recovery.

By the second week, Noah was transferred to the pediatric side of the hospital. The intensive care unit was safely behind him. He was kept in a large private room that had fresh oxygen pumped into it. He was happy to move as this meant he was doing very well and on his way to leaving soon. We had arts and crafts of all sorts throughout the room that Noah made; his creations in the midst of boredom. There were stuffed animals of all shapes, sizes, and colors; his friendly companions. He also had many get well wishes written on greeting cards that were taped to the walls. Noah was missed by his peers at school, his friends at home and many at church.

One day, special guests had arrived to visit. We had ties with law enforcement in our family and one of our dear friends shared Noah's incredible story with someone he knew in this community. Well, the visitor who was moved by our son's situation was a detective with the Los Angeles Sheriff's Office and he brought two other detectives with him.

Hi Noah," they all introduced themselves, "We heard that you were fighting through some huge challenges and wanted to come by and see how you were doing."

Noah perked up. He was so happy that someone other than family was there to see him. He shook their hands and they all stood around his bed. The detectives went on to tell him how proud they were of his progress and said when he was ready they would love to give him a ride in a real police car (since I worked at a different police dept., I recognized the jab – it was all in good fun). One of them handed Noah a die-cast, miniature sized police cruiser. We all chuckled.

After several minutes, they said their goodbyes and left his room.

"Wow Noah, that was so cool that they came down here to see you," I said with much enthusiasm.

"Yeah, I liked meeting them. Do they work with you, dad?" Noah asked.

"No, they work for a different city and they are part of the L.A. Sheriff's." I went on to explain the intricacies of law enforcement jurisdiction and the like. He didn't really understand or care for that matter. He was just happy I was there. It's no fun being alone while in the hospital.

By the third week, Noah was making slow progress. The TPN feeds administered by IV continued on a daily basis. Clearly, it was understood that it would be a part of his life until something else took its place. The fact was that he needed to eat – or, his body needed nutrients to survive. It was a little difficult to comprehend; no more food like he knew before. And he was a terrific eater.

Paula and I were very careful not to eat in front of him or discuss our meals as we visited him. He still showed little concern for his new diet restrictions, extreme as they were. Most of the time he kept himself occupied with puzzles, model cars, and laughing at whatever tickled his funny bone. Still, I noticed something in his gaze that was silent and stunned. He wouldn't say it, but I could sense his struggle with this new way of life. It didn't help that he was stuck in a hospital without his normal surroundings. His buddies were now pediatric nurses, doctors, and janitors who would keep his room clean. Not the best life for a nine-year-old, I'd say.

Noah was ready to escape the confines of Kaiser Sunset. With each day he tried to do more walking and short stints of standing. He took very short steps from one end of the room to the other, followed by a lengthy rest on his bed. A great exercise was to have him sit in a chair, instead of the bed, for twenty minutes. It was strange to actually see him get fatigued with the activity of sitting upright in a chair and he would ask for help to return to the bed once he had enough. His determination kept him persistent in his pursuit of complete rehabilitation.

He was only able to drink small amounts of broth at a time – not exactly a kid's favorite meal. Food was still too hard on his limited digestive system and would have to be slowly introduced moving forward. It was three or four ounces of beef broth for breakfast, lunch, and dinner. Sometimes he would prefer chicken or vegetable broth. How I wished he had a juicy double cheeseburger instead.

He was so thin. A combination of inactivity and the drastic change in his diet was the cause. Atrophy seemed to have taken over his physical structure. Yet, his bright smile filled the room when you were near and he welcomed you with kindness. He was thrilled to have visitors because Noah was a social butterfly. His grandmas, grandpas, aunts, uncles, and cousins would visit during the weekends and sometimes during the week.

As you could imagine, it just wasn't enough for him.

We described to Noah how interesting it was to stay at the Ronald McDonald House. The facility was like a hotel with a family feel to it. The enormous kitchen was a common place for all residents to share a few minutes as meals and snacks were eaten. We told Noah how the large refrigerators were assigned to each family and how we were able to keep food there. He thought it was a good idea to have a special place like this.

"When you're discharged you'll be able to see the house when we check out," I said to Noah. "The best part is the price. We are only charged eleven bucks a day."

"Wow, dad," Noah's eyes widened. "That's it?"

"Yup. What a blessing, huh?" I replied.

We were very grateful that there was such a wonderful facility nearby. The Ronald McDonald House was priceless. A very low-cost housing facility close by the hospital was a blessing to have. The house provided breakfast cereal and milk every morning for all of us to enjoy at no added cost. There were industrial sized refrigerators with enough space for every family to store a large bin of personal food. Even McDonald's coffee was available. *Are you serious?* Do you know how great that was for Paula and me?

We noticed there were certain evenings when groups of people or a small family would bring dinner for the residents. They served with a loving heart and their gesture touched us immensely. They had no motive other than to bring a meal and with it a smile. You cannot place a price on the heart of a volunteer. I guess you could say these special few are priceless.

The day before Noah's discharge we were met by the nurse care manager in his room. She had the difficult task of training us on how to care for him at home. His new life would require extensive around the clock care and we had to learn how to become a nurse, a doctor, a physical therapist, a counselor, and still be the best loving parent that we could be. It would require the deepest commitment – we were already committed to his life, so that was a no brainer. It would take 100% love – we had nothing else to offer him. It would take our greatest sacrifice – "Greater love has no one than this than to lay down one's life for his friends…" John 15:13 is right on point. Except, Noah was our son and we would without hesitation give our life for him. Yeah, we were in this fight together.

The nurse care manager brought some IV tubing, a large bag of saline, medical dressing change kits and several pair of gloves. We were eager to learn our new set of skills. This training meant he would be released from this temporary home and he could now move on to a new chapter. She slowly showed us all of the key materials and outlined a lesson plan. We

41

were provided with some written material as well, so note taking was minimal.

We must have been there at least an hour going over every single detail of his new IV central line. He had a double lumen version for alternate feeds; one side would be connected with infusion while the other remained capped off and closed. They would be switched every day and share the load.

He required a large bag of TPN solution that took twenty hours to infuse combined with a bottle of white lipids (it looked like milk) which required eight hours to infuse. Both liquids were connected into one line via a line splicer, but each liquid used a separate mechanical pump to infuse at a prescribed rate. The rate was prescribed with a specific amount delivered per hour and a certain number of hours for each. With the lipids spliced into the line with the TPN, the total infusion time did not increase the twenty hour period. It was down to a science.

She also taught us how to program each IV pump that was fastened to a five foot tall, chrome pole with wheels at its base for easy mobility. There were hooks on the top end for the TPN bag and lipids bottle to hang securely. The pumps were not very difficult once they were pre-programmed with the flow information, but we soon learned that changes were always made by the doctors and we had to program the rate info ourselves. Good luck with that one.

After an hour and a half, we were rubbing our heads. This thing and that thing, running this tube into this area – it was nuts. The dressing changes were tricky too because each time his port access was exposed extreme care was required to prevent the possibility of infection in his new line. Operative term: extreme care. The procedure required wearing a mask (not Casper or Frankenstein, but rather one of those cute light blue ones you see at hospitals everywhere), sterile gloves, a prepared room (no fans of any sort circulating air) and a huge amount of alcohol rubbing pads. We were informed that these kids have a tendency to become frequently ill from line infections and our level of care was critically paramount to prevent any occurrences.

Consider this: on one end we could see his central line hanging from the side of his upper chest area as it exited from the skin. It hung a few inches in length and was kept under a clear dressing called Tegaderm – a wonderful product by 3M. This line ran directly underneath the skin just enough for the human eye to see a raised line, like a tunnel, and it led upward to the side of his neck. This method of keeping the line between his skin and muscle tissue prevented any possible dislodging or movement. From his neck, the "tunnel" suddenly disappeared from view which meant it was fed directly into a major blood vessel, then through the vessel to a termination point near his heart. If a strain of bacteria was on the tip of his central line when an IV connection or disconnection was made or perhaps a dressing change allowed a "bug" to enter the line, it would be dangerous to his defense system, especially since the other end of the line was near the heart. It was sobering to think of the caution we had to employ when doing just about everything. Serious tactics were required.

After a long session with the nurse care manager, she reassured us both that we would do well. I guess we passed. If we needed any assistance, we had a large three-ring binder with the appropriate contacts and information in the event we needed help. She also said our first night at home would be a smooth transition because a travel nurse would be sent to bring helping hands. Once we heard this we both looked at each other and smiled (and a huge sense of relief had followed). Noah seemed to take it all in as he remained confident in our ability to handle this new journey. After all, he was part of the training process too. He would become the best quality control manager on this side of the Mississippi.

Before leaving the room the nurse also said she wanted to see Noah make improvements in his physical strength while recovering at home by taking short walks around the house. He agreed and said he would do his best. She also told us a wheelchair would be sent home when discharged, but the goal was to use it sparingly. Noah looked very weak in terms of muscle tone. He definitely was a different looking child just four weeks ago. It's amazing how much a little boy can change physically in a short amount of time.

Later that night while at the RMH, Paula and I discussed our detailed training and the impact it would have at home. It was daunting, but we were very tired of living the way had over the last few weeks and we were tired of seeing Noah suffer through these tough days while in physical recovery. I'm sure he was concerned, worried, afraid, confused, overwhelmed, and whatever else you can imagine a nine-year-old boy would be feeling. The healing process would be a physical obstacle and the emotional process was even more daunting.

The day had finally arrived. You can imagine the relief we all felt, especially Noah. He was ready to go; to check out and get on with life. He wore a smile from ear to ear and we helped him collect all of his belongings. He had an assortment of cards from many people whom he knew. It was wonderful having expressions of love sent to our son during this crisis. He also had gifts like toys, mind puzzles, and games. It was amazing how much he had received in just four weeks.

The nurse walked in to let us know his discharge papers were being finalized and all of the medical supplies, TPN liquid, and lipids required for the next few days would be ready at the pharmacy. Noah's medical pumps and IV pole were also ready for pick up. She reminded us that a home care nurse would arrive later that evening to set-up the equipment and run through his TPN and lipids infusion procedures.

At last, Noah was released from care. He was elated but slightly uneasy with his new life ahead. After all, only a month ago he was completely free from any illness or physical hardship. Now, he was a changed little boy. It would take a great deal of patience on his part to fight through the transition of being home. There were no doctors or nurses to summon for help – only mom and dad. Geez – no pressure.

The doctor who cared for Noah walked in to say goodbye and to wish us well. He was a very kind person and was in charge of the entire pediatric unit. You could see the years of service in his eyes and he absolutely loved his job – and children.

"Thank you so much doctor for taking care of Noah," I said to Doctor Johnson as I shook his hand.

"We really appreciate all you've done," Paula added with a warm smile.

"Thanks, doctor," Noah said as he stood slightly hunched in his shoulders. He clearly needed some physical exercise. PT – good for you, good for me!

And off we went. Noah was pushed in a wheelchair through the halls as he waved to all of the familiar faces – nurses, medical technicians, and doctors. It was like a ticker-tape parade, minus the falling confetti. He made many friends during his stay. We followed close behind and carried the last few bags of items not already packed into our mighty minivan. He was wheeled outside to the patient loading zone and I assisted our son into the vehicle. It was a sweet, sweet moment.

I looked back at the hospital as we drove away. I was overjoyed to bust Noah out of there, but I was so grateful in the life-saving medical care he had received. Starting with the genius surgeon, Dr. Appelbaum, whose dedication to his craft saved our son's life, to those in the pediatric intensive care unit who cared tirelessly for Noah's recovery, and with those who kept watching around the clock for whatever his needs were. Thank you! Thank you! It was surely a difficult time with tough days, but it would not be the last time Noah would be a patient at this facility.

We drove around the building to the pharmacy discharge pick-up office. There were boxes, bags, and medical equipment to load in the van. It began to sink in a bit more; we had a lot of gear and we were Noah's only hope away from this facility.

We drove to the Ronald McDonald House to check out and settle our bill. At eleven dollars a day, it was very affordable. It was a terrific blessing! We showed Noah around the lobby and kitchen area, while in his wheelchair. He was impressed with this unique place dedicated to supporting families during a crisis with medical illnesses.

"It would be nice to give back to the Ronald McDonald House. Wouldn't it?" I asked Noah.

"Yeah, dad. That would be nice," he replied.

My words were prophetic as many years ahead we would serve meals with our church and bring blessings with smiles to those who were hurting.

During the ride home, we kept Noah engaged in conversation. As is typical of a Los Angeles and Southern California drive, most of our time was on the freeways. We were about twenty minutes away from home when Noah began to complain of nausea. Then it hit us: he spent the greater part of the last four weeks in a hospital bed.

"Sorry honey," Paula's voice steeped with compassion. "We're almost home."

I kept watching him every few minutes through the rearview mirror. Like a trooper, he made it all the way home. I knew he dug deep during that transition home.

I hoped for a very warm and special homecoming. You know, the kind with party streamers, huge colorful balloons, and a large banner that reads: *Welcome home Noah*! But, we had our minds wrapped up in the onslaught of medical care training and such. The fact that he was home the week of Thanksgiving was a miracle in itself and our family had a truckload to be thankful for. We hoped for deep blue skies, but little did we know we really needed a handful more of umbrellas for the storms ahead.

**

637:15:55

The first night was a disaster, a nightmare, and a predicament all wrapped up into one. The very home care nurse we were told would be at our home did not arrive. After a call to the after-hours hotline (yeah, it was past eight-thirty by then) and several conversations later, we realized it was up to us to complete Noah's initial home set-up of his IV requirements. We were frustrated – big time!

Paula and I rolled up our sleeves and began sorting through the equipment pre-packaged into plastic, easy-to-open baggies. I pulled out our notes and literature so that we could make every step in this tedious process successful. After all, this wasn't just a complicated piece of furniture to assemble (aka Ikea) or troubleshooting a car's unwillingness to start properly. No, this was our son's life and his future. We had to get him hooked up as soon as we could to prevent him from becoming too much off of his TPN schedule.

He last received his fluids at the hospital just before discharge and he had a small window of being disconnected from it each day – four hours to be exact. Since he was on this "liquid-life" daily we had to make sure he didn't go beyond the four-hour timeframe, or he would start to experience symptoms similar to having low blood sugar. The TPN fluid had everything a body needed, including the proper amounts of glucose.

"Are you feeling alright son?" I asked with concern as I prepared the tubing.

"I'm fine dad," Noah said. "I just want to get hooked up quickly." He was clearly concerned with how the night was going.

Paula and I worked together. The pace was quick but done with precise care. We positioned his IV pole next to his bed and on it, both pumps were securely fastened. We had a waist-high table used to accommodate the layout prep for IV feeds and also for dressing changes. We made a terrific team.

It took us almost thirty minutes to connect his TPN, but the pump was not cooperating. The beeping sounds emitted after it began the infusion indicated a bubble was present in the tube. We had to stop the machine and access the chamber where the tubing was intricately loaded into the belly of mechanics. Yup, a bubble was trapped in the line and we used a method we had learned to clear it safely. Noah looked on with eager and tired eyes.

Once the tubing was cleared and repositioned, we resumed the infusion. So far so good. We watched for several minutes as the fluid was fed through the plastic tube mechanically and into our son's body. One of the reasons bubbles would be present was from cold fluid in the bag. It was very important to bring the TPN fluid to room temperature over the course of the day to prevent these bubbles and also to be sure the cold fluid would not interfere with Noah's body temperature. Since the fluid was pumped into his bloodstream, you could imagine how easy it would be to bring a chill into his body. But, our bag that night was just fine.

We primed the lipid fluid into another tubing line and fed it through the second pump. The end of the long tube was capped safely for connection into the existing TPN line later that evening. Since the lipids were only scheduled for an eight-hour infusion, we decided to connect it hours later just before we went to sleep. It's much easier to disconnect in the morning than in the wee hours overnight when I'm half asleep.

Noah was wiped out. He laid in his bed – his very own familiar bed and pulled his covers tightly up to his chin. He was at peace. We made sure his line was not interfered by his blankets or pillow. If there was any unwanted pressure on it or a kink was formed, a sudden annoying beep would sound to alert us. But, as for now, there was no alarm or need for concern.

It was time for him to rest peacefully. We cleaned up the mess of packaging, empty saline syringes, and empty packets of alcohol pads. One last peek at the pump and Noah, then we walked out of his room.

During this whole exercise which lasted at least an hour and a half, Luke, Noah's roommate, kept a watchful eye on our duties. He was glued to our every move as we performed the detailed tasks. He studied and he seemed like he memorized each step of the process. He was only three, but he was very bright and extremely aware of his surroundings. Luke's bed was in the opposite corner of the room. The room was not very big; ten feet by nine feet, not including closet space. With both beds, a dresser, small television, and an IV pole loaded with equipment, it made for a tight space. I wish we had a larger home, but I was thankful for what we had.

Paula and I exhaled a huge sigh of relief as we sat in our bed. Our room was across from the boy's room. We could easily hear the low humming sound of the pump. It was a steady and almost haunting rhythm. What a difference it was now versus life back in his hospital. We did not have to monitor the medical care being performed at Kaiser Sunset. Maybe we were slightly paranoid, but we heard horror stories of patients becoming sick from a medical care provider's laziness or lack of proper procedure. The last thing we needed was Noah to contract something else and add more drama into his equation.

We calculated what could happen next. What if his tubing punctured? What if his pump malfunctioned? The scenarios danced in our heads and we began to bounce ideas off of each other. Until, a sudden and strange sound interrupted, "beep, beep, beep..." The pump was alerting us to an error present.

We jumped off of our bed and quickly walked into the dimly lit room, thanks to the nightlight by Noah's bed. It had only been about twenty minutes since we connected him, but here we were again.

"Maybe it's another bubble," I whispered to Paula, trying not to wake Noah.

"Check the tube again as we did before," Paula replied. The line was cleared once again and the pump resumed operation.

"Are we gonna be doing this all night?" asked Paula. "This could be a long night."

I looked over at Noah and he was sound asleep. Yup. He was certainly used to this. Before walking out I turned to Luke and found him staring at me and at Noah as he lay there quietly.

"Go to sleep Luke. Noah will be fine," I assured him. He simply nodded and turned over.

Well, the pump became the annoyance of the evening by sounding off what seemed like every hour. After a few times, I just told Paula to stay in bed and I handled the tubing issues for the rest of the night. In addition to that, Noah had to pee frequently because of his lengthy infusion. His urinal was placed near his bedside, hanging from the IV pole. It was easy to reach and since he could not easily walk to the restroom with a fully equipped pole, this offered a simple solution. Every so many hours the urinal needed to be emptied. It was another task to manage through the night. And then there was the ostomy bag. Don't ask.

The morning had arrived, but it seemed like weeks were spent over those early morning hours. The lack of sleep made it difficult to think clearly. Paula and I checked on Noah first thing, although I saw on him with every pump/line correction. He was sound asleep and the pumps continued to run as scheduled. We checked the lipids bottle and discovered it was nearly empty. When the lipids pump completed its task, we turned it off and disconnected the tubing from Noah's central line (where it was spliced together with the other fluid). The TPN fluids still had approximately eight hours before the cycle was complete. It was a long time to be connected to a cumbersome IV pole.

Later that morning when Noah woke up, he needed our help to move his pole and pump down to the first floor of our townhome. All three of our bedrooms, girls included, were upstairs on the second floor. Paula helped him carefully walk down the stairs and I followed closely carrying the equipment. He ended up on the sofa in front of the TV. Our place was not very big; the kitchen and living room were pretty close to each other. We could easily attend to his needs from anywhere on the first floor.

He seemed somewhat content and it must have been attributed to the fact that he was home. Yes, he was back in his domain. The prince returned to his palace. You know, a lot of difficult situations are a bit easier to deal with when you can treat them at home. The familiar surroundings are comforting and allow for one to connect with certain stability. Yup, Dorothy was onto something. There's no place like home.

Paula offered Noah everything she could think of to make him comfortable. With his new way of eating, so bizarre and restricted, we had to be careful not to slip up and place a bowl of Fruit Loops in front of him or a fresh cut serving of mango and oranges (he loved Southern California fruit). I could imagine the look of disappointment that would suddenly appear if we made this simple mistake. No, instead it was small amounts of broth – beef or chicken. Yeah, it killed us. We wanted to make him a welcome home breakfast fit for a king.

"Can I get you something to drink Noah?" Paula asked while combing his hair with her fingers.

"No mom. I'm okay," he replied. The same rules applied with beverages – no sugar, no caffeine, no sweetener substitute (it caused diarrhea), no dairy products, no fun, no smiles, no Yellow Dye #5 (just kidding). Well, that pretty much ruled out all drinks except for magnificent water. Yup, good old H2O. Clear, fresh drinking water. It makes the soul strong and the body of a short-gut patient stronger. Hey Kool-Aid, take a hike!

I was crushed inside. How was Noah supposed to make it every day with these extreme and unrealistic eating restrictions? I guess with our help to support and care for him. *Whatever it takes, Roger,* I told myself. *If you have to somehow give him a part of your body or take him to another place where he will thrive or carry him when he can't walk, then that's what I'll do. No matter what.*

I guess only time will tell. We really had no idea what to expect. Each day was an empty canvas for Noah to paint his story upon. Through these next few days, we faced several challenges. Some hours dragged on like days during some of those times when he had pump issues in the wee hours of the morning. Sleep? Yeah right. I thought night feeds for an infant were a challenge. Not quite. Try IV feeds with continued pump problems combined with ostomy bag issues from a base (wafer) that wouldn't stick to his skin sufficiently and caused liquid poop to seep into his bed and sheets. Yeah, that was hard. We hoped for some relief and for it to arrive very soon.

**

"Happy Thanksgiving dad," I said to my father as he walked through the front door. We hugged each other, but he couldn't wait to embrace Noah who was on the sofa hooked up to his daily regimen of TPN. Peggy, my stepmom walked in along with Peter, my half-brother who was Noah's age (his uncle). Funny how that happens, huh?

Just days after Noah was discharged from the hospital we were celebrating Thanksgiving. What could be more of a blessing to our family than to have our Noah with us after such an incredible ordeal? Miraculous.

Paula and I had discussed our game plan for this special day. In times past she would cook up a storm with all of our favorites: cranberry sauce, turkey with gravy, and delicious mashed potatoes. This year, to be kind to Noah, we decided not to have dinner because he was not able to eat. To be fair to the other kids, my dad decided to take the kids out for dinner somewhere. We didn't want Noah to encounter the smells and sounds of preparing a delicious meal he could have no part of eating. That would be torture.

Noah seemed to accept the situation with the most incredible poise. His holiday dinner consisted of about a cup of hot turkey broth and water. Not quite the meal anyone expects for Thanksgiving. It was his meal nonetheless. I dreamed for a moment of him tearing into his own turkey leg and mashed potatoes, just like every year before. It's amazing what we can take for granted in life.

Paula and I had the same delicious broth Noah enjoyed. We were trying our best not to make him feel uncomfortable.

"I'm glad you're home, son," I said to Noah with an extra-large smile. You know, the kind that you order as super-sized with a helping of joy to go with it.

"Me too," Noah said with a look of relief.

And that, my friends, is how we spent our special evening. We enjoyed each other's company in the confines of our little townhome. There was nothing sweeter.

At the end of the night while in Noah's room, we began our routine of prepping the TPN bag and setting the table with medical supplies and all of the trimmings. It was always a big deal and required so much concentration. There was simply no room for any error and failure was not an option.

I thought about how tedious this regimen was and how difficult it will be moving forward. The intense steps required day after day and week after week would demand our very best. I immediately recalled how it was to have Noah confined to the hospital and how much we missed him at home. Normalcy is a precious thing. It wasn't long before I realized this could possibly be his entire life. Not just a few weeks or months, but years and decades. Wow. We prayed that our son would not have to endure such terrible medical issues forever. I also knew that if for some reason he did, we would remain right by his side.

The evening was not spent in our usual festive manner, but there was nowhere else I would rather be on that Thanksgiving night. Nope. Nowhere else. It was an act I can't describe. It must be the love bond between a parent and a child. I so desperately wanted to let Noah stand on my shoulders to see the parade, so to speak. Maybe, just maybe, I could do that for him one day.

5
SHORT-GUT LIFE

627:03:27

WE HAD OUR FIRST FOLLOW UP APPOINTMENT with Dr. Duh, a gastroenterologist dedicated to caring for the small gut, pediatric patients. He was kind, non-imposing and he was our son's new doctor. He had a great bedside manner and Noah liked him – that was huge! His knowledge of short gut related care was extensive and we asked so him many questions. After all, this was a whole new world for us. His patience in helping us get up to speed was unending.

It was now December and wherever we went with Noah, we brought along his wheelchair. His overall strength increased with every passing week, but walking was still difficult. I think he liked being pushed around in his chair most of the time. You know, getting that royal treatment and all. Although, he really wanted to be a wide receiver sprinting through complex routes and catching passes from his pops.

We tried to prevent Noah from becoming too reliant upon the use of his chair on wheels. In an effort to build strength in his body, we encouraged him to walk, stand and to walk some more. He was a champ about it, but you could see the discomfort in his face.

"You'll get there Noah," I said with encouragement. "One day you will run just like you did before."

"Yeah, I know," he replied. He was sure of it.

We scheduled an appointment at our local JC Penney portrait studio for our family Christmas photo. This was a very special moment for us and was the first portrait that included all of our children. Paula and I had a new perspective on life with the kids. We knew each day was precious and truly believed it.

We discussed how we should dress for the sitting. Should we wear formal clothing or keep it casual? A Christmas holiday background or a more subtle feel? After throwing ideas around, we agreed to have a look that was uniform: black sweaters and blue jeans.

We took several pictures in different poses. The mood was bright and fun. I knew whatever picture we chose would be perfect. After twenty minutes or so, we all looked at proofs on a large screen. We selected our family portrait and went home. Days later that same photograph of our wonderful family was framed and hung on the wall of our living room. It represented a moment in time we had shared. A moment just after a crisis, but came out of the other side together. It became a new mantra for our family: do it together.

You could see something special in Noah's eyes as he sat in the middle of the family portrait. He wore a sense of relief and hope. It was not merely a mask. No, instead it was a direct reflection of what he held in his heart. He would need that for the months that were to come.

**

I was contacted by a friend who worked for another police department. It was the same agency where my stepfather served as a motor officer for over two decades. He explained to me that many of the officers wanted to do something for our family and for Noah that would provide a donation towards our household's situation. I was honored to hear such news.

The officers of Huntington Park PD assembled a softball team and would play against officers from my department, Cypress PD. I thought it was a terrific idea and the game was set to take place in the city of Huntington Park – the city where I had grown up and lived for about thirteen years of my early life.

I attended the game with Brooke and Noah couldn't make it that day, so Paula stayed behind with him. The event was sort of like fundraisers you see for various charities. The members of both teams were sponsored or donated the fee themselves and these funds would be collected as the donation. It was pretty amazing to see officers from another department and from my own family of blue, even our chief, come together in an effort to do something for our family. These were many of the brothers I served with on the streets. I was so blessed by their gesture.

The game was a blast and once it concluded both teams gathered, friends and family who also came to watch, and one of the members of HPPD delivered a moving speech. I was handed the check and I felt the bond of brotherhood so strong in the midst of these law enforcement individuals. They made a difference on behalf of the Ziegler household and specifically honored our son, Noah. I thanked everyone for their support and effort on our behalf. I wish Noah could have seen their faces light up. It would have made his day – and he would have made theirs as well.

Not long after this event and from out of the blue, I received a call from one of the sergeants I worked with. I was still out on leave.

"Ziegler?" he said when I answered the phone call.

"Yes, sir. How are you?" I replied, surprised to hear from him.

"How's Noah doing?" He asked.

"He's a trooper. So much progress has been made and he is getting stronger every week. Thanks for asking." My words were delivered with appreciation.

"I'm glad to hear that. We want to help you with Christmas this year. I need to know the clothing sizes of your kids. We're going to have Santa visit your home the week before Christmas to bring their gifts." He sounded thrilled to deliver such tremendous news.

"Oh man! That's great." I felt like we had just won the lottery for the kids. "Thank you, sir. It means a lot to me."

I told Paula the good news and she was overwhelmed by the act of kindness. We felt like another family was there for us. In this case, a family of our law enforcement community. What a cool blessing we thought as we wrote down all of the kid's shirt and pant sizes. We just couldn't believe how awesome this was. How could we say thank you enough?

The special evening had arrived and Santa (one of the detectives) made his arrival to our home. He brought two others from our department to help carry the load of presents for the kids. I helped too and we made several trips back and forth from the police van to our living room where our Christmas tree stood. I was amazed at the mountain of gifts that surrounded our tree. They were piled upon each other in a large heap and was about waist high. Yeah, it was a really big pile! Shelby, Brooke, Luke, and Noah gave Santa big hugs and thanked him over and over.

When Christmas morning had arrived they each wore massive smiles as they exploded through each of the carefully wrapped presents. Noah remained in one place as I brought him the ones labeled with his name. When it was all said and done, something like twenty minutes later, the place was littered with torn colored paper and four exhausted children still in a state of bliss. It was priceless.

After about seven weeks, I returned to work. Paula suddenly had the burden of caring for Noah and for the household while I was at work. And it was a strenuous task considering our son's overwhelming medical care was so difficult to manage. These circumstances were easier to deal with as two full-time parents at home, but reality had set in. My vacation, personal and sick time had expired. Thank God there were those benefits in place with my employer. Of course, working for the city had many benefits. Our medical insurance plan was wonderful and it only cost a small amount each month. The city had a thorough plan for its employees.

I checked in with Paula and Noah often throughout my shifts with brief phone calls. Overall, his transition into short-gut kid life required adjustments, but he made huge strides since his discharge from the hospital just weeks ago. He also adapted quickly and seemed to have a certain comfort level with this new way of life.

One of the best parts of my week, ones I cherished so dearly, were the moments when I arrived home from work. As I walked through the front door, I was typically met by an eager Noah who pulled his IV pole on wheels behind him and wore the biggest smile a face could have. He traveled slowly and steadily, approximately 1.5 MPH – or less. Snails had something on his lack of speed. But, his fortitude and courage melted my heart as he consistently fought the entire distance to meet me at the front door.

"Hi, dad!" Noah said with great enthusiasm and a huge grin followed up with a massive hug. His body was very thin, but I could feel the strength in him increasing.

"Hi, Noah! How are you doing?" I quickly replied.

"I'm good," he said without hesitation, regardless of what he was enduring on that particular day.

He turned around and ventured back to the sofa, IV pole in tow and TPN pump attached. The mechanical, rhythmic sound of the pump filled the air in a subtle sort of way. I relied on that moment when I returned from an exhausting and hard day. Seeing him make that impressive effort was the wind beneath my wings.

This medical prison sentence was his new normal. His normal being the stress of monitoring the little details of every conceivable health risk associated with keeping a sterile central line. Normal being the kid in the house who woke up at 2:50 AM because his ostomy base leaked liquid-poop on his waist, his back, and in his warm bed. Normal being the nine-year-old who had to convince himself he wasn't the neighborhood freak all of a sudden. Yeah, this was his new normal. And as much as we tried to help bear that burden with him, Noah had to carry the weight of this stress with every waking moment and with each beat of his heart.

An important goal was to somehow introduce education back into his life. Because of his demands with IV pumps, ostomy care, diet restrictions, and other needs, he required a home school setting provided by an educator. The school district obliged and provided a teacher once a week during the regular school year. It wasn't much, but Noah dedicated his attention to those few hours a week.

It was Paula who typically took Noah to his appointments with Dr. Duh. Mainly because they were set during the morning or afternoon hours and I usually worked or tried to sleep after a long night shift (twelve-hour shifts required about fourteen hours total with briefing and overtime included). Her attention to detail and perseverance made for solid tools in her pursuit of caring for our son. It was obvious that she had a clear understanding of how to manage his medical needs and she became the authority in our family concerning every nook and cranny of all his medical care. She had amazing chops, indeed! It was amazing how much information she absorbed during doctor visits. Her medical knowledge increased every week and I knew Noah felt a sense of warmth under her blanket of protection.

Dr. Duh was light and kept a quick sense of humor. It was just what Noah needed. Rather than a daunting and ominous medical practitioner, his new doctor had time for laughs and for funny faces. Noah's giggle was perfected by now and it was his way to stave off the fear of the unknown. Don't be fooled, his laughter was genuine and not some façade.

Dr. Duh commonly referred to himself as the poop doctor. Noah thought that was just great. His detailed explanations were intriguing as he went on about the complexity of the small and large intestine. It all clicked with us and with our son.

Somehow we felt a sense of calm as we adjusted to short-gut life. This new way of life mostly affected the child (patient) we learned but spread a portion of its madness to other members of the family. There was no person unscathed. There was also a sense of routine through it all, but with a respect that at any time chaos could erupt.

Days passed and we couldn't see a light at the end of the tunnel, so to speak. Not that we weren't provided with a glimmer of hope at all, but we knew the only real way for Noah to get back to his former self was to get a new body – or by miraculous healing. Yup, bring out the cloning machine. I think they sell them on eBay. So, we managed through his reality with three other children and all of its twists and turns.

Noah became skilled in the art of "IV pumpology" and in central line management. He could remove the bubbles from his IV tube faster than you could say some long word in Spanish – backward. Okay, so it wasn't that fast, but he became more proficient than when he first started this ordeal. Oh, we didn't ignore the beautiful sounds of the pump alarm, pretending that it was some harmonious tune of stringed instruments. In contrast, we made sure Noah had a strong sense of caring for himself. It was our training philosophy. Think you can, think you can…and he did.

He proved to himself that he had control over so many details of this part of his life. We wanted to be sure that he mastered it. As he grew older, it would benefit his life to be so well adjusted. We helped him understand it was imperative to be self-reliant with his care because one day he would be an adult and on his own.

Now, we had spent quality time each night at about 9:00 PM. It was time for our dance with the tubes and sterile potions. We unpacked the medical supplies and talked about characters from Star Wars or what the Dallas Cowboys would do the following year. I could see that he was starved for buddy time. He really missed school, the social bug that he was.

After twenty minutes, he was connected and we began the dressing change for his central line. One could say that this part was tedious and they would be correct. But, you just do it and perform the task well because the last thing you wanted was a line infection. Those sorts of issues can make him very sick. Noah was the best quality control supervisor there was. Sometimes he would question me.

"Why are you only opening two alcohol prep pads instead of three?" he asked. Or, "Did you wipe hard enough and count to ten that time?" It was constant and I loved it. He would stare intently at my every hand motion as if I were a famous magician and he was trying to find my slip up and reveal my secret to the world. Good job, Noah.

**

102 degrees Fahrenheit. The fever was quick and made Noah look like a zombie. He laid on his bed lifeless as Paula placed cold hand towels on his forehead. We called the number listed in his medical folder. It was one of those "call when something happens" number to see what a nurse felt we needed to do. After we had called in his status and had a brief conversation, it was decided that he needed to be brought to the hospital. The fact was since he had a central line any possible sign of infection (like a fever) should be acted on immediately in order to administer IV meds. By doing so, the doctors could catch the infection early enough prior to having the bug (bacteria strain) infiltrate his bloodstream. The other end of that central line ended at Noah's superior vena cava (a major blood vessel into the heart). You can imagine how powerful the heart can pump nutrients and oxygen through the entire body via the bloodstream. Now imagine that same highway used by dangerous bacteria strains. It could mean sudden illness throughout the body.

Once we gathered Noah with his necessary medical information and complete medication cache (we kept all of the pills in a lunch bag tote), we drove him to the nearest hospital in our medical center network. It was late at night and we asked a relative to come over to watch the other kids as we made our way to the emergency room. Noah was clearly not his normal self and our concern was to get him treatment right away.

We arrived at the emergency room and checked in with the front desk.

We explained Noah's symptoms and they brought him into triage to check his vitals. His fever was still not budging and we really had no way to orally give him a fever reducer (ibuprofen or acetaminophen) because he had no way to absorb those meds. No intestine equals no absorption. It was complicated, to say the least.

By the time they brought him to a bed, he looked like a wet noodle. He laid on the bed and the doctor rushed over to him. After we briefed the doctor with all of the details, the staff drew blood and they gave him a suppository of acetaminophen to help with the fever. They also brought in IV pumps to connect his bag of TPN we brought from home and IV medicine to get into his system quickly. Then we waited.

After a while, his fever subsided some, but he was still uncomfortable. The lab results returned positive for bacteria and they continued to pump meds through the central line as often times the bacteria will remain in the IV tubing and breed. If they could prevent the spread of the bug and limit it to the tubing, they could sometimes save the precious line. In this case, they were successful.

After several hours, Noah was admitted into the pediatric ward for his continued stay. I was exhausted and Paula was delirious. It was the early part of the morning now and we had a difficult time keeping our eyes open. Noah was asleep and resting well.

This is where my intrigue of hospital cafeterias began. It's not that I love hospital food with a passion or delight in the average coffee they served, but it became a place separate from the room. A momentary escape, if you will. A place to regroup and refresh the eyes from the confines of four small walls. Keep in mind we already spent much time in the hospital with Noah's major surgery just a couple of months before, so we weren't mere amateurs – just not seasoned veterans by no means. No, not yet.

Well, after five days Noah was discharged. Thank you, Jesus. It was a harsh reminder of the shocking events that took place weeks ago. The doctors were able to save his central line, the precious lifeline to his TPN. That was great news! The thought of having another line installed (like a piece of equipment) was a bit torturing. For now, he was good to go. So, with gear in tow (medicine bag, a sack of clothes, and some magazines) we made our way to the minivan for our drive back home.

I didn't miss much time at work because I had a three-day week shift schedule and most of his hospital time occurred on my days off. This was a huge plus. In the real world, as we all know, parents must work and cannot just magically be at the hospital whenever their sick child needed care. Sick and vacation time must be used for these unexpected moments.

It became the ultimate balancing act for our family. This certainly wasn't the only occurrence in Noah's extensive bout with chronic illness we had to face. No, it was constant, persistent, and challenging. It was a blessing that Paula stayed at home with the children. In addition to having mommy home for the kids after school and form all of those wonderful traits in them, we had our very own nurse and caregiver for our sick son at all times.

**

Spring had arrived. Since life in southern California included awesome year-round weather, we could literally be outside any time. Noah was itching to throw the baseball with pops. By now he regained complete overall strength and he desperately longed for that playground fun with his school peers. Instead, his friends that lived in our townhome complex would visit when they were done with school.

Isaac was his best bud. He was in the same grade and he didn't treat him like a weird or strange, sick kid. Isaac was compassionate and amazed at Noah's plight. Noah kept his buddy informed with the latest TPN run rates (because they decreased regularly) and how important it was to maintain a strictly sterile environment around the central site. Isaac's eyes would open wide as baseballs and he was a great listener. The things nine-year-olds can be entertained with is quite funny.

Noah's teacher continued to meet with him at home once a week. We didn't see huge gains in his scholastic achievements, but we knew he was a very bright kid and all we wanted was to be sure he didn't get behind schedule. We hoped that he could return to school soon, but we knew that wasn't realistic with his serious health condition.

At this point near the end of the school year, Noah would miss his return to elementary school. The question was, would he be able to get back to school for the fall. The longer he missed being a part of the routine and normal pattern the more he felt isolated from the kids in his age group. He cherished each moment he had with his buddies at home or at church. But, because he also had his sisters and his brother at home, his social skills were always maintained.

Our other kids had compassion for their brother. Shelby, who was about two years older, had that motherly characteristic towards him. She always asked questions about his health and his bizarre new illness. Noah gladly shared all of the details with her and did so in such a way that made it seem alright to approach him about everything.

Luke, who was about five years younger than Noah, seemed to be the most inquisitive about his brother's condition. Being his roommate, Luke had a front row seat to every evening's medical routine. He was used to the IV pumps working their magic throughout the night, the sterile cleaning tasks we performed in their room, and the ostomy bag mishaps that frequently occurred between midnight and five in the morning. He studied all of the activity that took place like the first-year med student and every now and again asked a question to complete his understanding. Noah obliged with answers that Luke could understand, being a three-year-old child.

"Why do the machines beep Noah?" Luke asked.

"So that I can know there is a problem with it," Noah replied.

"A problem?" Luke said with a curious look.

"Yup. There could be an air bubble in the tube, so the sound tells us we need to fix it."

"Oh. So you can take the bubble out, huh Noah?" Luke said quickly showing that he made that connection.

"Yup," Noah replied with a grin.

Their exchanges were quite cute. The banter between young siblings concerning such serious topics was interesting. Especially how witty Noah was and how he used that great sense of humor. If I could have only recorded some of those great moments.

**

536:22:03

Earlier in the year, we were contacted by a wonderful person over the phone. She called to explain that she was from the Make-A-Wish-Foundation and Noah was offered a wish-granting opportunity. We scheduled a meeting at our home later that week. It was quite a surprise.

The doorbell rang and we knew it was our new friends from Make-A-Wish. Noah rushed to the door and greeted our two guests. They were very kind and couldn't wait to discuss this once-in-a-lifetime dream to Noah. We sat in the living room and began a friendly discussion.

One of the guests asked Noah how he was doing and he explained all of the details to them without hesitation. He described the post-surgery recovery, his many nurses who took great care of him, and how he has adapted to his new illness. They were taken back by his awareness and his remarkable recovery thus far. It was truly remarkable considering all that he had endured and it was amazing to see how well he carried himself through the fire.

"Well, Noah, when you had that life-threatening episode last year and were hospitalized, the staff who cared for you contacted us. They felt that you should qualify for a wish and submitted you as a candidate to our organization." Her grin was huge and she contained her enthusiasm, barely.

"We would like to offer you a dream of your own to select."

Noah's eyes grew large and his smile was priceless. "What do I get to choose?" he asked.

"Anything you desire that is located in the continental US. That is, from the east coast to the west coast. Because of your specific medical condition, we must keep your wish as safe as possible," she explained.

"That's okay," Noah replied, "I can think of a lot of things I would like to do!"

The wish granters, as they are referred to, asked Noah to select something he has dreamed of doing, someone he wanted to meet, experience a place that is magical, or whatever he wanted to do. They also said that if he wanted to meet the President, as many have done in the past, the waiting period was two years. We could see Noah's mind racing already.

"We're going to give you some time to think about it Noah, okay? We will meet again to hear what your wish is." She said.

"Okay. I'll be ready," Noah said quickly.

We thanked them both and walked them to the door. We said goodbye to our new friends. As we hurried back into the living room, we giggled as we huddled around Noah.

"What are you going to wish for Noah?" Shelby asked excitedly.

"Maybe you can ask for the Disney Cruise?" Brooke said.

"How about a rocket ship ride Noah?" Luke blurted out.

"Alright, let's allow Noah time to think about what *he* really wants," Paula answered. "This is his wish and only he gets to decide.

We were tickled. We were dancing. This was the best news we had received in a while and it pumped some new life into our son. With all of the lows he had experienced over the last few months, this was exactly what he needed. And what we needed as well, as parents and as siblings, to enjoy something fun and wonderful with our Noah. The fireworks were dancing in his head. Oh, I could see them. If it wasn't for the brightness shining from the living room lamp and from the bright kitchen lighting, his fireworks would be illuminating the night sky like brilliant shooting stars. *Go get 'em Noah*, I thought to myself.

A couple of weeks had passed since our meeting with the wish granters. Noah had made up his mind with no influence from any of his family members, or friends for that matter. He chose to visit the city that was the backdrop of his favorite movie during that time. What city? Well, New York City. What movie? Home Alone: Lost in Manhattan. Wow! We told him how great his choice was.

We met with our wish granters once again at our home. Noah presented his wish to them and they were very glad to hear his selection. They began to take notes concerning some of the events that took place in the movie. Noah told the tale well and they engaged in a healthy conversation concerning locations, important places, activities, and any other details that would encompass a trip that would bring this wonderful movie to life.

They explained that Noah would not be going on this trip alone, but he would be accompanied by the entire family. The kids began to cheer. Since Luke was at the tender age of three going on four, we decided to keep him home with his grandparents. The nature of the trip would require a constant change of venues, various modes of transportation, and schedules that would drive Luke up a wall. We felt that he would be miserable.

They told Noah the arrangements would commence right away and they would try to schedule this trip as soon as possible. It was early in 2003, so the New York heat and humidity was something to avoid, if at all possible. They also would have to coordinate heavily with Noah's doctor and consider all of his medical challenges. Every detail was noted. They had done this so many times before, so it was nothing new to them. No, in this area they were world-class experts.

Before they left, they explained our next meeting would be a send-off party for the whole family (immediate family and other relatives who would like to attend). We were thrilled!

Noah couldn't stop talking about it that night. As we connected him to fluids, our nightly ritual, his eyes danced and in his mind, he had already departed on his Make-A-Wish trip. The pumps were turned on and the noisy chirps couldn't keep him from dreaming big. It was nice to see him delight in something and keep his mind off of his daily reality.

Over the next several weeks, our prayers were to have Noah remain as healthy as possible. We knew there may be a small window of time for this opportunity. Because New York was such a long distance away, it would be detrimental to his health if he were to get sick during his trip. We "what if'd" the various scenarios of unexpected illness while in the Big Apple (because that's what parents do). We rattled off ideas and solutions repeatedly with each other and it only drove us mad.

Part of this process derived from constantly preparing for Noah's days and weeks during day-to-day life. We tried to be ready for the worst and yet hope for the best. It's a crazy way of living, but it also helped Paula and I map out situations before they ever happened – sometimes.

6
AND THEN LIFE HAPPENS

449:04:57

I WILL START BY SAYING THAT THE TRANSITION from Noah's urgent and life-threatening situation into a normal and daily family routine was the hardest adjustment to make. My rigorous law enforcement training and six months in the Orange County Sheriff's Academy definitely provided me with skills to endure stressful situations and to fight through many challenges we had faced. After seven weeks of time off, from the day I rushed Noah to the emergency room to the day all of my saved vacation, sick and personal time had expired, I went back to work. It was hard to leave him. No, it was painful.

Several months after my return, working the streets of Southern California, I met with the Police Captain at the end of my eighteen-month probation period. It was a long duration of stress as I tried to continue in my development within the strict guidelines and expectations of this police department, in addition to life with Noah's unexpected medical situation. I wasn't up to par based on conversations I had with my Lieutenant. But, I fought through the challenges and did my best.

It was a very sunny day in May when I was called in from the field to see the brass. I removed my sunglasses and entered the air-conditioned office. As I followed the corridor, my heart raced as I remembered a lengthy conversation I had with our Captain before the weekend. It was in reference to my probation period and my future. I lowered my radio volume as I approached his office.

"Good afternoon, sir," I said with a smile.

"Hey there Ziegler," the Captain replied. "Have a seat."

I agreed and sat in a stiff chair facing his large desk. I tried to read his facial expression while I waited for his next words. The Captain had a friendly demeanor and he tried to speak with a tender delivery, so as to soften the blow.

"You did not pass your probation period, Ziegler. I'm sorry to say that your employment will be terminated effective immediately," He said with a sense of compassion, but with official certainty.

64

My heart sank. This was the dream come true and a way for me to provide for my family in such a way I was not able to do before, both financially and with stability. But, it was over just like that. My mind raced several thousand miles a second. My heart began to slowly raise up through my esophagus and remained lodged at the back of my throat – so it felt. My eyes looked down into my lap as I sat in that chair. *What now?* I thought to myself.

I stood and shook the Captain's hand. I think I cracked a smile somehow as I thanked him for the opportunity. As I walked into the hallway it felt as though I was numb from the neck up; I felt strange. *What now?* I walked downstairs and entered the locker room. I began to remove my uniform and each piece of equipment. My sidearm, an HK USP .40 S&W pistol now unloaded, was placed into the holster and left on the bench. My shiny badge rested beside it. I turned those items and other property over to the training division sergeant, followed by a series of paperwork and a final handshake. I was stunned.

I walked outside the station and carried my personal gear in a large duffle bag. I loaded my car with my belongings and sat in the driver's seat. I sat there for a few long minutes….it seemed like several days. I kept staring at my family's faces in my mind – one after another. I saw Noah's face and his huge smile. I was disappointed in myself. How could I let this happen? What about our medical insurance? What will happen now with all of the hundreds of dollars a month in medical care costs? I had so many questions and had no answers. *God, what is the next move?*

I gripped the steering wheel, tightly. I felt a huge lump rise up in my throat as if it were my heart once again trying to escape this desperate pile of flesh. I could feel the tears well up in my eyes. Noah's face kept filling my mind…his image, over and over. I was extremely frustrated and upset. I reached for the keys and started the engine. The radio instantly resumed playing music because I left it on when I had arrived at the police station parking lot earlier that morning. Immediately I heard a familiar song on the radio; it was Clay Crosse and one of my favorites. The upbeat song filled the sedan as the chorus began. The lyrics were powerful and cut right into my heart:

"You need to know there is a road for you. And not just for tomorrow, but your whole life through…" the words to the song pierced my heart. I sensed time had stopped as if this particular moment meant something remarkable. It continued to play, *"…You need to know with every step you take, consider the choices that you make."*

Wow. It was as though God had whispered directly into my ear. I was dazed and pondered those words. I must have looked like a mannequin in that driver's seat; frozen as I clenched the steering wheel with all of my strength.

I wiped my tears and swallowed my thumping heart back into my chest. I began asking God for direction and for comfort. I knew this would be staggering news to Paula. I was numb and began to drive away from the police station. It wasn't a tender moment or a solemn sense of goodbye. No, it was bitter and felt like rock salt packed into my bleeding wounds. Still, I drove thinking about those words in that song. *There is a road for me and not just for tomorrow, but for my whole life.* What road? I could only see the road directly in front of my life and not beyond the turn.

I made it home, parked on our street, and killed the engine. I must have sat there behind that wheel for a while, staring at our dining room window. I finally found the courage to get out of the car and walk to the front door, gear in tow. Yet, this time it was different. This time, there would be no shift the next morning. No, the gear would be permanently stored.

I opened the door and walked inside. And, without skipping a beat, there was our little patient shuffling over to me as fast as he could.

"Hi, dad," Noah always had a smile when he greeted me. There came Brooke, Shelby, and Luke also.

"Hi, daddy." It was a concert of hellos and I desperately needed that medicine. Those moments can never be taken away from a father. They are kept deep down in the secure chambers of the heart where nothing can destroy them. I had many of these treasures securely hidden away. I made deposits constantly because I had everything a man could want in life; a beautiful, wonderful wife and the best children in the world. There's nothing like a man's family. It's his treasure.

I spent the next several minutes with Paula discussing the details about what took place earlier. She hugged me and began to cry. But, it wasn't for our circumstances. No, she told me she hurt for me because this was my dream and that she knew I was crushed. Her words soothed my pain. Her comfort and compassion were like sweet honey to my lips and softness to my ears. I knew we would make it through this together. Little did I know we would lean on each other so many times through this long journey ahead. We experienced some serious crisis moments and difficult life issues, but who doesn't? It was a foreshadowing of things to come. Or, at least more storms we would face. This was merely our training ground in our present for serious battle in our future.

**

427:00:45

June had arrived. This meant that Noah's Make-A-Wish trip was at hand. It was a wonderful time for our family to enjoy something positive after recent events. For Noah it was a breath of fresh air to his fatigued lungs, so to speak.

Our friends at Make-A-Wish contacted us and said the wish party would take place at our local Dave and Buster's restaurant. It was scheduled on a Saturday in June and held in a private room was reserved just for us. The atmosphere was exciting. The private dining room was decorated with colorful balloons, wild streamers and other wonderful decorations. We were very impressed and Noah's face lit up like a full array of Disneyland fireworks. Pop, pop, Kaboom!

We were handed an envelope with all of the wonderful tickets and events they had planned for our family to enjoy. The itinerary was spread over five days in exciting Manhattan, New York. We were also handed a very large amount of cash tucked inside an envelope. This would pay for all of our meals, tips, taxi rides, and other miscellaneous items we needed. Overall, it was a very generous package that some incredible company had unselfishly donated for Noah. I still get emotional thinking about how amazing it must feel to give to a complete stranger, a child no less, an enormous life inspiring event in the form of a Make-A-Wish dream. It was perfect and touched our hearts. I hoped that one day I could do the same for others.

We stayed for a while in our private party and discussed the upcoming NYC trip with our parents and with Paula's sister Yvette, who also attended the event. Noah was dazzled with the maps and brochures of all those exciting places he would visit. His dreams would soon become realities and he deserved every ounce of it.

The party concluded and we thanked our wish granters with big hugs and warm smiles. They also gave the kids Dave and Buster's loaded game cards to play their hearts out. Noah, Shelby, and Brooke ran away like bandits fleeing from the scene of a crime and headed towards the game area. We walked around with Luke and helped him play exciting video games. Since he was only four, we decided to keep him in the care of Grandma Romie and Grandpa Mike during our upcoming trip. He didn't seem to mind, but how much could a four-year-old really understand about NYC?

That entire evening was filled with a buzz of the trip. The air was filled with electricity and Noah couldn't wait. There was chatter about the Statue of Liberty and millions of cabs running through the busy streets. We tried to paint a picture for the kids based on the movies we had seen and of course through Noah's favorite movie that inspired this trip.

We ended the night with the same routine of IV connections and

TPN/lipids. I believe Noah slept very well that night. I'm convinced that he dreamed about so many wonderful adventures he was about to embark upon; a new land and skyscraper surroundings. No, not visions of sugarplums. Rather, visions of Central Park excursions and FAO Schwartz toy store extravaganzas. I'm sure in his mind it was a blast. *But just wait until we get there son. It will be a life event so big and one you'll never forget.*

7
MAKE-A-WISH: NYC

"Come with me, and you'll be, in a world of pure imagination."
-Willy Wonka

422:04:33

IT WAS A SUNNY DAY IN LATE JUNE and the limousine was parked outside of our townhome. Noah was going to enjoy a first-class ride to the airport. Shelby, Brooke, and Noah were all ready to go. All of our bags were packed and Noah's medications were secured in a special carry-on bag. The wish granters also gave us a soft-walled cooler on wheels with an extendable handle for his six large bags of fluids/lipids. Our doctor made sure we were supplied with all of the appropriate tubings, cleaning pads, gauze, tubing attachments, etc. for our long trip away from the comforts of home. The challenge was to be 3,000 miles away from his medical team and have enough on hand to administer his daily regimen of liquid nutrition without skipping a beat. Organization was paramount.

We shuffled to the limousine and our driver was very helpful with our luggage. He wore a smile and made Noah feel very special. I guess he was impressed with how well the driver handled all of our luggage, open and closed the doors, and did everything with courteousness. We stepped in and sat in the luxurious, stretch vehicle reserved for movie stars (wink, wink). Shelby, Brooke, and Noah thought it was the best car ride. Paula cracked open fizzy soda cans and poured them into short glasses for the kids, ice cubes and all.

Our wish recipient was overwhelmed with the amazing VIP treatment. Noah turned to me with a huge smile and said,

"Dad. You should tip the driver a hundred bucks."

"Oooh, good idea Noah," I replied. Then we both chuckled.

We arrived at John Wayne Airport and our driver helped us unload our bags at the curbside. The skycap service took them from there and checked in all of our luggage, except for Noah's medical roller bag. It was kept close by so that we could be sure to have all of his critical supplies on hand. You know, it would be tragic to have them not make it with our luggage and end up somewhere else. That bag was his life support. No, it had to stay with us at all times.

We were told to make our way to the American Airlines Lounge. This was reserved for pilots and not open to the public. Noah was thrilled yet some more. He was treated like royalty, as we all were.

We had enjoyed refreshments as we waited for our flight. There was a concierge person who met with us and explained that Make-A-Wish handled the arrangements for Noah's trip. She went on to say that we would be given special boarding privileges before any other passengers. All of the kids were smiling ear to ear. It was like they all won a lifetime supply of their favorite ice cream.

After a while, we were escorted to the terminal and boarded our plane. It was a 6-seat wide, single-aisle down the center type of aircraft. We had seats in the same row and the sixth seat was reserved for Noah's medical roller bag. Perfect.

We waited for the rest of the passengers to board and then we began our flight to the Big Apple. Wow. It seemed like it was only yesterday when we first met with the Make-A-Wish staff in our home. Now we were well on our way. Just a handful of hours with non-stop flying and we would arrive at our destination. It was so amazing to be a part of this wonderful organization and witness the dream fulfillment right before our very eyes. Of course, this being Noah's dream made it extra spectacular.

He sat next to me and we have a smooth flight. You could see the excitement coming out of his pores, but also a sense of calm. He really had no clue what to expect, other than what his favorite movie showed and what he was told by the Make-A-Wish team. He knew it was going to be the most amazing trip of his life thus far and for that, I was blessed to share in his moment.

There we were, as the song goes, *"Leaving on a jet plane. Don't know when I'll be back again..."* Although, our trip would last five days and then we would return back home. If we could accomplish our goal, to safely help him make his wish to come true, then it would be something he would never forget.

After we landed and gathered our gear, including Noah's medical rolling bag, we scrambled into the terminal and looked for our driver near the luggage zone. Once we had our luggage and met our driver, we were led to our second limousine. A thirty-minute ride into downtown Manhattan brought the excitement to a heightened level. Noah, Shelby, and Brooke were glued to the windows gazing at the passing skyscrapers lit like Christmas trees at night. It was electric and fantastic.

Our driver parked in front of our hotel: The Doubletree Inn, right smack in the heart of Times Square. Whoa! It was like we were stars in a motion picture and Noah was cast for the leading role. We made our way, luggage in tow by a hotel attendant, to the front desk. After tasting the wonderful chocolate chip cookies handed out while at check-in, we were informed that there was an error with our reservation. It seemed that our suite was taken by someone else. We explained that this was Noah's Make-A-Wish trip and they immediately offered us an upgrade to the Presidential Suite for the first two nights. We looked at each other and felt like royalty.

The elevator climbed the length of the high rise building and arrived at our level. "Ding," the doors opened and we walked down the hall to our special suite. Drumroll, please…Tada! The door was unlocked with our VIP key (wink, wink) and we were in awe by how impressive the suite was. *So, this is how important people live*, I thought. We all hurried from room to room and the "oohs" and "aahs" were sung in unison. The window views from every room overlooked the Times Square area below at W. 47th St. and 7th Ave. All of the brilliant flashing marquee and advertisements were like fireworks across the sky.

We felt like we were on top of the world. In a way, we sort of were. I turned to my son,

"We made it," I said. "How does it feel, Noah?"

"I'm hungry," he quickly replied.

"Alrighty. Let's go get some food."

So, we fly from one coast to the other, spend half an hour in a limousine, get to our four-star fancy hotel, and our first meal was…Sbarro Pizza. Yeah yeah, I know. This is the same food you get at the local mall, right? Sure it is, but I'm telling you it was probably the best pizza we had in a long time. We all joked and laughed at the table as we ate. We all shared reasons to explain why the pizza tasted so good. Was it the water? Or, the special ingredients only available in NYC? We all got a kick out of that one.

It was about midnight and we all were exhausted but spent a little while strolling around the streets. We still had some nervous energy to expend. The night was very humid and it felt like 80 degrees. If this was any indication of how the weather would be, we would have to keep a watchful eye on Noah. He didn't do well with heat and dehydration would easily crush his body in a flash. Since he basically didn't have a small or large intestine, he couldn't simply drink fluids to hydrate properly like most others. This would be a difficult challenge for us. We just hoped that he wouldn't end up sick in the local hospital because they may not have the expertise to care for him.

We got back to our grand room and we felt like cement bags that could barely move. Still, the energy of being in the Big Apple was electric. We settled everyone into bed, including the star of the week who was connected to his nightly infusion via portable CAD pump. Paula and I turned off our grandioso master bedroom lighting and enjoyed the bright glow of the NYC lights outside of our huge panoramic window. We let out a collective sigh…we finally made it.

**

We were reminded that our bodies lived in a time zone three hours behind when the telephone rang at 8:00 AM – Eastern Time. I staggered around the king size bed to locate the phone in my strange but royal surroundings.

"Hello? Yes," my voice cracked. "Oh, hello Sergeant. Okay, we'll be ready. Thank you."

Sometimes a completely wonderful, yet unexpected moment occurs that enhances an already magical time. A connection through a close friend of the family told us a couple of weeks before our trip that he would try and do something for Noah while in NYC. Well, that check was just cashed. He coordinated a personal tour with two detectives from the New York Police Department Counter-Terrorism Unit. Wow is right! That was so cool. We had to be ready to go in about an hour's time and meet them down on the street in front of the hotel.

We quickly squeezed our jet lag and tiredness out of our bodies and met the detectives on the street. There they were in a blacked out, very large unmarked Ford Excursion. We made our introductions and climbed inside. Like in a hit crime movie, the detectives spoke with a heavy New York accent (no really, they had accents) and asked Noah what he would like to do first. They went on to outline the itinerary scheduled for the next few hours.

Noah decided to head over to the NYPD helicopter hangar first, located outside of Manhattan. Since there was thick vehicle traffic clogging the roadways, the detectives decided to drive in the shoulder with police lights a blazing (no sirens) to safely pass the commuters. It was way cool! Noah felt like he was royalty or something. During the car ride, they told him stories of what they prepare for and typically encounter on a daily basis. Since 9-11's terrible attack, the awareness levels of the local law enforcement bureaus were heightened.

After several minutes in the SUV, one of the detectives pointed to a random building in the distance that looked somewhat abandoned.

"Hey Noah, that's our office," he said with caution in his voice. "Now, you must not tell anyone. Okay?"

"Oh wow, I won't say a thing," Noah promised. It felt like we were with R2D2 holding such sensitive information that could bring down the Empire.

We spent the next hour or so with the NYPD Aviation Unit and some helicopter pilots. Noah sat in the cockpit of a chopper wearing the pilot's helmet and all. He toured the facility and learned about some of its history as well as the special diving bureau's importance. They capped off the tour with a low flying helicopter "fly by" with sirens screaming. It was a stellar grand finale for Noah.

Next was an early little lunch at Coney Island's Nathan's for their one of a kind hot dogs. The detectives parked the SUV on the sidewalk (why not?) and gave Noah more red carpet treatment. The dogs were delicious and were worth the extra drive. After a great lunch, it was time to get back to the city and end our special time. It was a short burst of time spent with our new friends and, like all fun times, had come to an end.

We exchanged our goodbyes and expressed our heartfelt appreciation for their generous act and kindness. We reminded them both that this trip will make special memories for Noah, for our family and we would never forget this. They gave Noah a special patch worn by personnel in their unit and wished him well through his journey. Noah's grin was mighty big as he waved goodbye and watched them drive away.

We spent the rest of the day with a volunteer tour guide who worked with Make-A-Wish foundation families. He showed us by way of walking, bus & subway some of the local sites and tastes. Noah handled the hot & humid weather pretty well, but it made him (and all of us) fatigued by the early evening. Our time ended with our friendly & personal tour guide. We will always remember Sam and his stories of growing up in this wonderful city. Noah was wiped out as we arrived back at the hotel. But, the instant beautiful surroundings of the Presidential Suite seemed to work its magic. We prepared him for his nightly infusion and made sure he was okay. He really enjoyed the first day of this great trip.

The next three days included sites of the Statue of Liberty, Battery Park, Chinatown, Little Italy, and some souvenir shopping. We ate, we laughed, and we took pictures of everything we saw. One of the days we saw the Lion King on Broadway. It was amazing. Noah, Shelby & Brooke were enthralled with the live singing and theatrical stage presentation. The emotion of the story was played out so very well and we didn't want it to end. I could see the enjoyment in Noah's eyes and in his facial expressions. During the play, he didn't think about IV feeds or concerned about his missing intestines. No, he was transferred temporarily into a state of bliss.

All he had to be mindful about was capturing every wonderful detail right before his eyes.

We walked out through the lobby of the theater afterward and picked up a musical CD of the performance and a full-color brochure. Souvenirs were nice to bring home.

A taxi ride from the theater brought us to Rockefeller Plaza where we sat in the outdoor atrium (this is where they have the ice skating rink in the winter). We had a terrific menu of lunch items to select from and it was Lobster for me. Noah and the girls got a kick out of the bib placed around my neck in preparation for my surf and turf. My delicate taste buds were not disappointed. We sat there comfortably and enjoyed every second that slowly crept by. We knew it would be one of our last special moments, so we quietly took it all in. Noah's eyes danced in full view of the surroundings as he slowly ate his wonderful, outdoor lunch. You could get a sense of his mental filing system being pleasantly overwhelmed with numerous details. Every now and then he would point out something to us that he captured with his eyes, like a brand new discovery. Man, was it sweet to see his wish come true!

By the end of our stay in the Big Apple, we were exhausted. We spent our last evening casually hitting the sights of Times Square. The girls looked for a cute find and Noah got a kick out of goofy Statue of Liberty sponge hats and obnoxious touristy t-shirts. He would have none of that for himself though.

Instead, he wanted to see what the ESPN Zone had in store for him. We all walked into the cool sports-themed experience and Noah found the area that interested him the most: video games. Now, these were not your typical games you'd find just anywhere. Rather, the type reserved for special entertainment restaurants and fun-zone atmospheres. He was on the hunt for that special one. One by one he would seem interested, but then continue on in his quest. Gotcha! There it was: an interactive boxing game. He turned to me with an enthusiastic smile and said,

"This is the one, dad."

"Okay, Noah. Let's see what you've got." I sounded like a prize fight manager and he was my highly tuned athlete.

We read some of the directions and then Noah grabbed the left and right-handed, separate controls. He gripped them with both of his hands, which mimicked the boxing gloves concept perfectly. He faced the screen (his opponent) and held up his hands in the ready position.

"Now don't let him take you down, son. You've got to be smarter than he is and tougher," I assured him with my best confident-filled speech.

"Alright. He's going down," Noah muttered as he began his intense stare-down with his fierce enemy.

The bell rang for the first round. Noah sort of stood there motionless and uninspiring, to say the least. *Bop. Bop!* The jabs were precise and quick to land on Noah's head.

"Duck, Noah! Keep your head bobbing!" I shouted.

By now, his tongue hung slightly out of the left side of his mouth and his movements were more deliberate. *Swoosh. Swoosh.* His jabs struck the menace square in the face. *Pop. Pop.* Two more to the opponent's head and Noah had more confidence. As the round progressed, Noah was doing his best Ali impersonation: feet were dancing and his body was like a slick dolphin cutting through an ocean wave. Noah ducked down then shot upright. Danced to the left then jumped back to the right. He was doing it. By the end of the round, he was thoroughly exhausted. His arms hung limply by his side and his mouth panted for air. He smiled and wiped the beads of perspiration off his forehead.

"You okay?" I asked.

"Yeah. This is great!" Noah replied without a hitch.

Ding. Round two. Noah wasted no time. He went in for the kill. *Jab, jab, jab,* and a punch to the midsection. *Punch, punch, punch,* and an uppercut to the chin. Boom! His opponent hit the canvas and the audience cheered (the game was pretty realistic). Noah was ready to deliver another barrage of blows to the dizzy fighter. Then, like a madman, the fighter came at him with fury and rage. *Pop. Pop. Pop.* Three punches were delivered to Noah's head. My son danced and kept delivering make believe punches towards the screen. *Left, right, left, right.* Then, *smack!* Noah took another blow to the head and fell to the canvas. We both screamed at his boxer to get up like it would make all the difference. The referee counted: *eight...nine...ten, you're out!*

"Awe, no way!" I said. "I think your boxer could have gotten back into the fight and won."

"Yeah. Me too," Noah answered, as beads of sweat poured down his face. His hands fell limp to his side and he had no more energy left in him. He clearly needed a drink of water...or a couple of gallons at least.

Paula and the girls met us as he finished playing.

"Wow. You look exhausted my son," Paula said as she stared down his tired physique. He smiled and explained how tough the boxing game was. She remembered to check his central line, located on the right side of his upper chest. The Tegaderm dressing was already working its way off from the sweaty skin beneath. This was a problem. We had to get that dressing changed, but more importantly, sterilize the site as soon as we could. An infection could do him in and the quickest way to get sick was through that central IV line.

We gathered ourselves and made our way back to our hotel. We were all sticky and tired from the humid blanket of hot weather outside. Even after five days of living on the east coast, summer thickness, we were not used to it. Noah was pretty much shot. He collapsed on the sofa like he just ran a marathon. His life was sucked out of his body. We handed him a drink and cooled him off with cold water and hand towels. He looked better after several minutes. We prepared and connected him to his nightly regimen of TPN fluids. This would put some additional fluids in him as well. He looked happy as if he had accomplished something on his list of great things to do. It was time to end the trip and get back home. The girls felt the same way.

The next morning arrived much too soon. Paula had a great idea of waking up at the crack of dawn, walk down to the NBC studios, and get a glimpse of her favorite morning TV show: Good Morning America. After she wiped the sleep from her eyes, she quietly made her escape. She went so far as to make a large sign and held it up while in the audience, in hopes of having it be seen all across America. It read: *Visiting NYC for Noah's Make A Wish*. Back home, her mother recorded the show for us to see. It was a special moment and she did it in the name of Noah Ziegler – short gut syndrome patient extraordinaire. Who's your mama?

The highlight was when she took a photo with one of the television show's anchors: Robin Roberts. Thank you, Robin! What a great addition to our portfolio of pictures.

**

The terminal was stuffy and seemed to be consistent with the humid weather outside. Our plane was due to arrive very soon and we were ready with bags in tow. Noah looked and felt a bit tired. I guess the boxing game was the final straw; it dealt him the final knockout blow. Little did we know that Noah was brewing a serious line infection in his weakened body. It commenced a powerful chain reaction of events that became a physical downward spiral.

We stepped into the plane and found our seats. After all, passengers were secured, we taxied towards the runway and gave our attention to the safety measures dictated by the flight attendants. Shortly after, the powerful jet reached its takeoff speed and we climbed sharply into the horizon. The Ziegler clan was headed for the west coast and ready to return to our home. Paula and I were a little nervous. We had a sense that our son was hitting a wall. You know, that barrier between where feeling good ends and pain and sorrow begins. Where a struggle finds life in its simplest form and grows consistently into an organism that overshadows with gloom. THAT wall.

By the next day, Noah spiked a fever. Hospital time. They ran blood tests as part of standard procedure for kids with central lines and the results came back positive for a bug. Man, was this really happening? We felt relieved and bummed at the same time. Relieved because he could have experienced this a few days earlier while in a different state across the country, and with a different team of doctors. I'm not saying he would have received any less quality of care compared to the care back home, but just that it becomes more complicated when physicians handle an unfamiliar patient with odd conditions. Like missing your entire small and large intestine. Now that's an odd condition.

We spent the rest of the day and night with him at the hospital. It became almost normal to be there. In that environment, we felt kind of at ease with the hospital smell and irritable fluorescent lighting. Well, not really at ease, but maybe just more adjusted to these surroundings. It became easier to be comfortable with being uncomfortable.

Noah was treated for his line infection, but they were not able to save it. This meant a new central line had to be placed somewhere else in his body. After about two weeks he was finally released after a new "appliance" was surgically inserted. I always got a kick out of the medical terminology used to describe these devices. Appliance? Really?

Homebound once again to start a fresh, new summer. We had unanswered questions though. Like, where will my next place of employment be? Law enforcement or another field? How would Noah do over the next few years with this strange condition? Would he be one of the few to last fifteen years with TPN infusions before the liver disease comes into play? Or, would he face that terrible path a lot sooner? It made us crazy and we wrestled with these possibilities constantly. Our brains would twist and turn down paths of unending puzzlement. Yet, we knew that God held our very lives, even Noah's frail condition. It was by His hand our Noah was blessed with the survival of that radical surgery, not so long ago. Thank you, God.

We remembered and we stood at the face of the unknown with a strong sense of hope. The kind of hope that is supernatural. The kind that defies the odds. The kind that keeps our hearts close to Him, the One who holds our very lives in His hands. Again, thank you, God.

8
PITTSBURGH: A NEW HOPE

I think some people dance while in fiery trials and some people just burn. I don't know which one I will be, but when it happens please be by my side with a jovial song and bring an extra-large fire extinguisher.

158:02:12

NOAH'S DOCTOR SAT VERY STILL in his chair; he was calm but serious. He searched for the right words to say and then delivered them with caution. It was at this moment when we learned Dr. Duh wanted to maintain the same course of care. He hoped that his very small jejunum (a handful of centimeters long) would grow. Grow enough to achieve some semblance of a normal bowel and have the ability to absorb nutrients. By way of this miracle, Noah could have the TPN fluids discontinued if absorption was restored sufficiently.

We believed his words and his expertise but hoped for a breakthrough soon. We were near the end of 2003 – about a year after his life turned upside down with that life-saving surgery and unexpectedly thrust into short-gut life. But, we wanted more for him. Was that wrong for us to expect something more, something amazing? Yes, we are incredibly blessed to see him every day and we are able to hold him through this tough road. We knew there were those who didn't make it through such horrible circumstances and we had the capability of living with him. Living...with him. Oh, how we all can easily forget to live...*really* live.

Here we were facing these incredible odds. How can the bowel grow? Paula and I discussed these and other medical perplexities for hours. It seemed like we always had these lengthy conversations about Noah's situation and would often end up even more confused. We could not come to any conclusion other than God knew the intimate details of these circumstances – He knew everything. It made more sense to lean on Him for peace. It was difficult, but trusting Him with this complex diagnosis and viewing these heartbreaking challenges through His eyes was peaceful.

**

The IV pump began to scream. There must have been an occlusion in the tubing.

"I'll get the nurse mom," Noah said in an automatic response as he laid in his hospital bed. He reached over with his hand and held the pillow talk device. His eyes focused for a few seconds then he pushed the appropriate button to summons his nurse. Paula peered over the top of her magazine and glanced at the machine attached to the IV pole next to his bed. Noah was admitted for an infection in his IV line....again. His fever was somewhat low grade, but we moved swiftly when we noticed the visible signs of sickness moving in. The IV pump was administering antibiotics in his central line. The nurse walked in and cleared the occlusion in the tubing and reset the pump.

"You need anything, Noah?" She was kind and attentive. "Some water with ice chips?"

"Sure," Noah said.

"Mom. Anything for you?" The nurses would always ask us if we needed anything as well.

"No thanks. I'm fine right now," Paula was content at the moment.

It was a routine conversation that repeated in our lives far too many times. We became professional patient parents in a strange sense. The pay was not that great and the benefits were less than stellar. You see, we didn't earn vacation time or get to plan a special week or two out of the year to escape reality. No, there wasn't a casual Friday, but we could wear just about anything we felt comfortable in. There were no promotion levels to achieve or corporate ladders to climb as well. And the hours...geez, terrible! Sometimes 24 hours a day, non-stop.

Noah didn't care about things like something to drink or read when he was admitted for these episodes. Typically, he was so sick with a fever, or pain in his stomach (caused by a twist in his duodenum and small bowel – called an ileus) that he focused on his discomfort. This time, it wasn't so.

Paula and I became very familiar with the hospitals where Noah was regularly treated. They became his second home and the staff became his second family. The most common facility was about twenty-five minutes away from our home and it was a smaller hospital. The pediatric ward was able to treat most of his basic illness needs, like a bacterial infection in his line or a dehydration episode caused by his lack of large intestine and very low absorption (the weather had a lot to do with one). When he faced more serious issues, he was taken to the large facility located in Hollywood,

California ("Sunset" as we knew it because it was right off of Sunset Blvd). That was about an hour away. A couple of times he went to the Bellflower facility and it was about a forty-minute drive from home.

After another two week stay at his *Chateau de Hospitalet*, Noah was cleared for home. We packed up his things, which included his favorite VHS movies and any additional fun items we may have picked up at the gift shop, and made our getaway. Homebound and en route. Noah enjoyed those rides home and we often had the window down to let the warm, Southern California wind gently brush up against his face and his through his hair.

By now, the end of summer was approaching and we tried to accomplish as much as possible with the kids. Trips to the local beach were only six miles, an easy drive, and we made that a regular event. Shelby and Brooke maintained close bonds with their girlfriends and kept a constant state of normalcy. Even when the storms came with hospital stays, they always kept in close touch with their dear friends. Luke was so young that he seemed to be concerned only with a video game his brother happened to be crushing or he played with his favorite toys. That is, crushing in the sense that Noah was killing it or defeating the game – you know.

Noah, well he had his best friend, Isaac, over almost every day. We all lived in the same townhome complex and we were close friends with their family. Isaac had two brothers and two sisters, so our kids always played together and had a blast with them. We also attended the same church, which was a very short drive as well.

By the end of summer, it was time for the youth group's camping trip. Our church was very large and had a wonderful youth program for all ages. Noah really wanted to go, so Paula and I had discussed the complicated intricacies of sleeping in a tent with all of his medical gear and medicines. Yeah, we were a go for launch. We planned for the worst and hoped for the best. The goal was to get Noah to that camping site and keep him living life as before his illness. The girls were also a part of the fun and Luke stayed with family members.

The first night was tricky. The trip would last for only a weekend, but it would be plenty of time to explore nature with medical equipment and constantly monitoring his care. The most difficult task was managing his IV fluid maintenance since it was still administered over twelve hours and with two large pumps attached to an IV pole. Not the best equipment to have with you during your family camping trip. No matter. It was quite an experience!

Where else could one enjoy the abrupt beeping alerts and the soothing mechanical sounds of machines running through the calm evening? Under the midnight sky littered with stars a twinkling, there we were nestled together in one big tent. It was tricky but well worth it.

Noah felt a little – no, a lot uncomfortable toting that large pole around the other kids from the youth group. There must have been at least fifty other campers there from our church. He decided to remain in the tent while connected, which kept him rather isolated for those twelve hours. Hey, I totally got it. We ran his fluids from 8:00 PM to 8:00 AM so that he could be up and around with his pals in the morning. It worked out well and it was very important to him. He wanted to make sure he created a normal life pattern and as close to the one he lived before his calamity.

By this time, I returned to the workforce. I ran into a buddy I had worked with five years earlier, while at our church one weekday. I clued him in on how I had lost my job and how Noah had been very sick. He was amazed and was moved with compassion by what he heard. Bryan, who was sent by God, hooked me up at a company where he was a supervisor. They needed one person to fill a void and I was their man. Maybe it wasn't the exact job opportunity I was looking for, but during times of duress, any blessing is huge. HUGE.

Now keep in mind, it was the end of summer and I was working at my brand new job. I had your typical Monday through Friday office hours schedule and had to learn a new industry: commercial and residential lighting. I worked directly under Bryan and we had that groove going in the office. It seemed like we never skipped a beat. Just like our last place of employment, we worked very well together. He paired me with Ben, another great friend I had worked with at the same previous company where Bryan and I were colleagues. *Hmmm, seems like a reunion here.* Needless to say, I felt very comfortable and welcomed by my new employer.

Over the next several weeks, we noticed Noah's overall health begin to change shape. I mean, his frequency in hospital visits became alarming and his liver numbers (monitored by continuous blood work) slowly became elevated. He also had many run-ins with his ostomy bags. They continuously leaked at all hours of the day. Those times when we heard him call out "Daaaad" at 2:45 AM, we both knew what that meant. If there was no beeping pump alarm, it meant that he either wasn't feeling well or that he started getting that moist sensation in his bed from a leaking bag. Keep in mind that this was liquid fecal matter…poop…excrement. Poor little guy.

The days became longer it seemed. Noah's daily needs stretched the hours a bit more. There were so many new issues that arose, it became constant monitoring of his health.

Paula was the best manager of his health care. Her dedication was fierce and her motherly love was the solid foundation behind it. She was either on the phone with a member of the doctor's office, ostomy care, home nursing team, medical insurance, social programs for any assistance, education professionals, and more. When she wasn't on the phone, she was organizing all of his medical supplies, taking him to his medical appointments, making sure he met with his home-based teacher and monitored his central line site (any dressing issues or signs of skin irritation). I guess you can say she was the most important person in his life when his health mattered. He just didn't realize it. It was her passion and drive that really helped him to keep going.

Another interesting exercise was keeping him clean. Now, he wasn't a dirty child. Rather, it was the importance of maintaining a clean central line site to prevent infection. The part that concerned us the most was how to bathe or shower him while water-proofing his IV port. You would think there would be one of these "kits" thrown in with every monthly shipment of ostomy products. I mean, they provided special adhesives to keep the base tightly on his skin, adhesive remover to break the impenetrable bond that the adhesive created (does anyone else find humor in that?), custom openings to mate with his stoma, all sorts of sizes in bags, etc. Why not invent, create, design – take your pick, a watertight seal to work with all various central line sites. His was located on his chest, so do we wrap seventy-two layers of plastic wrap around his torso? Yup, tried that – didn't work. How about taping plastic squares onto his skin to cover the area? Yeah, that leaked too. *Now stand still son. I'm going to spray a polymer-based silicone heated to your body's temperature so that the seal can be semi-permanent, but not adhere to your top three layers of skin cells.* It seems like we always tried to come up with inventive ways to overcome that obstacle.

Another type of threat we faced was a brutal infection. Whether IV line, skin or topical or those nasty internal infections, any one of these obstacles proved to be a worthy opponent. And when you have a child missing his entire small and large intestine, the last thing you need is a whopping infection to contend with. Well, it was always a concern. Once during a hospital stay, the staff reminded us that these types of infections were often the source of serious illness or even death. This weighed heavy on our minds as we navigated through the obstacle course of illness and health maintenance. There was always something lurking just around the corner.

**

12/31/03. It was almost time to ring in the New Year. Except there were no firework explosions, party favors, or celebrations to enjoy. Noah was in the hospital yet again and was admitted at the large hospital in Hollywood – Kaiser Sunset. He had a liver biopsy performed the previous day by his GI doctor to measure how much damage existed (caused by the daily TPN and lipid infusions). Apparently, his clotting factors were very low and he had bleeding episodes from his nose and his stoma (often visible through his ostomy bag). It was determined that he was at stage three liver failure. This was terrible news.

As a result of the liver biopsy, a hematoma episode developed in his abdomen just above his liver. That meant internal bleeding. The scan revealed the bleed to be the size of a softball and he was getting blood infusions to maintain his levels. The severity of his liver problems began to manifest in a critical situation. Time was not on our side. He was scheduled for surgery the following day to resolve the problem. He faced yet another surgery, although much easier than his twisted-gut issue over a year ago. Our nerves were on extra high alert.

Here we were facing a new year of challenges for Noah's health in 2004. How would this year be for him? With the dark cloud of growing liver issues and bleeding episodes, it looked like a year ahead filled with storms and trials. More storms and more trials.

We held on to hope constantly. We learned to encourage our young Noah and remind him that we would always fight for him and be by his side no matter what. Rather than be frozen or paralyzed by the circumstances he faced, we pushed through the despair and into hope's existence. We also reminded him that God created him so wonderfully and with great complexity. We called upon God for help and we knew His presence was real.

I would often tell Noah, in jest, that we should have ordered pollen allergies instead of small intestine twists and short-gut syndrome. As if we were able to place these orders on a menu of life when babies are born. Silly. But, we chuckled through these tough times when those silly moments were available. They were not always there. Sometimes in its place, there was pain, suffering, and white-knuckle desperation. Have you ever felt this?

Paula and I left his room and told him we would be right back. It was almost midnight and it was time to grab a few snacks for the room – New Year's Eve, ball-dropping style and get a mental break from the dreary hospital setting. We drove to a nearby convenient store and wandered the aisles in the hunt for chocolate cake treats and the like. One of our favorites was the infamous Hostess Snoballs. Yeah! A pink coconut spongy-shell that tightly covered round, perfect chocolate cake and crème-filled delight. We scored. We made our way back to the car and sat in the parking lot for a few minutes. It was now 12:05 AM. We wished each other a happy new year and kissed. We couldn't believe we were actually in a parking lot at a Hollywood 7-Eleven store with Noah in the hospital again. To our left, a car with a driver who looked like a shady character. To our right, a homeless looking individual asked for handouts. The setting was depressing, to say the least. It was far from a romantic spot on top of a scenic overlook, atop the hills high above the twinkling city lights. We joked about how we had spent many major holidays in the hospital with our son, up until this point in his medical journey. Add this one to the list: New Year's Eve in the parking lot of one of America's favorite convenient store. Nice.

We had the pleasure of reuniting with someone while at Kaiser Sunset. A doctor we had met during Noah's intestinal surgery in 2002. Her name was Dr. Nanjundiah and she was brilliant. No, really....brilliant. Was it a coincidence? Not at all. It was all part of an incredible plan and we had no idea at this point.

She remembered Noah like he was her own patient. She recited the details of his condition and it impressed us. Here it was about a year later from that November 2002 day and she recalled those vivid details stored in her memory bank. Then those words came out of her mouth, like a soothing medicine on an aching wound,

"You know mom and dad, they do intestinal and liver transplants in Pittsburgh Pennsylvania." It sounded like a fairy tale. One that we've never heard before. Almost like a forbidden story kept secret by an overprotective parent of young children.

"Pittsburgh?" We said as Paula and I looked at each other. "We didn't know this was an option."

Dr. Nanjundiah, also a pediatric gastroenterologist, said that she had recommended this specific facility and had transferred patients to Pittsburgh for this type of surgery. We learned that the pioneer of liver transplantation, Dr. Starzl, still practiced in Pittsburgh to some degree. We were impressed and thought this would be worth exploring with Noah's doctor.

"Thank you, doctor," we said to our new friend. "That gives us a sense of hope right now. Where is your office?"

"I usually work from my office in Garden Grove (very close by) and some days at Bellflower," she replied with a smile.

I felt a sense of a calm, nurturing sense about her. She really knew what was going on with Noah and had experience in this field. Outstanding!

We made the decision to change doctors once Noah was discharged and we were back home. You never know what lies around the corner in life. As it has been said, you only see the turn up ahead, but not the road that it leads to. With the current state of critical liver disease upon Noah, we saw this new relationship with Dr. Nanjundiah as being Noah's best chance at navigating through a complex medical situation. She represented a new hope. We scheduled a follow-up visit with her soon after our conversation in Hollywood.

Her office was much closer than what we were used to. Noah liked her and she took to her star patient, as she named him. We brought her up to speed on all of Noah's adventures. She was amazed at how brave he was and at how much we had endured with so many critical episodes. We instantly felt like we were in very capable hands.

Dr. Nanjundiah explained her deep interest in learning the latest about small bowel research and current success rates concerning the transplants performed in the country. Her concern for Noah was that he was at the stage of his liver disease that did not include the luxury of time. She maintained that he should have been recommended for liver and small bowel transplantation several months earlier. We got a sense from her that it had become critical to get the help for Noah that would not just get him healthier, but the kind of help that would save his life.

She told us she would make contact with the transplant team in Pittsburgh, PA and begin making the necessary preparations. We thanked her and walked away from just one meeting holding onto a new hope; it was tangible and burned deep within. It was also overwhelming to think about having your son receive a new organ, well, new organs – especially so far away from home.

On the way home, we asked him how he felt about his new doctor and this new talk about organs. He seemed very open to the idea, even at nine-years-old. Noah was very aware and could understand the details of his circumstances. It was amazing to see such awareness and he didn't seem scared. He felt like this new chance would be a way to stop having these bleeding issues and all other symptoms. We talked about one day having no IV ports, no TPN, no fluids infused overnight and so many other inconveniences that littered his day.

That night we spent the last half hour with Noah going through his nightly ritual. The bitter stench of the alcohol pads became like perfume in the air – you get adjusted to it. The wiping, cleaning, swabbing, & sterilizing steps for his central line were automatic but taken very seriously. We programmed the pump for a new nightly delivery system. We were so ready for a chance to get Noah the help he desperately needed. Would we be able to get on the list for organs soon? How would the next several weeks look? More hospital visits? Probably. Yeah, definitely.

**

158:07:41

March 2004

Noah's bleeding episodes increased and became worse in duration. We were at Kaiser Lakeview, about twenty-five minutes from our home, and he was a frequent resident there due to his ongoing health issues. The latest blow came just after a liver test was conducted through blood work. He was brought in due to a bleed in his stoma and the fluid seeped into his ostomy bag. It was difficult to locate the source of the bleed at home and we didn't want to remove the bag or base too much in an effort to minimize the irritation. We applied pressure to the area as we drove him to the hospital. The blood clotted in his bag and looked like a small organ, sort of like a kidney or something similar. We were very alarmed and asked the doctors to contact Dr. Nanjundiah as soon as possible.

The results were in and one of the doctors we really liked was rounding on him. He was kind and connected with Noah on a neat level. He was concerned – in his voice and in his facial expression. Almost as if he had to deliver some extremely tough news. Yeah, it was quite a pill to swallow. His words were calm as he told us that Noah's liver numbers were very elevated and he was at a point where the only option was organ transplantation. His liver was not recovering well and he strongly recommended that they move to the next step: referral to Pittsburgh.

We knew it was coming. This was no secret. But, the day – the very moment – you hear those precise words, they seem to cut deep into your tissues and settle into the cavernous chamber of our hearts. Reality weighed down on our chest like a sack of bricks. We were numb and a bit uneasy. Yeah, we had insight by Dr. Nanjundiah and that this would be necessary, but it became a sudden reality. Paula and I were stunned and Noah was a bit shocked.

This became something additional to face; a new obstacle to overcome and yet this was by far the scariest one he would face. The questions in his mind swirled, I'm sure. This was not like the more common surgeries that we heard about like kidney transplants. No, this was a whole new world that was kept in secret. It was kept this was only because the world we lived in didn't include people who ventured down this path and we didn't have anyone to share their wisdom from a patient's point of view. This was a direction filled with many unknowns.

I remember leaving the hospital to run a quick errand. While away from

Noah I called my dad. For some reason, it was overwhelming to deliver the words.

"Hey, dad. We're back in the hospital for Noah's bleeding problems. They've gotten worse," I said.

"Oh man. I'm sorry. He's been going through so much lately," he replied.

"Yeah...there's more," I tried to gather my thoughts and communicate, but my long pause was too obvious.

"What is it?" he sounded extra concerned all of a sudden. Probably from my delay and from my flat tone.

As the words fell out of my mouth I began to sob.

"Noah needs...a...transplant...now...," my words were staggered. I was barely able to drive as rainfalls fell from my eyes.

"What?!" My dad was taken back.

"Yeah, the liver numbers are very bad and his eyes are getting yellow. It's liver disease. At some point, he will get worse and they are trying to get him to Pittsburgh for an evaluation. This is his only chance. The TPN has just destroyed his liver." I wiped tears from my cheeks with one hand while I gripped the steering wheel with the other. I was officially driving under the influence of heartbreak.

We spoke about the hospital that performs these surgeries and how amazing it sounded. I told him there were others in the country, like the University of Nebraska and even UCLA, but none were as successful as Pittsburgh Children's Hospital.

I called my mom and told her what was going on as well. Every family member was shocked like we were. No one could believe that his health was in such peril. We hoped that Noah could last through the TPN infusions for several years before reaching this state of urgency and illness. Every child responds differently and he was one of those who declined rapidly. Time was now against us. If I could take time and lock it up for at least a few years then release it, I certainly would.

We spent the next few days with Noah as the doctors gave him a variety of meds to help stop the bleeding and get him back on his feet. The blood infusions became a regular thing. Dr. Nanjundiah gave us her best doctor-patient speech about her promise to take care of our son. She was loving and genuine. We knew that he was in the best hands under these circumstances.

She began the process of sending her recommendation to the pediatric small bowel and liver transplantation team at Children's Hospital of Pittsburgh. The detailed documentation, the countless phone calls, and her sense of urgency – she was spot on. Basically, Noah was required to have a complete surgical evaluation performed in Pittsburgh, which lasted several days, and only when completed would he be placed on the waiting list. The waiting list is just that – a list people wait on for a chance to live. If we could be in Pittsburgh within twenty-four hours and make this happen, we would have done so. But, the red tape and formalities take much time. Again, we had very little time.

Despair tried to creep in. It was not invited and definitely unwanted. Still, it's voice disguised by normalcy and a familiar face tried feverishly to make its way into our hearts. We still gripped hope by its wings – I called it white knuckle faith – and believed with an intensity that Noah would get through this. We held on to God and our faith had been tested not too long ago and we were not about to jump ship at this point. Give up? Negative. That was not an option.

**

The kids were all tucked away for the night. It was nearly a week after his most recent hospitalization discharge and the recent days seemed to weigh on us. Paula and I sat up in our bed late that evening. We talked about the details of something that did not take place yet. So many details to explore and so little time. How long would he be on the list waiting for the call? How will we be able to keep the other children in Pittsburgh during this time? How will I keep my current job and be able to be in Pittsburgh as well? So much content to digest. It was like swallowing chunks of steak whole without chewing them; this was nearly impossible to swallow. How will this all unfold?

We discussed these matters for hours that night. All the while the muffled sounds of Noah's pump played in the background. It reminded us of how critical our son's life was; so fragile and delicate. His life was now dependent upon another person's organs. That was a mind-blowing concept.

More weeks had passed and Noah's bleeding episodes continued. They were like mini-gushers and became increasingly difficult to stop. His clotting factors were terrible. We encouraged him through each and every moment while applying pressure to his stoma site. That seemed to be the main culprit of focus, the stoma area. We often would talk about something else in order to keep his mind off of the obvious. He always kept a bright outlook. He was so brave through these most difficult times. We were so proud of him.

By April, his condition grew worse and his skin glowed with a pale yellow tone; so were his eyes – now yellowish in color. His liver numbers were telling the story of a tortured organ trying to hold on for dear life. If we could only see how much damage was done, we could get a sense of how much time he really had.

He was admitted for yet another uncontrollable bleed. Once at Lakeview, it was decided by the doctors to send him over to Sunset. They were better equipped for surgery if he had another hematoma. Paula rode with him in the ambulance. I drove our minivan to meet them in Hollywood.

Our little Noah wasn't doing well. Dr. Nanjundiah was able to cauterize the site and stop the bleed, but we could see the sense of danger behind her eyes. We left the room with her so that we could discuss the situation away from Noah.

"Mr. and Mrs. Ziegler, I'm afraid we are at the most critical time for Noah. I have made the necessary recommendations to Children's Hospital in Pittsburgh and they have agreed to receive him for a surgical evaluation. I will make another call to them right away and let them know we must act now." Her words spoke directly to our hearts and carried a weight with them that felt like a wave crashing down.

We asked so many questions and she had all of the answers. She was on top of this and that made us somewhat at ease. She steered the ship into uncharted waters and had the experience we needed to feel comfortable with her decisions.

We talked to Noah and brought him up to speed. He was kind of happy to go visit a new city, even though it was for a very scary thing. We reminded him that the testing was needed to evaluate his physical capability of handling this important surgery/recovery and to determine his place on the waiting list. We only hoped it would be as short of a wait as possible. He was nervous about the whole process of multi-visceral transplant surgery; it was a mammoth obstacle. We repeated those tender words to calm him: "God is bigger than this situation and He will always be with you Noah."

One other concern Dr. Nanjundiah had was the five-hour flight to Pittsburgh would be very long considering his current state of health. He would be transported via air ambulance, which was a medical Learjet, and she hoped his bleeding would not be a hindrance for the long-distance flight. We had both agreed that Paula would fly with him and I would travel via a commercial flight to meet them at Children's Hospital, across the country.

We made arrangements for Shelby, Brooke, and Luke to be watched during the five-day trip. Our family helped us out with those critical moments when we needed to rush Noah to the hospital and that was a blessing. They stepped in to help during this latest need for this critical evaluation too.

The next day we got the word; we had a green light. The flight was scheduled to leave the very next day and Paula packed her things in a small carry-on bag. Her other belongings were packed in a large suitcase that we both shared. We spoke to our children and made sure they understood how important this was for Noah and that it would only be less than a week before we would return. They understood and were also very brave for their brother. You could see it in each one of them, they quietly cheered for their brother. In their actions and in their devotion, they stood on those front lines with us to support him through it all.

I drove Paula back to Kaiser Sunset because Noah was touch and go with his bleeding issues. It was a very long and emotionally draining day. But, lately, that was all we seemed to experience.

The following day, transport day, I gathered the kids and drove them to see Noah. We spent the time with him laughing and tried to remain upbeat. He remembered his plane trip to New York and how much fun it was, but he still felt excited about flying in a small Learjet.

"Oh yeah, Noah. These are almost like the fighter jets that protect our skies with combat-trained pilots," I said with big eyes.

"Yeah," He said with a chuckle. Noah got a kick out of that.

"But your jet probably won't have missiles and guns. You know, no need for that sort of stuff for medical planes," I added.

"Yup. Not gonna shoot anyone out of the sky I guess," he was quick with a smile and faster with a witty response. He was amazing during this crazy stress.

We said our goodbyes and I told Noah and Paula I would see them the next day in Pittsburgh. The hospital made all the arrangements for my flight and our hotel. We were now on the verge of a huge and significant mark in his fight for health – for life. Sometimes we take for granted our health and rarely do we ever have to fight to get it back after losing ground to a life-threatening illness. We were about to embark on an amazing journey across the country to meet with the most successful liver and small bowel transplant team in the world. In…the…world! We felt like we were about to get a rare chance at receiving a really big blessing…and it couldn't come at a better time.

**

134:00:50

"Thank you," I said to the bus driver as he pulled the lever that opened the hydraulic door to let me out with two large suitcases in tow. I clumsily exited the 28X (Airport Flyer as it was named) and made my way onto the sidewalk in the middle of Oakland, Pittsburgh. It was a busy college town, home to The University of Pittsburgh, also called "Pitt." The campus was spread out over several city blocks and I saw clumps of students busily walking to and from their classes. I remembered the bus driver's directions for my short walk to the hospital. Noah and Paula already had arrived earlier that day.

I walked for three blocks and entered through the northeast entrance, near a busy street. After asking for directions to the pediatric center where Noah had been staged, I finally made my way up several floors and through an older system of buildings joined together. I entered his room and found him on the bed with a big smile and his typical upbeat greeting. There was Paula right by his side. I hugged them both, relieved to finally reach them.

"How was the ambulance flight?" I asked.

"It was long and very bumpy," Paula replied. "The turbulence was bad in spots and we had a stop in Kansas for fuel, but Noah did well. There were no problems for him during the flight. It was just very tight in the cabin with all of the medical equipment and his gurney."

"Wow, Noah," I said to my son with excitement. "Sounds like you had a special flight, huh?"

"Yeah, it was kind of cramped because I had to stay in my bed the whole time. Not like our flight to New York," Noah said with a grin.

The doctors began their assessment with blood work and scheduled Noah for a battery of tests. We had little time to get fully acquainted with our new surroundings, but hospitals are very similar everywhere. The staff was very welcoming and friendly. Our main contact was a GI doctor, Dr. Peters. He was very informative and helped us understand the details of their process of testing and assessment. Noah was comfortable and willing to comply without a hitch.

After a few days, we had the official word. Noah would be the recipient of a small bowel, a pancreas, and a brand new liver. The surgeons said they would have expected to see him several months earlier because his condition was very serious. Because of the advanced liver disease and related physical problems, Noah was placed at Status 1 for his blood and tissue type. It was the highest level a patient could get placed, anywhere in the country. This was serious and we realized how extremely important getting these organs became. Now what?

We were also invited to attend a class for parents with children scheduled for liver and/or small bowel transplant surgeries. The meeting lasted a few hours and there were two other sets of parents who also attended. The class covered many topics including the history of this world-class, successful program. We were amazed at the incredible details surrounding this somewhat rare medical condition and their surgical advancements used to bring a lasting resolution to these children. We were impressed with the program and with the staff's dedication to excellence.

The pioneer of this specialized surgery began this groundbreaking procedure at the University of Pittsburgh. His name is Dr. Thomas E. Starzl and he is a brilliant physician with a big heart. His first transplant patient received a liver and did very well many years later. Over the years, there were groups of patients joining the ranks of those who received liver/small bowel organs and Noah would become part of the third generation of recipients at Children's in Pittsburgh.

At the end of the week, we left the hospital with a game plan and a direction. This all we could hope for. Well, a successful transplant would be nice too. Our stay in Pittsburgh was rather short but filled with training, overviews of care, short and long term post-transplant information and everything else in between.

When we arrived back home and settled in, we had a nervous thought flood our minds. Where would we be when that urgent call for organs happened? *It could be today*, we thought. Our minds played various scenarios of when the surgery would take place. We racked our brains with this and that, constantly churning details of all possibilities surrounding this life-changing event. It was nuts and we were certifiable crazy parents. What'd you expect?

All the while, Noah continued to have ongoing bleeding issues. His liver was not going along with the program and definitely didn't operate on the doctor's timetable. Isn't that funny how we start to think that our internal organs have behaviors as humans do? Almost to the point where we wanted to name them. Huh, the things you do to cope through the craziest of life's storms. Like I said, certifiable.

**

It was now May and all we could do was pray for the call. We were in a dangerous game of pin the tail on the donkey; the tail being a stick of dynamite and the donkey was a block of C4, so it seemed. Days were slow to pass and our desperation grew deeper. You could see the worry in Noah's little face daily. We patched up bleeding stomas, pinched-tight bleeding noses, and got regular labs to monitor his blood counts. His liver wasn't producing hemoglobin fast enough to meet the demands of his bleed episodes. It was constant stress.

We cried out to our Lord and asked for help. The situation required a spiritual intervention. Our church family rallied around us and helped to keep us on this side of sanity.

There's a verse in a song that says, *"Where does my help come from?*

My help comes from You (God). " And we believed with our whole heart and mind that we were in God's most precious and capable hands. He orchestrated countless details from behind the scenes and we could see His hand moving. Sort of like the Wizard of Oz who hid behind that dark curtain and maneuvered the controls to amazing wonders. Except God is the real deal and He held our very lives within his palm.

As human beings made from this crude flesh, we often groan and complain about everything at some point. We were uncomfortable having to witness our son endure these hardships. We hurt with him and for him. We wanted nothing more than to take his place and restore him physically to sound health. Oh, how we can take our health for granted.

Flesh and blood. This is what we are. But, there's a soul that is buried inside and it cries out to live. We heard Noah's soul cry out like a loudspeaker glaring over an unruly crowd, "I want to live!!" We heard it through his eyes – his calm and weary eyes. Weighed down with deep concern, the fear began to penetrate his gaze. But, in between his smiles and happy faces, we knew his will to survive existed at the very core of his foundation.

**

The sunset colored the skies with many shades of orange and scarlet red as we drove right into its canopy. The freeway traffic was moving well and we were almost at Kaiser Sunset. It was one of those heavy and scary bleeds that demanded urgent attention at the big hospital.

"You okay Noah?" I asked as we sped down the freeway.

"Yeah," Noah replied with a towel pinched over his nose and head tilted back. It was almost routine at this point and a little ridiculous to say the least.

We checked him into the pediatric intensive care unit and they began their triage. This had the makings of a long stay. I could cut the frustration with a knife.

Dr. Nanjundiah arrived the next day.

"Hello. How is my star patient?" Her voice was calming and upbeat as usually.

"Hi doctor," Paula greeted her and began bringing her up to speed. Although, we kept in close touch with our doctor over the phone and it was certainly nice to have that open line of communication.

She cauterized his nose and had a look of concern on her face. We've seen that look before. She began to tell us that she made the call to Pittsburgh and alerted them of his dangerous symptoms that continued to worsen. The intense bleeds, combined with the declining liver, were a great cause for alarm. The Pittsburgh transplant physicians made the decision to transport Noah to their hospital and wait there for the call for organs. Paula and I looked at her with huge eyes and knew this was now becoming very serious. We were thrust into DEFCON 2 and the plan was to get Noah to Pittsburgh as soon as possible.

"Mom," said Dr. Nanjundiah, "Will you be going with Noah to Pittsburgh?"

"Yes," she replied without skipping a beat.

We only had this one option. There would be no possible way both of us could be there with him. I had to stay behind and work. You know, keep the income coming in and maintain the insurance. It was a very tough decision to have Paula, mother, wife, my best friend, be sent away into the great unknown with respect to timelines and Noah's future. The family unit would be separated, stressed, and stretched through the strenuous times ahead.

"You need to go home and pack a bag for your trip," said the doctor. "We need to make the flight arrangements for tomorrow." We agreed and asked Noah what he needed from home, aside from the basics of clothing and such. He was ready. His mind was already made – he will get this surgery and get better. He wanted to move on physically and be a normal kid once again. It was his vision, like the tale of Pinocchio, except Noah wanted to be rid of the illness of short-gut syndrome and liver disease. Didn't Pinocchio get to be a real boy in the end? I think so.

For Noah, he wanted to sprint in the park and catch long football passes without wearing medical equipment on his back. He wanted to run and not get weary. He hoped for the days when he would not have to hear those annoying mechanical pumps churning through the night. He desired the day when he could eat a banana split and pay for it only with a bad tummy ache. Just a taste, again. Just to dance through the meadows and cut loose the chains of bondage from this oppression.

He hoped and he also believed. This was his time. If it meant he had to be away from his siblings and away from his dad, it would be tough but he would pay that price in order to live again. Oh, to live again. How we forget what it truly means to live.

A short time before this latest trip to the hospital, Paula and I had discussed who would care for Shelby, Brooke, and Luke. The plan looked good on paper so we asked my father and stepmother. They gladly accepted the role of caring for them while Paula was away with Noah in Pittsburgh. Since they lived in San Diego, the drive was a short two-hour jaunt from our home. My understanding of Noah's waiting period meant that I would be very touch and go; I was on high alert, stand-by as well. My employer was gracious enough to allow me the time needed when I was called to travel and be with him on short notice. There was no feasible way I could keep our children with me back home knowing all of this. After all, with my emotional strain and possible urgent departure, we believed the kids really needed to be with others during this difficult time.

The bags were packed and we drove Paula back to Sunset later in the afternoon to be ready for a very early departure. I carried the luggage as Paula held onto Luke's and Brooke's hand, while we walked through the brightly-lit hospital hallway. Shelby helped by carrying her mother's small tote bag that contained many snacks and goodies. It was becoming surreal at this point. I knew it would be extremely hard to say our goodbyes.

We spent an hour or so with Noah and Paula. We laughed about funny things Luke was saying (he always had something colorful to say). We reminded the girls and Luke that they would be in very good hands and we would be able to speak with them as much as they wanted. The question that burned in our conversation was, when would they return? We had no significant answers. This would be a season with an unknown conclusion. We literally could wait for a week and receive that call for organs or wait several months. I didn't know how much time Noah's body had left, but it was obvious that he didn't have the luxury of months.

It was time to leave. Shelby and Brooke hugged Noah tightly and Luke smiled for his big brother as he wrapped his arms completely around him. It was a precious moment and a bit overwhelming for the girls. They were old enough to understand the element of danger Noah now faced. The kids hugged and kissed Paula tenderly. She began to tear up and tried to pour that last bit of love into her wonderful children. There's nothing like a mother's love for her children. It's sweet, powerful, and so beautiful! I gave Noah a big hug and told him I was proud of him.

"Take good care of your mother, son," I said with a warm smile. "I will come out to see you very soon."

"I will, dad," Noah said.

I embraced my bride, my true love. This was hard. I needed to be by her side through this mess, but I was not able to. Life is very unfair. I wanted to make this all go away and walk Noah and my family safely into the peaceful sunset. But not today. Where's the fairy tale ending? Where's the part where the end credits roll upwards on screen playing a light-hearted song and you just feel awesome? Man, this was tough to bear!

"I love you," we both said to each other. The tears fell and sometimes that's the poetry of love that expresses devotion. It was proof, not that we had to show the world, but it was a consequence of our love for each other. I was crazy about her.

"Bye, baby. I'll talk to you in the morning," she said.

I took Luke by the hand and walked with the kids back through the hospital. As we walked back to the minivan and climbed in, I told them how fast this week would pass and Noah would be getting his transplant soon. We all were crying and the ride home was solemn. I tasted hope in the midst of sorrow. I could see images of Noah jumping for joy and our family reunited once again. I just didn't know when these images would manifest into reality. There was hope and we held onto that with both hands tightly.

When there was no one there to pick up the pieces from our shattered hearts and despair tried to become a permanent resident within our family, we cried out. We held up our hands to Him who sits on the throne of grace and we asked for mercy. For in those moments where our pain seemed to have shattered our hope, God's mercy and grace saved the day. That's what He does.

9
HOSTAGE

Life just isn't fair.
It sure is a lot of wonderful things, but fair it is not.

81:05:38

THE FLUORESCENT LIGHTING IN THE LARGE ROOM hurt Paula's eyes. It strained and added to the headache she was fighting. She rubbed her forehead with her fingers, massaging the pain away from her head. She sat at Noah's bedside in the Intensive Care Unit at Children's Hospital of Pittsburgh waiting for a doctor to arrive.

Finally, one of the interns walked over to them. The huge room contained at least fifteen beds, each one only separated by a curtain. The headboards were set against the wall and the foot of each bed pointed towards the center of the room. Unless the curtain was drawn every patient's bed was visible to everyone, which made privacy something you had wished for.

"What can I do for you?" a very young doctor greeted Paula at the foot of Noah's bed.

"Hi, doctor. I just wanted to know when my son will be getting his blood infusion," Paula was his best advocate and always expected the best from the medical staff. She also asked for the day's game plan.

"We are waiting for the delivery from the lab. It shouldn't be too much longer," she answered then turned to our son. "You okay Noah?" the doctor asked with a smile.

"Yup. Just want to feel better," Noah wasn't shy about telling the staff how he was doing.

"We'll fix you up in no time, Noah." The intern turned and walked away.

"I'm sorry you're not feeling well Noah." Mom's words were soothing to him. It was like a gentle breeze on a warm, summer day. "I'm here and will not leave until you are better." Paula sat up in his bed right beside him. She ran her fingers across his long bangs and continued to reassure him that he would feel better.

It was now three weeks since his medical transport brought them to his temporary home. Sure, it wasn't the likes of a fancy, five-star Marriott Hotel by the sea, but they knew exactly how to keep our son alive.

The ICU was busy as Paula sat with Noah for hours at a time. She had a room at a nearby hotel, compliments of the insurance company, and she used its shuttle service for transports to and from the hospital. If there were private rooms with an extra bed by Noah, she would probably sleep there more times than not. The limited space was cramped and made it difficult to sleep overnight in the upright chair provided.

There was no call with organs and no way to even contemplate when it could occur. The problem was growing and becoming more and more serious. Noah was having so many complications with his liver and the bleeding issues continued daily. Sometimes multiple bleeds in one day. He became jaundice – yellowish tones in his skin color appeared over time. He was definitely so much weaker than when he had arrived.

"I'm going to step out and grab some coffee, Noah," Paula leaned over him and said quietly.

"Okay, mom." He was tired from another eventful, medical crisis-filled day in the ICU. It became the status quo.

She walked through the large, wide open room with her eyes forward as she passed all of the other children's beds and stepped through the door. There was a flood of emotion that waited to meet her eyes if she were to unexpectedly catch a glimpse of another suffering child. As she made her way into the elevator, she glanced at the time: 7:30 PM. The day passed by like cold molasses and it was only coffee that could help her stay alert now.

The pre-summer air was warm, but still cool enough to be comfortable. The local Starbucks was only two blocks away and made for an easy walk downhill right into the main street area of Oakland. It was a college town with a hub of restaurants, fast food, and coffee joints. She pulled out her phone and called me. She always made sure I was informed with updates; at least two or sometimes three times a day we spoke.

"Hey, baby. How's Noah today?" I asked her. This was the first time we had heard each other's voice that day.

"He's hanging in there Rog. He needs blood infusions frequently and his liver is not looking good. The surgeons are hoping for organs very soon so that he can be strong enough for the surgery." Her voice was flat and she sounded beat. "He keeps asking for you."

"I miss both of you so much," I replied as my heart sunk to my feet. "This is the most difficult time for all of us. You know, being so far apart. The kids have been in San Diego for a few weeks and I miss them too.

How are you holding up?"

"I'm okay. I just hate being so far away from you and my other babies," said Paula. "I just hope Noah can get better soon and we can come back home…and be a family again."

I held the cell phone as I stood outside my office building. I had about thirty minutes left in my day. I stared into the surrounding buildings and into the sky, trying to find the words that could make it all better for my sweet wife. But, without a warm embrace or without a tender kiss on her lips, my feeble words were lifeless. I could almost hear falling tears slowly trail down her cheeks. Like an avalanche toppling down a snow-covered mountain peak. Yeah, there were tears alright. She was trying to be strong and she certainly was, but her heart was breaking for more than just Noah's condition. We both had ailing hearts that were crushed by these circumstances.

She bought her coffee and began her walk back up to the hospital, still on the call. We ended our conversation as she reached the main doors of the facility. We spoke a few hours later. Usually, our last call was made around ten or eleven each night before she collapsed on her bed.

Her nights typically ended with a hotel shuttle ride back to her empty room about two miles away. The Residence Inn, where she lodged, was a recharging station – not a home. Even during those late night hours, it became nearly impossible to rest and unplug her mind from the day's events. She fought heartache constantly, being on the front lines of warring with our son. The battles were intense as she engaged with his illness and waged war against time.

Only the heart of a mother can have the capacity to fully comprehend the depth of love for her children. No one else can understand the breath and life of sacrifice. No one. And Paula was no different. Her heart was strapped to her chest because each time she held Noah's limp hand or gazed lovingly into his weak eyes, her beating organ was stressed and seemed like it was about to explode. I imagined it was strapped externally to her sternum because it allowed a medical professional the access to pound on it in the event of failure. I might be a little dramatic here, but trust me on this one. She was driven by her love for him and not by the support of an automatic sympathetic nervous system. No, it was pure will. When she remained at his bedside, day after day, hour by hour, it took supernatural power to keep her and to sustain her. Yeah, a mother's heart is special and unique. Noah had the best weapon in his arsenal and he had no clue. He had his mother loving him, guarding him, and fighting with him through his toughest moments and through his extreme circumstances.

**

The doctors made their rounds every day. It usually looked like one experienced doctor with tenure followed by a small group of attending physicians. They moved from one patient to another reviewing the illness or medical condition of every child and discussed their previous night's progress or declining status. I understood how they could easily become cold, hard, and lack human compassion on a certain level. It takes a special professional to accomplish the task of keeping sick children alive and little did we know that we had an amazing team dedicated to such enormous feats.

They were our heroes, in the flesh. They didn't wear bright colored, skin-tight costumes to conceal their identity or have flashy names like Master Blaster or Doctor Vroom. No, but instead each one wore a long white coat with a small name badge in most cases. Sometimes they were "in the zone" and didn't seem very approachable, only because they kept so much patient information in their heads at any given time. They worked with fierce passion and moved with purpose throughout the intensive care unit.

Paula shared with me that her mother and Mike (Romie's husband) had booked their travel dates to spend a week with them in Pittsburgh. I was relieved to know that they would be visited by close family. It became increasingly difficult to have Noah and Paula so far away. It was unbearable at times for me, but to think how she was handling this on her own just killed me. My suffering heart was pale by comparison.

May was coming to a close. We quickly learned, as parents waiting for their child's life-saving transplant, that long holiday weekends brought more opportunities for life. Not to sound negative or sick, but the nurses reminded us there was a higher percentage of partying going on during these weekends and the statistics showed an increase of casualties. We were not looking for something tragic to happen, but rather that our very sick child would be healed miraculously.

Our reality was that Noah required a donated liver and small intestine. The only way for this to happen was for someone to have a fatal accident and unfortunately, it had to be a child. This idea was terrible to embrace; it just didn't sit right to us as parents. We could only imagine the horror of losing one of our children in an unexpected tragedy. Our hearts could not bear the thought of having to make that decision, to have our deceased child become a donor. It was a solemn and sobering thought, indeed. And on the other side of that tragic moment was our little Noah, waiting for his moment to live. No, it wasn't fair that someone had to lose their life in order to save our son's. In case we already didn't know – life just isn't fair. It sure is a lot of wonderful things, but fair it is not.

Memorial Day Weekend came and went. There was no call for organs, as they say. Instead, there was more suffering and daily blood infusions for our son. *What would June bring?* We thought. *Could this be the month for everything we had hoped for?*

June began with grandma Romie and Mike visiting Noah and that was a great lift for him. Paula said they had arrived and stayed very close to the hospital. They chose a rental car, so they were able to get Paula out of the confines of the hospital for mental breaks. Her jaunts were short as Noah was just too touch and go with his condition worsening. But, those moments were vital for Paula.

Noah's new visitors sat patiently at his bedside during their stay. They made Noah smile and laugh some. They both knew from conversations with Paula just how sick he was, but nothing could prepare them fully for actually seeing him in that state. Paula's mother had a great sense of humor and Mike always had a great story to tell. They spent most of their time in the ICU with him and from time to time Paula would spend an hour or so with her mom away from the hospital. During these moments Mike would accompany Noah.

Noah enjoyed having visitors. It was a special distraction from his typical daily routine while imprisoned in the ICU. This strange cold place had become his temporary home. Who wants that? Especially a child who only wants to smile and make his mark in this world. Yeah, visitors were a treat; he was definitely a social person. He didn't know it, but he would continue to fight from that same room…for a long time.

**

My cell phone rang in the middle of the workday; mid-afternoon and I was working on several things at my desk. I looked at my phone and saw that it was Paula. I quickly answered it as I walked outside of the office building. My desk was not too far from an exit door.

"Hey, babe. How are you?" My senses were heightened some as I greeted her.

"I'm okay." Her voice was strained. "Noah's is not doing well today. He became very sick overnight and had a rough morning today. They had to induce a medical coma and put him on a ventilator. He doesn't look good Roger. You better get here as soon as you can."

My vision sharpened as I heard those words beat against my brain. The pounding was vicious. I focused my eyes down at the pale asphalt and her words echoed…replayed over and over. I was stunned like a baseball bat was swung full force to my stomach…THUD! I had to recover because I had to get to Pittsburgh immediately.

"I will see who can help us and call you later," I replied. Now I was on a mission.

Money was not flowing into our bank account these days. Our expenses included supporting two households and on one salary. I earned an average income that I appreciated, but it was far less than what I had earned while working as a policeman. We stretched our dollar to match our situation, but somehow on paper, it never worked out. That was a miracle in itself. Noah's illness incurred expenses that were constant. Those who have chronically ill children know what I mean. So, to have $600 laying around for an immediate flight across the country was not a reality for us. I made a call to my church. They were supportive in all ways through Noah's sudden illness and the staff told me to call them when a need would arise.

A short time later, I had a round-trip ticket, permission from my employer to suddenly leave and not have issues with my position (they were simply amazing), and a ride to the Los Angeles International Airport. I called Paula and told her I would be arriving late that night on a direct flight. She was relieved and so was I.

"How's he doing?" I asked.

"He's had no changes since we last spoke. They are watching his monitors closely and started some additional meds. Just be ready to see him this way, Rog." Her words struck my heart. "Just be ready. It's going to be tough on you."

Hours later, my flight landed in Pittsburgh. Paula made arrangements for my curbside pickup once I arrived. She made some friends at a local church who were glad to help (the same non-denominational fellowship we attended back home). Tom and Bernadette picked me up and drove me to the hospital that late evening. Their gesture simply blew me away. God was moving in the hearts of those who loved and served Him, even those who lived across the country and so far away from our home in California.

Paula made lasting friendships through this nearby church, Calvary Chapel Pittsburgh. She was visited by the pastor and his wife (Kevin and Krista), the youth pastor and his wife (Tim and Jan), and Tom and Bernadette. It was a blessing to have complete strangers in a foreign town open their hearts and do nothing but give of themselves to Paula and Noah.

I finally arrived at Children's Hospital many hours after Paula's phone call. I thanked my new friends, said goodbye and made my way into the entrance in haste. I picked up a couple of funny toys while at the airport terminal. I couldn't wait to show Noah the special glasses I found that make your eyes look like tiny tunnels from the outside. They were thick, black-rimmed and goofy. Laughter was a powerful tool.

I found the ICU on the sixth floor and I walked into the large dimly-lit room. I glanced around quickly and saw Paula in a corner next to his bed.

She looked so sad and tired but relieved at the same time. She walked towards me and we embraced. I missed her deeply and couldn't stand being away from her and Noah. She turned and led me to Noah's bed surrounded by a pulled curtain – our only means of privacy.

There was my son. Noah was asleep with a device that covered his nose and his mouth. It fed him oxygen at a steady pace and there were monitors that kept track of his vitals. My heart tugged and broke completely in half for him. I was stunned and paralyzed. I couldn't say hello to him and see him smile. It wasn't Noah. No, this was not the boy who I last saw in Hollywood just over a month ago. Paula encouraged me to talk to him. Even though he was in a medical coma, she wanted to keep his mind engaged.

I kneeled down to his side and reached my hand to the crown of his head. Gently, I said hello and told him I was there right beside him. I quietly told him I wasn't going to leave until he was better. Man, was it tough. It took everything inside of me not to lose it and burst out into a rage. That was one very hard night for me to endure.

Paula and I held hands and sat there for a while. Yeah, it was late, but I never felt more at home than right by her side and by Noah. That moment was filled with melancholy and heavy moods, but still, we had joy within the moment. We were exhausted, but it was a true joy to have each other. And nothing was going to take that away from us.

The next morning, we called the hospital as soon as we woke up and checked on Noah through his ICU nurse. There were no changes in his condition. As we had our morning coffee and a little breakfast, our hearts decompressed slightly. The power of sitting with each other was evident and we sorely missed having each other to lean on. Her eyes were sad and it matched the condition of my heart. Noah was in such a different place than he was a month earlier and it seemed that he was on a steady downhill slide – in the wrong direction. It was a heaviness that weighed on us both. To know that she was there every day with him was just incredible. The hardship she endured without me and our other children was a testament to her strength. Yeah, she is truly one-of-a-kind amazing.

We made our way to the hospital via the hotel shuttle. One huge benefit of our insurance plan was having the nearby Residence Inn accommodations. Many other families whom we met didn't have this same resource and had to either pay for these costly expenses or stay at the local Ronald McDonald house.

We hurried to the ICU and arrived at Noah's bed. We both kissed his head tenderly and wished him a good morning. It was still a shock to see him lifeless and non-responsive. Paula began to tidy his bed (blanket and sheet perfectly covering him) and checked the monitors. She was educated with her new surroundings; breathing rates, oxygen saturation levels, heart rhythms, and the like. Her focus was precise and her intention of becoming the very best patient advocate was evident. I was so very proud of her. If I was able to nominate her for exceptional mother extraordinaire every week – forever, then I most certainly would. *Excuse me, nurse, can you please tell the director of surgery that Paula is here and will be able to spend a few minutes sharing her insight with the team? Thank you.* Okay, so I thought strange and exaggerated things, but I truly believed she should be given praise for her devotion and efforts.

Two days had passed and Noah had improved. The intubation device was removed and he was groggy for a while. When he finally was able to understand, he cracked a smile at us. My heart began to mend. His lips were dry from the plastic tubing and the area of his mouth that closed around it became slightly chapped. Paula was right on point making sure she applied a gel-like moisturizer to begin lip healing. We told him stories about how I hopped on a plane in a flash and was having difficulty with the humid weather adjustment. He wouldn't know – all he knew was the stale confines of the ICU.

As the days progressed, he gained his strength back and was pretty upbeat, considering the circumstances. I enjoyed my time so much, but I knew I had to return to work. I didn't want my employer to think I was trying to avoid returning to my post. All the while, I thought about how strange and difficult this separation was. It was a recipe for a family and marriage disaster.

I made my arrangements for the flight home (compliments of our church) and called the office to let them know. The last several hours with Noah and Paula were extra painful, emotionally. It just didn't seem right. We all know life isn't fair. It just seemed like the odds were already stacked against our family and the stress of being apart added extreme complexity to the situation.

There I was, just as the song goes… *Leaving on a jet plane. Not sure when I'll be back again.* Really, I didn't know, but I knew that it could be for that amazing moment when Noah would get the call for organs. The plane taxied off the runway and I felt empty inside. I was built for my family, for my wife. We were a unit separated during a crisis and the pain it inflicted stung deeply.

**

The room was still dark at 6:30 AM. My alarm shattered my sleep and I looked around our bedroom to see if anything had changed. I hoped that the last couple of years were just the nasty effects of an intense nightmare and that I would suddenly awake to see Paula asleep in our bed. No, that wasn't the case at all. Her side of the bed was empty and I only had Spike, Noah's Mini-Pinscher/Chihuahua mix, tucked away under the covers.

I jumped out of bed and again realized that Paula and Noah were still in Pittsburgh, and Shelby, Brooke, and Luke were still in San Diego. It was another morning reality check. A week removed from my quick jaunt to Pittsburgh and I thought I would not make it past 6:00 PM that day. If I felt like this, how did Paula feel right about now? I rolled into the shower and prayed for her day as well as for Noah. I thanked God for his amazing mercy that was new again…every morning it's new.

As I drove to the office with the rest of Southern California in Orange County, I made a quick call to Paula. After all, it was about 10:30 AM in her world.

"Hey, baby," I said with a perk in my voice (talking to her was the best part of my day).

"Good morning, my honey," she replied. "I'm just getting ready to call for the shuttle and visit with Noah."

"Great. Tell him I love him." I said.

"I will."

We discussed how Noah had now waited for almost two months and things were not getting rosier. We shared how much we missed each other and how great it will be when we are all together as a family again. That kept us going. It was our goal and our dream.

The day crept by at a snail's pace as most do while in the ICU. Noah had a nice sponge-bath from Paula and she took extra care to be sure his hair was combed. You know how mothers are. She was also present for when the doctors rounded on Noah and she would always ask the correct questions, but with discretion while in front of our son. This time, they asked if they could speak with her in the hallway.

"I'll be right back Noah," she said with a smile.

"Okay mom," Noah said.

The doctor and Paula made their way into the neighboring hallway outside of the ICU and discussed Noah's status. The doctor explained that his heart began to show signs of congestive heart failure and his liver functions continued to decline. Her eyes trembled with tears and she kept her composure as he continued.

"Mrs. Ziegler, we are going to do everything we can to keep him well for as long as it takes until his organs become available," the doctor said tenderly. "We are monitoring everything and working directly with the transplant team to ensure Noah has the best chance of successful transplant surgery."

She heard more about his liver struggling to maintain his blood levels and how the bleeding issues were more difficult to treat (stop the bleeding). The blood infusions were administered nearly every day and they continued to order B-positive, CMV-negative for him. It was understood that he could not develop CMV prior to his transplant as this would increase certain complications. So far, there was a heavy supply of his blood at the nearby blood banks. Thank you, Jesus!

Paula gathered herself before she went back to Noah. It was like a pounding wave of pressure that struck against the walls of her life. She fought back the fear of losing our son, but when the physicians updated her with Noah's bleak report it became nearly impossible to maintain a grip onto hope. Crashing waves against her life seemed to bring her world to a crashing halt. Yet, she held onto our Lord for strength while the pitch-black clouds prevented any ray of light from piercing through. She held on for Noah so that he could see her mom fight this with him. So that he could see her spirit and imitate her actions. She was never leaving his side.

I can't tell you what Noah was thinking during these difficult days, but according to Paula, he did his very best to wear a smile. When those moments of pain, or discomfort, or critical care were required (like trying to stop an aggressive bleed), he tried to remain calm...and he usually did. He watched funny movies and SpongeBob cartoons often. It was his way to bring something familiar into his new toxic environment. Clearly, he was engaged in a battle for life.

Later that week, the doctors made their rounds and Paula was there with Noah. They made their way to Noah's bed, from one patient to another, and the leading physician began to spill information to the interns who surrounded him. He went on to say that the patient (referring to Noah) was experiencing congestive heart failure and other related organ complications. Paula immediately turned to the doctor and interrupted him sharply.

"Excuse me. You don't need to say these things around my son!" Her voice carried volumes of weight, as Noah's ambassador and advocate. And as the woman who gave birth to him, she made it very clear to the physician that he overstepped his boundaries.

After the group walked past his bed and onto the next patient, Paula leaned over to Noah and apologized to him for what they had said. She hugged him gently and loved on him for a while longer. Her words were soothing and brought comfort to our son. She was a master at her craft and so brilliant during these tremendous trials.

Soon after, she called for his nurse and explained to her how terrible the exchange was during the rounds. The nurse apologized and said she would mention something as well to the staff and to the head nurse. It was through this conversation that Noah's head transplant surgeon, Dr. George

Mazariegos (Director of Transplant Surgery), was made aware of the incident and visited with Paula and with Noah.

He carried himself with poise and compassion. His smile instantly made everyone who met him feel like he was family. As he spoke, he assured them that our son would be well taken care of and see to it personally. He explained his role in working directly with the ICU team to ensure Noah had the best opportunity to have a successful transplant surgery, once the organs became available.

Paula was relieved but shared her concerns with Dr. George about the ICU rounds and how inappropriate their conversation was around Noah. He agreed. In fact, during the next team meeting with all physicians – ICU and transplant – Dr. George brought Paula with him and gave stern warnings concerning the inappropriate details shared by her. She felt like a lamb in a room of hungry wolves (although no one was threatening her), but Dr. George was her guardian, her protector, and was her number one fan. She kind of has that effect on people.

**

Days merged into one long span of dreadful time. Deep into June and there was no call from the transplant office; there was no hope in the form of a phone ringing with that special news we had been conditioned to expect. With every phone call, we salivated emotionally as if it was the very one we were waiting for. Still, there was no news. No news was not good news.

Paula's daily reports about our son wore on me. The physical separation made the pain worse for me and also for Paula. It was her lack of having her husband at her side and her children loving on her that increased her pain. We didn't think it would be this long of a wait. After all, Noah only had so much time before all options expired. The thought was torturous.

We encouraged each other, but sometimes the words just didn't flow. I could see the strain in our marriage develop. A hairline crack here and there caused by intense stress was a side effect of this ordeal. We would do whatever we had to in order to keep our son alive – anyone would, but sometimes the price of such actions can cause collateral damage without direct intentions. I loved her with everything I was made of and I knew she had the same devotion towards me. We desperately needed to be together to fight this. On the same ground, on the same soil.

The situation with our other children also carried a certain weight of stress as well. Because they lived with my father and stepmother two hours away, I didn't have the luxury of seeing them as much as I needed to –

which was every day.

The weekend was my opportunity to share special time with them. I felt like a co-parent and it was strange to feel this way. Initially, I decided to drive to San Diego, pick them up, and bring them back home – to their true home. During those moments I sensed a mild disconnect in our relationship. It was unintended, of course. The strain of these circumstances consumed me. As much as I tried not to show it, I was stuck in a deep depression and I didn't know it. My wonderful children – Shelby, Brooke, and Luke, did not deserve this. It was not their fault either.

My father told me the kids had a difficult time adjusting when I would pick them up and have them home for the weekend, so I kept my weekend visits with them in San Diego. Some close friends were kind enough to watch Spike and keep him company during those weekends. We made the best of our time with fun outings to places like the zoo or the movies. Still, the tone was sometimes somber.

During one of those Friday evening drives after work while on the Interstate 5 highway, I experienced something that nearly forced me off of the road. I played the radio to keep me company on the lonely drive and one of those songs suddenly played. You know, the type of song that was written just for you and the lyrics cut into my world like a red-hot knife carving chilled butter.

My hands gripped the steering wheel tighter as the first few lyrics were sung to me:

"I'm down on my knees again tonight,
I'm hoping this prayer will turn out right.
See, there is a boy that needs your help.
I've done all I can do myself."

I was stunned and mesmerized by those words. How did he know? It was like he knew our family intimately. The song continued and so did my emotional experience.

"His mother is tired,
I'm sure you can understand.
Each night as he sleeps
She goes in to hold his hand,
And she tries
Not to cry
As the tears fill her eyes."

Too many tears welled up on my eyes and I had to wipe them quickly,

111

so I could maintain my lane on the dark highway. My heart pounded like it was forced to pump additional blood into my extremities for some unknown reason. As the song played, I pictured Paula and Noah over 2,400 miles away in the hospital ICU – struggling to make it through.

"Can you hear me?
Am I getting through tonight?
Can you see him?
Can you make him feel alright?
If you can hear me
Let me take his place somehow.
See, he's not just anyone – he's my son."

I was overwhelmed by this time. This was my prayer I continuously sent up to heaven. These were my very words I conversed with my Lord while I sat alone in my bedroom, time and time again. Because He was real during those times, not just when the days were bright and the butterflies danced in the sun-kissed air. No, during these times of crisis and despair, our God showed up and I felt him. He carried me and He helped me get through that lonely drive to see my children. Like so many times before, He carried me.

Thank you, Mark Schultz, for recording such a moving and powerful song. I firmly believe it was written for me, for that particular drive to San Diego...and afterward.

**

"Mom, my back is hurting," Noah said.

"Lets' help you get out of bed and into the chair," answered Paula. "We have to keep you in and out of bed as much as we can."

It took several minutes to help him move his IV lines safely out of the way (he was always connected to a few pumps) and ease him out of the bed. His body was weak and becoming frailer. She helped him carefully stand and transition into the chair next to his bed.

He had an unrested look on his face; a worried gaze as he watched something funny on the TV screen. He fought through discomfort in his bones, tissues and against fear constantly, I'm sure. Although he didn't talk much about it, sometimes he would say the organs were taking too long and he may never get them. Why should a ten-year-old say such words? I'll say it again, life just isn't fair.

It was Paula who delivered the right words of comfort and helped him see there was hope. In fact, she was the official ambassador of hope and continued to share the powerful message with Noah, as only a mother is able to.

It was during these weeks where it became day by day for our Noah. The fighter inside of him kept his will to survive in top form. It was the physical breakdown in various areas that reminded him he was definitely under devastating duress.

It wasn't much longer before Paula called me with that sense of urgency in her voice. She told me I had better get on a plane as soon as possible. Noah was not doing well. Why did this have to be so difficult? I wanted to pound my head against the wall in extreme frustration, but that would only be stupid. It was a combination of anger and desperate fear that surrounded me. This was my world.

I called a dear friend who I worked with at the police department. I still kept in touch with Sandor after my release. He and his wife, Faith, always offered to help in any way. In my shaky tone, I told him what Paula had said and he immediately paid for a round trip airfare to Pittsburgh. No questions and no need to pay it back. They were selfless and awesome all wrapped up into one wonderful couple.

I immediately packed my bag and arranged for someone to care for Spike. My ride delivered me safely to LAX and I boarded the red-eye flight. I called Paula to let her know I would be there first thing in the morning. I sat on a very empty plane and waited to pull away from the terminal. There were three people who sat directly in front of me. It was obvious they knew each other as they talked and laughed in their conversation. *I wish I could share the same upbeat emotions*, I thought. After a few minutes, one of the guys led them into a prayer for a safe plane trip and I immediately joined quietly. It was soothing as his words comforted my heart and I felt God's peace at that moment. When he ended the prayer I agreed and said "amen" and added "thank you" for that encouragement. He turned back towards me and smiled.

For a moment, just a few seconds, there was a peace that covered my brain and warmed my heart. It really was something that could not be fabricated or imagined. No, it was as real as the shirt I wore on my body. That's the peace that surpasses all understanding referred to in Philippians 4:7. It reads: *"And the peace of God, which surpasses all understanding, will guard your hearts and minds through Christ Jesus."* I had no family with me, I didn't have my wife in the seat next to me, and my best buddies were nowhere to be found – yet I knew God was right there with me. His presence was felt and I gazed out of the small window and glanced towards the black, night sky. I smiled. As if I audibly heard His words of comfort, I responded in my heart – *thank you, Lord. Please be with Noah right now and send him this same comfort.*

It was about 5:30 AM at the Pittsburgh airport terminal. My head was foggy. I hurried past the closed retail stores at the airport mall and made my way to the outdoor transportation zone. Just outside was the 28X bus stop, where I waited. The muggy air clung to my skin.

I hopped on the next transit and eventually made it to Children's Hospital. I had one carry-on bag with me and rolled it through the empty streets early that morning. My heart raced as I got closer to Noah and Paula. The elevator rushed me to the sixth floor and the doors finally opened. I quickly walked through the halls and made it to the ICU. *I'm here.*

The few nurses that were in the large room smiled my way as I approached his bed. I met Paula and squeezed her gently in our embrace. Reunited and it felt so good. I reached down to Noah and he was again in a medically induced coma. He was fighting a nasty bacterial infection and his breathing was labored just before they connected him to the ventilator. I gently hugged him and wanted to steal him away from this prison and rescue him from this torture.

I made it. There I was, at the place that made the most sense for my existence. It was my real home, although I sorely missed Shelby, Brooke, and Luke. Still, the hospital was now my home base and I didn't want to leave. He laid there peacefully getting the IV medications infused that helped to destroy the enemy bodies inside of him. It was the same circumstances, just weeks later.

I noticed his skin was a little more yellowish than before. His tummy was bloated, the doctors referred to the condition as having a distended belly, and Paula explained that the liver disease had caused it. *God, please heal him and comfort him. Touch him like only you can and restore him. Bring peace to his mind and give him wonderful dreams. Take care of our little boy. Hold him. Keep him. Watch over him. Amen.*

A few days had passed and Noah was recovering very well. He was off of the ventilator and his sense of humor returned. We talked and laughed. Our goal was to keep his mental state outside of the confines of the ICU. He wanted to run and catch that touchdown pass with full strength. He wanted to be home already. Enough was enough. He wanted to click his heels together like Dorothy and instantly be transported to his bedroom. I guess Paula was Dorothy and I was – well, take your pick...the Cowardly Lion, the Tin Man, or the Scarecrow. Huh, it's funny but I think I was a part of every one of those characters in some way. If I only had a brain, strength of heart, and an extra measure of courage!

It was early July and we strolled outside in the garden. I pushed Noah in his wheelchair and he had a few pumps running important fluids and meds around the clock. So, we brought them too. Since the IV pump stand was equipped with small wheels at the base, we were able to place it right behind Noah's backrest and kept it in motion with his chair. He was mobile. Yes, he had movement. *Houston, we have no problem.*

We visited the garden and certain parts of the hospital grounds, like the gift shop. He held toys that lit up and looked through certain books. It was just a small way he could remove himself from ICU confinement, both physically and emotionally. We had to pass by the candy and treats swiftly because he was not able to eat anything. A small piece of candy would cause so much turmoil in his gut and perhaps cause a nasty bleed at his ostomy site. He pretended it didn't bother him, but I knew he dreamt about having those delightful things again. We were careful not to eat those sorts of things around him and he didn't whine about it at all.

July 4th arrived and we talked about having another huge weekend opportunity for higher percentages of getting organs. At some point, we forgot about celebrating holidays like the Fourth of July as we always had, but now teased the thought of having organs for our son. It was strange, but parents with extremely sick children are not normal. We lived in a different realm than most others. No, it wasn't fireworks and family get-togethers, instead Paula and I encouraged each other with the hope that Noah could very well get his surgery any minute and come out of this nightmare. It's funny how this life changes us.

By July 6th, there was no news from the transplant surgery team. There were no parades for Noah and no celebration for his recovery yet. Don't unpack the streamers and balloons folks, not yet anyway. It was tough getting through these several hours. Our hopes were dashed by reality. How much longer can he last? We prayed for time, but we prayed more for his miracle.

It was then that we had a tough setback – a huge blow. We were called by the ICU staff to let us know Noah had a negative reaction to something and his vitals were not strong. Paula and I made our way to the hospital as soon as we could that evening. We arrived to find a team working in his corner trying to stabilize him.

"What happened?!" we asked the doctor frantically. Then the words hit us like a falling sequoia tree.

"Noah had low blood levels that required our support with another infusion. When his nurse went to retrieve the bag, she accidentally returned with the wrong blood type. After it was administered, his body immediately began to reject the infusion," the doctor explained.

"Are you serious?!" Paula answered with a serious look in her stern eyes. We were floored and could not comprehend such an error could be committed by such a highly functioning medical team. The wrong blood type meant his body went into shock and set him back physically. He was struggling for hours and it made for a very tense evening for us. We prayed and prayed through the night. God brought this little boy so far there was no way He would let him go now, right? Of course not. We held on to that hope tightly. Hope was all we had. We grabbed hold of that braided rope, that lifeline sustaining us as we hung suspended on the side of that cliff hundreds of feet above the ground. We clenched it so securely until our knuckles turned white and we lost feeling in our fatigued hands – never looking down. That's how tightly we held on.

We sat next to Noah as he was asleep. The fresh, correct blood type was being infused into his IV, among other meds. We were emotionally spent, exhausted. The calm was before us and the fury had passed. His monitors showed a struggle in his body still; a fight that ensued by his organs to keep going. Like I said, it was a setback.

We were with him long past midnight. Our level of exhaustion exceeded our physical endurance and we were allowed to sleep at the hospital to be close by our son. There was a dorm style area in the lower level that had small rooms for the resident physicians and other staff to sleep in. We found our way to the small rooms and collapsed. We hoped that nightmares would not follow us into our sleep, but little did we know the horror was waiting to ambush us in the morning.

**

40:05:15

My eyes opened and I looked at my watch: 7:15 AM. I looked over at Paula's bed and it was unoccupied. *Where was she?* Maybe she was in the restroom. I fought back drowsiness and climbed to my feet. I searched the hallway area and restrooms – no Paula. I washed up quickly and decided to make it up to the sixth floor. I'm sure she was there to check on him already.

I walked into the ICU and found Paula sitting at Noah's bedside. She had been crying and I knew something terrible had occurred.

"What's wrong?" I said softly but with urgency in my voice. "Is Noah okay?"

"He's alright, but we need to talk with the doctor. He's on his way to see us," she said as her eyes were swollen with pain.

A familiar ICU doctor approached us and greeted us with a warm smile. "Can we please talk outside?"

Noah was asleep from a heavy dose of meds and we walked out to the hallway. My heart pumped rapidly in anticipation of his delivery.

There was some good news and some very bad news. The good was that they had received a call from CORE, (Center for Organ Recovery and Education), with a match for organs. Great! Right? Well, as the call came into the ICU, the head physician had to determine whether or not Noah was able to qualify for the surgery. You know, physically ready. When he checked his latest chart evaluation and set of vitals, it was determined that he was not a candidate for the transplant. That was the bad news. It felt like my hands balled into fists and tightly squeezed them in total frustration, but I don't think they did. I held Paula close and we both couldn't believe our ears. Not now – not like this.

The doctor apologized profusely for the nurse's error the night before. This was the cause of Noah's missed opportunity and it didn't sit right with him either. But, to us this was devastating and utterly not acceptable; that a simple error like infusing the incorrect blood type could be made at this level of acute and intensive medical care was beyond comprehension. I felt numb to the world and to my immediate surroundings. This did not just happen, right? The horror show continued except now we had to swallow the harsh reality of missed organs. That was the part that stung and felt like a Samurai sword had penetrated my pericardium, but stopped shallow of my heart to keep me somewhat alive for the front row seat to my disaster. Am I being a bit dramatic? So, you would be yawning and uninterested right now if it was your child? That's what I thought.

Missing this chance was a kick in the pancreas. Our winning lottery ticket was thrown into the fire, so it seemed. As long as we've been here waiting, keeping death at bay and not see one lick of an organ come Noah's way was dreadful. When would he possibly have another chance? Another several months perhaps? The thought sucked the life out of my brain and the details were too much to process.

After several of our questions were met with the doctor's best answers, we returned to Noah's side. It was solemn and quiet. The beeps and flashing monitor signals bashed my brain and reminded me with clarity that he was not getting his organs today as he should. Almost as of his surroundings were mocking our calamity.

We looked at Noah with different eyes now. The moments were now even more precious as we felt like this was more of an uphill battle. Huh, like it wasn't before? Paula sat next to him and quietly kissed his cheek. She expressed her motherly love in tender ways that melt steel.

"I love you, Noah," her whisper carried thick, passionate emotion.

Shortly after our meeting with the ICU doctor, Dr. Peters, Noah's GI doctor, came to see us. He always was the most gentle and kind person. In the wake of the disaster, he brought with him a sense of peace.

"Mr. and Mrs. Ziegler, I just learned of the news and I wanted to come by to let you know how sorry I am and to check on Noah," he said. We greeted him with our best smiles. He walked over to Noah, like a guardian angel, and sat next to him on his bed. Noah was asleep, so with tender words Dr. Peters quietly spoke to our son. He really cared for him and he only wanted the best possible outcome for his life.

"Can we take a walk, mom and dad?" he said.

"Sure, doctor," I answered. We walked out of the hospital and into an area that bridged both Children's Hospital and Presbyterian Hospital, where adult transplant patients were seen. It looked like an open garage where ambulances and other emergency room drop-offs were made. We walked over to a long bench and we had a seat in the warm summer air.

I sat on one end and Paula just a few feet away. Dr. Peters sat on her other side and said quiet, calming and reassuring words. I heard him speak but carried my eyes out into space away from them both. With every few words he spoke, my throat tightened and my heart pounded almost audibly. I could hear Paula's sobbing begin and her words dripped in anguish. She tried to speak clearly, but pain overwhelms simple speech sometimes.

As I stared into the distance, I felt drops of fluid form in the corners of my eyes. I began to shed pain through my face and I clenched my fists as they were at my side. I pictured Noah laying there in desperation. I couldn't get his innocent face out of my head. I swallowed back more pain and sadness. Dazed, I allowed my tears to roll down onto the sidewalk. My eyes studied every drop crash into the pavement. And in my mind, I realized our son was held hostage by this ongoing nightmare. My heart broke for Noah.

I heard waves of sobbing from my sweet wife. Her heart must have been crushed. I could barely hear Dr. Peters console her. It was a huge blessing to have him here with us. How many doctors would sit by our side with us during this devastating moment? Not many. I respected him for his genuine concern. Anyone who devotes a portion of their time and themselves to help our family is someone I highly regard. Dr. Peters was one of those special people in our lives.

After several minutes of just decompressing outside on that uncomfortable bench, we stood up and embraced each other. Our marriage continued to receive blow after blow from a barrage of unseen cannons. We endured and remained together as one through our family disaster.

We both thanked him and walked back to Noah. We had to collect ourselves and regain our composure for that next moment he would be awake. We didn't break that piece of news to him. It would be too much to bear. No, we saved that one for a later day.

The aftermath seemed to fade into our next area of focus: another opportunity for organs. Here we were mid-July in a desperate wait for that call. Time seemed to slow from what was already a snail's pace to a dead crawl. I'm not sure what a dead crawl means, but to me, it seemed like that snail was tied up to a harness and was forced to pull the weight of a fully loaded 747 airplane across the Sahara desert…in the rain. That's how slow this became.

10
ELEVEN CANDLES

5:03:25

AUGUST WAS PRETTY NICE in Southern California. At least where we lived. Blue skies with high clouds created a perfect canopy that stretched as far as one could see. I wondered how the weather would be during the next couple of months in Pittsburgh. It was humid and rainy in July, but maybe we would get some relief in the coming weeks.

The days ahead for Noah were exciting and yet bittersweet for us. We were just a few days away from Noah's eleventh birthday. He was a little excited about the coming celebration. His mind was more focused on daily battles with pain, discomfort and severe symptoms caused by end-stage liver disease. He wore deep shades of green and yellow on his skin. His belly was swollen like he had swallowed a large watermelon whole. His skin showed a roadmap of veins like a traffic pattern of the busiest part of Los Angeles. All of his breathing by now was labored. Probably due to his increased liver size placing unfair pressure against the walls of his weak lungs. He had a constant convoy of mechanical pumps with large syringes feeding his vascular system life-sustaining fluids…constantly. They were stacked in vertical formation on two IV poles adjacent to his bed.

Was this my son? He resembled the bright-eyed and vibrant, laughter-filled second child who lived in our home. His speech was so labored that we had to carefully listen to every spoken word in order to understand him. His voice cracked and sounded like his tank was always out of gas. I wanted to pick him up, carry him on my shoulders and escape, but I couldn't hold him up like that anymore. He had to be assisted by nurses to turn him from his left side onto his right, and so forth. Those days of getting out of bed were long gone. He was now a permanent resident to his hospital bed.

He began to see images of things that were not there. A sort of mirage as if he was stranded in a vast desert raging with intense heat and his mind produced visual distractions. It was called ICU psychosis and it was a very

120

real condition for those patients who were held captive by this hospital setting. The stress had now caused severe emotional trauma.

His corner of the ICU had several toys and plush animals that sat behind him on top of a shelf. There were bright colored animals and a very large stuffed animal from Shrek – "Donkey." This beast was large and took up one whole seat on one of my flights from California. It made him smile when I delivered it earlier that summer.

But, that oversized plush character couldn't compare with the contraband Paula had smuggled into the ICU. She held in her lap Noah's Sea Monkeys on their transport from Los Angeles. They were in a small habitat, water and all, and they survived the leer jet's five-hour flight. Noah loved to see them swim around in their container and he thought that was cool. Yeah, it was all fun and games until the infectious disease doctors learned of this illegal material proudly on display in their facility.

She also brought in an amazing group of lightning bugs. We had never seen these delightful bugs before and they danced with intermittent light that glowed in his corner of the room. Yup, also contraband. She was a renegade and no one could stop her from making our son's day brighter and happier. If that meant she had to sneak in a Rhinoceros into the unit, then so be it. She would find a way. I loved her for that. I was the rule follower and she was quite the opposite. Now isn't that something.

I flew to Pittsburgh with Shelby, Brooke, Luke, and my dad to celebrate Noah's birthday. My mom also flew out earlier with my sister-in-law, Yvette, but Yvette had to return home before his party. So, our family was present – my parents, (Paula's mom couldn't make it a second time because she had visited earlier in the summer), and all of our children. We were ready for a birthday bash like none other.

The situation was about to get real. Noah was not doing well at all and, unless those organs came very soon, he was not going to make it much longer. The thought of losing him caused a tornado of distress in our hearts. Our minds would wrestle with that idea of losing this battle and our precious little boy leaving us. It was crushing.

So we took that stress and made arrangements to have a birthday bash outside in the garden area. There was a nice park-like setting with benches and foliage surrounding the little haven of peace. It would be perfect. The alternative was to have it indoors if the weather was too hot or rainy that day. Our friends from our local church supported us and supplied a ton of resources. Darla, one of these dear friends, offered to make a special cake for Noah. She asked him what he would like and he ordered a custom SpongeBob, ice cream cake.

"Wow!" said Darla. "You've got it, Noah. You are going to love it!" His eyes sparkled with the thought of tasting cake again. It had been months since he last enjoyed any food.

The plans were set and we had ourselves the making of one grand party for our son. Having my mom and dad with us made it extra special too. Of course, seeing all of our children together was simply outstanding. They couldn't wait to help make it one of Noah's best days ever.

We spoke with the ICU doctors to make sure Noah was cleared for the outdoor event. They allocated two of the unit's nurses to accompany and monitor Noah during the festivities. We asked our new Pittsburgh friends to be there too. The more the merrier. After all, it was important to have Noah supported and uplifted as much as possible. We went shopping for several party favors and decorations galore.

Another key individual who was selfless was Frank. He was part of the Child Life Program at the hospital and he was one of the supervisors. His role was to make sure he brought rainbows and sunshine to these wonderful children and to their families. This was achieved through many visits with toys, games, special visits with a friendly puppy, or maybe tickets to a local sporting event (for those who were well enough to travel outside of the hospital). Needless to say, Frank was outstanding and he made Noah laugh frequently. He was one of our son's bright spots in the day. So, when he heard of this gala event planned for Noah, he jumped on board with his team to provide their sunshine on this big day.

2:04:09

Thursday, August 19. It was Noah's official birthday. Hooray! We scheduled his bash on Friday when there were enough hospital resources available and it didn't seem to bother him at all. Of course, we did our very best to provide birthday cheer and love to him on this exact day, but all of the trimmings were set aside for what tomorrow would bring.

Just one day away from his glorious bash. His vitals were stable but he was fighting a nasty bacterial infection in addition to all of the other issues resisting his ability to stay alive. The infection was in his femoral artery and it was very difficult to treat.

Some of the nurses would stop by his bed and begin to cheer him on as he drew near to the party. He would grin as best as he could and show a glimpse of his old cheerful self. But he was tired. Tired of fighting. Tired of hanging on when there was little hope in his mind. He remained on point and focused to make it to that finish line, but the mileage of ICU trauma-life was wearing him down.

It was the longest fight of his life and of ours too. We could sense years draining from our very lives. The stress made fun of us both and mocked us with the reality that surrounded us. Sometimes a child in the unit would not make it in his or her fight and it sent a chill through our bodies. The constant barrage of negative circumstances beat against us. We pressed on. We held Noah close and spoke the most sincere and encouraging words of life into him. We prayed over and for him, as well as many from our church we had become friends with. They would come, visit and share their love with Noah. They delivered more hope as well.

The time capsule of the ICU was no respecter of persons. Minutes and seconds passed like hours and days within the cold walls of the unit. Some patients had short stays, just a few days, and then released to the recovery floors. Some patients spent their time like punishment in a prison cell with twenty-five years to life, so it seemed. It felt like this for Noah. There were moments when we prayed for a turn-around in his health from one hour to the next. Just make it to the next hour, son. Just another 60 minutes – fight…fight…keep fighting.

And then there were moments that delivered more pain and suffering. Those moments felt like we were in a battle to see him through shorter time periods. These uphill moments were spent digging deeper and running faster through a hurricane of rage. Uphill on a mountain of snow and ice. Uphill climbs with several feet of mud and rushing water in downpours of torrential rains. Yes, these desperate moments became fights from minute to minute. From second hand to second hand. From beating hearts to beating hearts. You could count the pulses like a beating bass drum smashing against our weary brains. Minute to minute, our little Noah clawed his way through the lowest point in his life. He carried on his shoulders the burdens of this medical nightmare because we couldn't carry it for him, but we wanted to. I begged God to carry this burden for him. Please get him to through the next sixty seconds, I pleaded with our Lord.

We kissed him goodnight and said special prayers with him as we did every night. He was in good hands for the night. Oxygen was good. Pulse was good. Saturation was fine. He was ready for sleep. We thanked the evening nurse who was assigned to him like we did each night before. The kids said goodnight to their brother too and we left for our hotel.

After we settled down and rested our heads on those soft pillows, Paula and I shared our excitement with each other about Noah's special day. We had prayed that he would make it to his eleventh birthday for the last several months. And that was going to be another answer to prayer – again. In fact, even more special than this prayer, was the one we lifted up with Noah for the last few weeks. This was a prayer to receive his life-saving organs on his birthday. It would be the best birthday present he could ever have…ever. The gift of life is one that outweighs anything by comparison. And we asked for this together and we believed for this miracle together. Wouldn't that be amazing? Yeah. It would be perfect.

**

1:02:12

We gathered at his bed mid-morning and began to cheer him on. His nurses, both assigned to this birthday detail, already made the arrangements necessary to have his meds ordered in advance. The outdoor garden area was decorated with festive goodies and the guests began to make their way into the courtyard in anticipation of Noah's arrival.

It would take a miraculous effort to pull this feat off. Paula and I assisted both nurses as they prepared our son for liftoff. The last few tubing enhancements and modifications were completed. We dressed him and began to help him sit up in bed. The soreness and discomfort caused an uneasiness to overcome Noah. He looked like someone else's child and nearly unrecognizable. His war-torn body barely held together.

"Take your time son," we encouraged him as he remained in the seated position for several minutes. He tried to catch his breath, but his diaphragm was being heavily persuaded not to breath by his enlarged liver.

"Ready," he said as we were in position on each side of him. We helped him ease his way to the edge of the thin mattress and moved his feet over towards the cold floor. Mom put on his special birthday slippers and we waited for his next signal. When he was ready, we eased him ever so slightly, inch by inch towards the edge of that bed and faced him towards the empty wheelchair. As we held his body, his feet slowly descended to the floor and he looked very exhausted.

"Almost there Noah," Paula said.

"Okay," he replied. We held up his waist and supported all of the IV tubing connected to his body in several areas. He took baby steps as we help him up. We couldn't carry him, because his body was just too delicate. Touchdown – he made it. The nurses positioned two IV poles with what seemed like an army of fifteen medical pumps attached and working at several different rates independently – one pole on his left and pole one on his right. I looked at the clock – twenty minutes had passed. It took twenty minutes to get him from his bed into the wheelchair. It was quite a feat!

The nurses pushed the birthday boy through the hallways of the hospital and Paula and I followed close behind en route to the party location. It was electric like a Disneyland Main Street parade. You could sense the excitement building in him. It was subtle, but we could feel it. We made our last turn around a corner, then through the outer doors and finally we reached the courtyard area. Frank, grandma, grandpa, Shelby, Brooke, Luke, and all of our friends were cheering for him as he made his grand entrance.

The music played uplifting songs and the colorful balloons floated in the air. He grinned as best as he could and tried to wave at everyone. It was fantastic. There was nothing else like it. The greatest Super Bowl in NFL history could not compare to the immense elation we felt that gloomy and hot afternoon. The mood was overwhelming in the best sort of way. He needed this moment like he needed oxygen. So did Paula...and dear old dad.

The gifts were opened by our other kids as Noah had very little arm and hand strength. His smile and grins were few and were distanced between looks of pain and suffering. The thick humid air fell heavy on us. Instead of an exuberant Noah, we experienced the tired and weak child we have known throughout this summer.

After a long forty-five minutes, during which Paula kept cooling him with a cold towel on his face, we asked him if he was done and ready to resume the party in our back up location. He agreed. A quick "all hands on deck" team effort and the party was relocated into the cool confines of the hospital. We had a large conference room set up with all of the goodies in no time. You could see a little relief in Noah once he felt the cold air press onto his face. The air-conditioned room was a blessing.

We continued our onslaught of fun and laughter, making every minute count. The best was saved for last. Darla brought her prize cake in from the freezer and set it on the table directly in front of Noah. The large yellow cake was amazing, decorated just like SpongeBob Squarepants. Noah's eyes suddenly rolled back into his head and he passed out...just kidding – sorry. He was overwhelmed with joy and could not wait any longer for the tasty treat to hit his taste buds. Remember, he has not been able to eat or drink anything for weeks upon weeks. The doctors had to keep him in this state to prevent working the gut and to help minimize bleeding episodes.

But, today was his day. He was in charge. He called the shots...to some degree. Cake? Go for it. Fork in hand? Check. Mouth salivating? Yes, it was. All eleven candles were lit and set ablaze. Then the singing commenced. It was loud and proud – happy birthday vocals were rocking it! As we neared the end of the happy tune, Noah anticipated the last note and began to exhale at his very best. With the help of his siblings, all candles were blown out. When all the smoke had cleared Noah was ready to dive in. He received the honorary first mega slice.

All eyes were on him. His first bite thrilled his senses. Aaaaahhhh. The flavor was better than expected. Second, third bites…he stormed through that piece of custom-made delish in a blaze of glory. Way to go son. We cheered him on.

Now, the aftermath. He was exhausted and ready to get back to his bed. We thanked everyone for all of their love, support, and gifts they had brought. In a very quiet voice, Noah said thank you too. His breathing was much labored. He was in some pain now because of his lengthy, upright seated position.

We wheeled him back to the ICU and our family and friends helped with the honorary clean up duty. The birthday boy was brought back to his little piece of ICU world and was carefully helped back into bed – again, carefully. After reconnected with monitors and all vitals checked, he was ready for a night of rest. We tucked him in and stayed with him for a while. We told him how proud we were of his fight and his courage. We also reminded him that God has not left him. Even though it seemed so dark and desperate, he never left our son. We prayed with him and kissed him goodnight.

As we left the ICU we felt relieved that Noah was able to enjoy himself for a change. We hoped for this day to arrive and for us to see our son live to see eleven. These are the conversations we had since his illness became overwhelming to manage. While some were planning family vacations and discussing sports activities concerning their children, we cried about having the realization of having to transport our son's body back home if he didn't make it. I mean he was right there at death's door. It was serious. So, today's event was nothing short of spectacular and filled with a few hundred-thousand wonderful memories. Little did we know, Noah had less time in this fight to stay alive.

11
PATCHWORK KID

"What you leave behind is not what is engraved in stone monuments, but what is woven into the lives of others."
-Pericles

0:08:00

MY EYES OPENED VERY EARLY the next morning to the sound of my alarm. It was 4:30 AM – zero dark thirty as they say in the military. I turned my head towards Paula and in the darkness found her peacefully asleep. It was a cherished moment to see her resting; it was sheer bliss. Especially knowing how much she has poured out of herself during the last few months. I didn't want to wake her, but I had to pick up my father at a nearby hotel and drive him to the airport with our rental vehicle.

I walked quietly into the bathroom and washed up, then made my way through the next room where the kids were asleep. I managed not to interrupt them and left our hotel room. I walked past the front desk and greeted the night shift person. I grabbed a quick cup of coffee in their lobby area and walked quickly to our rental minivan. I called my dad to make sure he was awake and ready to go. And that he was.

He stayed at a hotel not far from the hospital and I was there at the curb in just five minutes. Pops was standing curbside with his luggage in tow.

"Good morning Rog," he said with an upbeat tone. "How are you doing this morning?"

"Hi, dad. I'm doing well," I replied.

"How was Noah last night?" he asked.

"Oh, he did well once he was put back into his bed. He was wiped out," I said.

We had a great early morning conversation on the way to the airport. He encouraged me in the Lord and said that God had His hands on Noah and on our family. We laughed about the funny moments we had shared during his time in Pittsburgh – as short as it was. Luke always did something that cracked us up.

He was really taken back with Noah's illness and was saddened by how sick he was. I could tell he was trying to be positive about the situation, but I completely understood how grave this was becoming. We didn't have much time left.

I dropped him off at curbside for departing flights and gave him a big hug, then he disappeared into the terminal. It was nice having both of my parents with us during this time and seeing him leave was a bummer. My mom was still with us for another week, so that was great.

I returned to our hotel at around 7:00 AM, after making a stop at Walmart for a couple of things. Twenty-four-hour stores were amazing. I asked the front desk for a shuttle ride to the hospital as I made my way through the lobby and back to my room. I figured I would leave the van for Paula, the kids, and my mom. Shelby, Brooke, and Luke were still sound asleep. A little sugar overload and emotional highs from yesterday tuckered them out.

0:05:06

I walked outside and saw the shuttle ready to go. Since it was a little early in the day, there were no other passengers on this ride. I climbed in the front seat and greeted the driver. He was a friendly person with a kind smile. We were able to become familiar with all of the shuttle drivers because of our lengthy stay at the Residence Inn.

Our drive was only two miles to the hospital. I began small talk about how incredible Noah's birthday party was – when something happened. It was like any other day, but something changed, something was different. Our conversation was interrupted by my cell phone ringing. I was a little shocked at how early someone was trying to reach me. I pulled it out of my pocket, looked at the screen and saw a 412 area code number – local to Pittsburgh. For a millisecond I thought there was a problem. Now what?

"Hello," I quickly answered.

"Good morning, Mr. Ziegler?" an unfamiliar voice said.

"Yes. This is he." My heart began to thump nearly slamming my sternum.

"I'm calling you because we have received a call for organs, for your son, Noah." Her voice said with a smile. You can tell when the person on the other end of the phone is smiling. At this point, my mind was laser-focused on those words she just delivered into my ear. She could have also said that I just won the global sweepstakes lottery and would earn 3 million dollars a month for life or something, but I wouldn't have heard it. As far as I was concerned, the call was over and she had already accomplished her goal to inform me of the most miraculous news I could ever receive –

he has some organs! I answered in utter joy and amazement.

"What?! Are you kidding me?!" I sounded like a game show attendee who just received one of those free cars or something.

"We haven't told him yet and he is still asleep," she added.

"I was on my way there to see him, so I will see you in a few minutes. Thank you! Thank you for calling!" I was on a cloud or something. My out of body experience had just taken place. I had just been elevated to another dimension or so it seemed. I told the driver who was now celebrating with me in that shuttle as we drove to the drop-off point.

I dialed Paula right away. She answered in tears; she was crying and barely able to speak.

"The nurse called me a few minutes ago and told me. I'm so happy Roger! You have no idea." She couldn't contain herself and I could hear Brooke and Shelby in the background too. This was the call we had been waiting for. A chance. A real chance.

"I'll meet you at the hospital babe!" I said with excitement. "I love you."

"Okay. I love you." You could hear the tremendous weight that was lifted off of her shoulders, in her voice.

You couldn't put any price tag on this moment. It was truly priceless. No money, no experience, no prize, or anything else of value could have been placed on the scale to compare with this moment. This moment...this one right here!

We pulled up to the hospital and I thanked the driver. He told me to send his best to Noah. I jumped out like a paratrooper in a hot zone. Before entering the hospital I decided to make a few quick calls. I called my mom next who was also already awake and was getting herself ready to see Noah. She was jumping up and down when I broke the great news to her. She sounded like she also won one of those cars too.

Next, I dialed my dad's cell. Maybe he hasn't taken off yet and would be able to answer. His voice message answered – straight to voicemail. I left him a message and told him about the wonderful news, but wanted so desperately to tell him directly. *I'll wait for him to call back when he lands*, I thought.

My last call was made to Pastor Kevin. Both he and his wife, Krista, were so instrumental in blessing us over the last few months that we felt a close bond with them and their small, but mighty church in Pittsburgh. I also left him a detailed and enthusiastic message.

I hurried through the main doors and into the elevator. I was giddy and filled with excitement. Sixth floor. I raced out of the elevator and scurried through the halls near the ICU. I walked in and walked directly to Noah. He was asleep still and doing fairly well.

His nurse met me right away and made sure we spoke far from his bed. She explained that since the donated organs were not yet harvested, we couldn't say anything to Noah. At least until we knew it was a green light for surgery. Oh man! How was I supposed to keep quiet? Noah was about to get his life back and I had to keep my mouth closed? It was crazy and I was ready to explode. She said one of the transplant doctors would be by soon to discuss the details with us.

Okay. So here I was; the father of a helpless boy who has been fighting for his life during the entire summer and I had knowledge of a possible life-saving transplant but had to hold it inside. It was madness. I asked her how he did over the course of the night and she said he did well. Except for the femoral artery infection and near kidney failure, among other incredibly serious symptoms (you know, end-stage liver failure and congestive heart failure – just to name a couple) he was in top shape. You gotta laugh at how bleak this was. It was unreal and this was simply a miracle that he would be allowed this type of intense surgery.

0:04:23

Paula, my mother, Luke, Brooke, and Shelby had arrived. They wore the biggest and widest smiles; their faces illuminated the dimly lit room. Since it was early and very quiet in the ICU we kept our voices down to a loud whisper and bottled up our enthusiasm. Noah was still asleep and I told the crew away from his bed about the secret we had to keep. Still, we had a mini-celebration in our own three feet of space in the hallway. No streamers required.

We finally met with a doctor who briefed us. Since it was a confidential level of secrecy, we were not allowed to know any of the donor's details. As the doctor began to explain some of the details of how the organs were harvested, we began to feel the heaviness of the crisis the other parents must have experienced. I mean, in order for Noah to have a chance at life, someone else had to die. That was the cold, harsh fact of the matter and it brought our sense of appreciation to a whole new level. We began to ache for those parents who lost a child. It was sobering.

We were in a holding pattern as the surgeons verified the organs were viable and healthy for transplantation. Nothing was assumed and nothing was left unchecked. So, we continued to wait with bold eagerness.

Noah's eyes opened and saw all of us surrounding his bed. He was wondering why we were all there so early. We said it was a continuation of the previous day's birthday celebration. He bought it. We kept our little secret very well. We kept repeatedly watching the clock and frequently asked the nurse for any updates – no news each time. We waited some more. We were professional waiters. We excelled in the art of waiting. Waiting alumni, you could say.

0:01:48

Two hours had passed and we were jumping in our skin. Yet visibly calm to Noah, our minds raced with the idea that this could be his day. The nurse had said they had to keep him NPO – no oral anything. That included ice chips, which he had grown accustomed to enjoying. But, this time he was annoyed with the morning's restrictions and was getting a bit grumpy.

It was 11:00 AM and there was no word. I looked at Paula from time to time with that look in our eyes. We knew the background to this moment and felt the intense pressure mounting. How long does it take to harvest organs? Well, with incredible precision and detail, it can take several hours.

11:30 AM. Still nothing. There was a restlessness developing among us – except for Noah. He was irritated and uncomfortable. I didn't know how much more his body could take. This was his best he could be…in this minute right here. He would not improve beyond this one point in time, but rather continue to spiral down a black hole of physical despair. Minute by minute, he descended into the next phase of disease as if right before our eyes. Minute by minute, 11:46…11:47. It was torture to witness and we had a front-row seat.

All of this summer's fighting and clawing just to make it to the next day wore down Noah's guard. His defenses were weakened. His vision was clouded with little hope and with an ongoing threat. He mustered a smile only on rare occasions and tried to be present with us. He tried his best.

0:00:29

Then, like a flash of lightning, Dr. Mazariegos walked into the ICU. He approached the nurse directly and said something to her for just a minute. Then he made his way to Noah's bed and to our little assembly around him. I could see it in his eyes, almost behind them, I knew what he was about to say. I will never forget.

"Noah. You have organs and are cleared for transplant surgery," he said with relief. I instantly punched both of my arms and fists into the air. *Yesss*! We were elated. Paula began to cry the best joyful tears in quite a long time. I turned to Noah with my hands still stretched up high and we all rushed to his side. His countenance immediately changed and he rolled up all of that emotion into one single gesture: with his right fist clenched he pumped back his elbow to his side like he just hit the game-winning grand slam in the World Series. It was awesome! I took in all of the family's emotion as we embraced. Brooke was crying profusely – she had the tender heart. My mom was wiping tears from her eyes too. We all had shed months and months of stress and despair in one minute. My heart was thumping in my chest from pure adrenaline. This was the best moment in our lives – the very best.

Dr. Mazariegos and a nurse began assessing Noah's IV lines for transport. He paused and leaned over Noah's head for a few moments. He spoke softly into our son's ear and reassured that he would do his best for Noah during the surgery. His voice was serene and soothing, in an atmosphere shaken with death and disease. Noah listened and nodded his head over and over in agreement. He couldn't say much because of his lungs pressed down upon by his enlarged liver and surrounding tissues. I loved the connection the doctor made with Noah in this tender moment.

We watched another nurse join the team and helped to prepare our son. It was crunch time. We asked the doctor about his current infection and he said it was still present, but it would not be a factor. He also said this was the best opportunity he would have for this transplant and they would take some risk in light of the circumstances. In parent's lingo: Noah didn't have many days left and if not now then not at all. After all, he was supposed to be scheduled the next day for a line to be placed in his femoral artery. This would be used for the coming dialysis treatments for his failing kidneys and it would also mark certain disqualification for any transplant surgery. Talk about dodging a huge bullet. He was just days away from being removed from the organ waiting list...forever.

But God. Yes, but God had another plan. His hand intervened at just the right time. At the final hour, He showed up. Well, He was here all along. There is no other way to explain Noah's survival; he made it through this toughest of fights. No, he was carried by His Lord. Like the famous footsteps poem, written by an unknown author, Noah was carried when he could no longer walk. And He carried both of us as well, weary parents and our children too.

You see, Noah had prayed to receive organs for his birthday. God sees the incredible details in our lives – even a birthday wish from a little boy, who suffered through a dark summer in Pennsylvania. Now, this was his moment; a chance to live.

0:00:07

12:23 PM. The doctor briefed us on the entire procedure and what timeframe we should expect. We gave him our cell phone numbers so that we could receive updates throughout this marathon surgery. They anticipated at least twelve hours. Wow! We both knew he would be in the best hands. This highly respected liver and small bowel transplant team was regarded as being number one in the world – the entire planet. You got it – THE best.

0:00:02

We leaned over Noah as he was being wheeled into the main hallway towards the operating room. This was it; here we were at the starting line to the rest of his life. The team of medical specialists stopped the convoy and paused just before the large, red doors opened and they took our son away. It was our moment for hugs and kisses. He was nervous and scared. He looked up at Dr. Mazariegos and asked if this was going to hurt. He assured Noah that he wouldn't feel anything and that he would be asleep through it all.

Now, it was that special point of release; to let Noah go and place him into the hands of this gifted surgical team. After all, we had hoped and longed for this opportunity for months and for tearful weeks. The countdown had brought us down to zero. No more waiting and no more hoping. The future held a new beginning and new sights ahead on Noah's life. The future was now.

We told him we loved him so much and that we would be praying for him. Then, we watched him and the team disappear behind those imposing red doors. No more waiting and no more suffering. The countdown had expired to zero.

0:00:00

I wanted to absorb everything about this moment because we wouldn't see him until sometime after midnight. It was going to be a long day ahead. So, we did what every family would do waiting for their child to endure a lengthy and arduous life-saving transplant surgery – we went shopping. What, you say? Yup. You're right, sounds crazy huh? I'm telling you, there's no way to explain the peace Paula and I had experienced. We weren't worried or concerned the least bit. No, all of those feelings were bled out of our souls over the last year and a half. It was time to enter peace mode. It was a peace that surpasses anyone's understanding and could only be provided by our loving God. It was miraculous and it was real. The greatest positive thinking mindset could not compare.

We believed that our wonderful God would have our son in His care and would bring him through this next several hour ordeal. We believed and we held our heads up high knowing this day had arrived. It was Noah's day and it was long overdue.

We piled into the minivan and drove to the mall, about twenty minutes away. We found a restaurant and assembled at a large table. I turned to each one with a smile; Paula, my mother, Shelby, Brooke, and Luke. It was like we were in a dream; we were giddy and had to pinch ourselves repeatedly. Yeah, the endorphins were at an all-time high this afternoon. We ate and talked about how our son would become a brand new person. I glanced at my watch and noticed about two hours had passed...no word from the surgical team yet. No problem.

We decided to do some school shopping for the kids since the semester was right around the corner. Another hour had passed and there was no call. Further along into the afternoon, the kids continued to enjoy themselves – mostly the girls who tried on colorful blouses and adored all of the shoes on display. It all went so well. Then, my cell phone rang in the four o'clock hour.

"Hello," I nervously said.

"Is this Mr. Ziegler," a kind voice said on the other end.

"Yes. Yes, it is. How is he doing?" I asked.

All of my family's eyeballs were immediately fixed upon me while I was on the call and waited for any clue I would deliver.

"Yes, he is doing very well. We just completed the removal of his liver. Since there was so much inflammation, the doctors took extreme care. All is going as planned."

"Thank you very much," I sounded relieved.

"We will call you again with another update," the nurse said.

And just like that, we felt another wave of happiness and at the same time, we were amazed at the complexity of this procedure. These doctors, these transplant surgeons were superhuman to us and were engaged in saving our son's life. What an amazing concept!

We continued our excursion at the mall and by now I had received calls from my father, who was so elated, from Paula's mother and her siblings, and from Pastor Kevin. It was so nice to express our appreciation with our close circle of loved ones and to share this moment with them. We had to find a way for us to communicate the latest news with our circle of family and friends back on the west coast. Daily phone calls to multiple people would not be realistic.

By early evening we had returned to our hotel room and relaxed for a while. Then another call was received from the nurse who reported that everything was going as planned with Noah and there were no concerns. Through each stage of the surgery, we continued to hear from the team. It seemed like every two hours, which made it nice to have continual feeds of progress. They would update us in real time.

After dinner we grew anxious to see our son, so we decided to wait at the hospital for a while. We began to feel the effects of the long day. I remembered that I was up extra early that morning to drive my father to the airport. It was time for caffeine.

By midnight, we needed another breath of fresh air. We figured the surgery would be nearing its end soon. We made our way into the summer evening and walked a few blocks into the heart of Oakland. We casually strolled passed small storefronts and fast food joints, most of them were closed. Since it was a college town, the local hangouts included a couple of bars and small eateries. We found a convenience store and perused the aisles in search of instant awake, immediate rush, or body-slam adrenaline fixes. And there it was: No-Doz capsules. Yeah, that'll do.

It was now 2:30 AM and we were barely hanging on. Just then a familiar face broke through the ICU. It was Dr. Mazariegos and he looked exhausted. He asked if we could speak with him in the hallway. We agreed and stumbled together outside of the ICU area. He began to debrief us on the lengthy surgical procedure and he started by saying that Noah did very well. He was in the post-operation room recovering nicely. Dr. George continued to explain the complexity of removing Noah's liver due to the rejuvenation and regrowth it made desperately trying to survive. As a result, it was four times the normal size. No wonder Noah's belly was huge and distended. He also said they had to reduce the size of the donor's small intestine because of the trauma that existed in his abdomen. There was no way they could fit the entire donated bowel, but he was able to receive about five precious feet. No large intestine was used; this was not part of the procedure offered by the transplant department. As his voice calmly delivered the news, his body subtly swayed forward and backward just enough for us to barely notice. Exhausted was not the word to describe his physical condition. No, it was definitely something beyond exhaustion.

We thanked him and hugged our hero. And that he was – our hero. Both he and two other transplant surgeons, Dr. Soltys and Dr. Sindhi, were the greatest medical practitioners that walked this earth – according to the Ziegler household. Yes, even those supportive cast members in anesthesiology and the other nurses who did their part in making this super procedure a success were our heroes. We thanked him some more and watched him walk back to through the halls of the quiet and empty hospital.

We returned to our own little world in the unit, where Noah's bed was parked before leaving over thirteen hours before. We both sunk into our chairs and waited for his return. The laptop we borrowed from the hospital was my companion. I used it to record these amazing events and also to send email messages back home.

We connected with a wonderful patient update system offered by the hospital. It was called Carepages and it used email lists as a method to connect to everyone we wanted to reach in our group of family and friends. With every entry I made into the system, a message was sent to all of those who had accepted this link. We absolutely loved this convenient system. All of our friends and family were able to view and even post messages back to us. It was brilliant.

I glanced at my watch – it was 3:15 AM. My body was stiff and cried out desperately for sleep. Sitting and waiting became a career. I kept looking up at the doorway of the ICU. I hoped to see my son each time but had to continue to wait.

Then, breaking the early morning silence, a medical team had appeared and wheeled our superstar into his piece of hospital real estate. They carefully positioned the bed head first, locked the wheels, and then quietly left the room. We immediately stood to our feet and leaned over his lifeless body. He was peacefully asleep and would be in this state for a while. I contained myself, but it was difficult not to break out into a loud cheer for his victory…for our victory.

My first entry into our Carepages system tells the moment like this:

Aug 23, 2004 12:05pm

WE'VE GOT ORGANS!!! It gives me great pleasure to say that on Saturday, August 21, at 12:30 pm, we got the green light from Dr. Mazariegos (the lead transplant surgeon) for Noah to go into the O.R. with both matching and good organs...

...He was done and wheeled back to the ICU at 3:30 am on Sunday. The surgery was very short compared to what they had expected. It went very well with no complications. When we saw Noah, his skin coloring was back to his normal color. The yellow from the jaundice was gone. His chest and stomach no longer had the roadmap of veins he had before and had shrunk down to the size it was over a year and a half ago. Amazing results just out of surgery! The doctor told us that Noah's old liver was one of the worst they've seen and gave us a Polaroid of it. It was black from decay and weighed 7 lbs. It was over 4 times the size of what Noah should have. They also had to remove his spleen due to its increased size.

He has been heavily sedated and is on the ventilator (a very low setting). In fact, this morning the nurse told us that Noah's blood pressure was spiking because he was reacting to his surroundings (the noise around him, the nurses working right beside him, etc.) and they had to give him an increased dose of fentanyl to keep him calm. He wants to wake up and get on with his new life. He is such a fighter! His recovery so far has been excellent.

The docs are very pleased with his progress. He is expected to be paralyzed with meds for a couple of more days and in the ICU for 1 1/2 weeks. He will then be moved up to the 7th floor where he will stay in a normal room recovering. Praise God for His blessing! This has been such a difficult three months here in the ICU with so many lows. Now Noah can experience life as he had before.

We are told to expect Noah's recovery to be about 6 months from post-op. Maybe 6-8 weeks in the hospital, and the rest as an outpatient. Noah will have rejection, but better to have it now than a year from now when it can be very dangerous. Remember, we are at the very best facility in the world for an intestinal transplant. They have done more of them here for the last ten years and have the best success rate. They know what they are doing.

I'll be updating his progress this week. We want to give you a special verse today: Ephesians 3:20 says, "Now unto Him (God) that is able to do exceeding abundantly above all that we ask or think...". God is awesome and is unstoppable! Thank you for your diligence in prayer over the weekend. Your prayers were answered.

Until next time,

God bless you.
Roger, Paula, and Noah (the kid with a new life)

12
UNSTOPPABLE!

AN OPPORTUNITY TO LIVE BEYOND the worst summer of his young life – this is what Noah now held in his hands. He received the most precious gift anyone could ever give – the gift of life. Now he could see beyond the dark cloud that once overshadowed him and focus on a future that was real. This was an amazing opportunity for our little boy.

Our nightmare was over. It was terminated by a lethal dose of perfect hope. Suddenly, we could exhale. Incredibly, we could dream once again.

We were excited to see a transformation of Noah's physical state; from weak and fragile to a body of building and reshaping. It was a slow process and his first steps were to heal and be healthy enough to be transferred from the ICU to the seventh-floor transplant wing.

Paula and I shared a tremendous relief. Our demeanor was that of exhausted winners who crawled over that elusive finish line. I'm sure you have been there at some point in your life. It was like sacks of bricks were finally removed from our shoulders. All we could talk about now was our son - his future and his life. It was freedom he would experience. Some, but not all issues would be dissolved and that was a tremendous value added to his life-account.

Although, it didn't take long for another crisis to appear. Two days after the transplant we were informed by the ICU doctors that Noah experienced serious issues that required immediate surgery. Another wave of concern hit us both. Would this be a minor setback or something that would jeopardize his chances of keeping these precious organs he fought so hard to receive? We called the various prayer chains that had been faithfully lifting up Noah and our family over the last several months. This was our weapon of action against the hostile enemy. This was our offense and our defense. We held onto the mercy and grace of our Lord. We may have been temporarily defeated, but we retained the future victory – no matter the outcome, because of Jesus. Yeah, it was because of Him. He was unstoppable and he held Noah in His tender care.

Aug 24, 2004 11:15am

Hello everyone. We had our first scary moment yesterday. At about 7:00 pm, we received a call from the ICU doctors telling us that Noah's pressures had dropped, his lips were pale, his tummy was distended, and that he needed to be rushed into the operating room for internal bleeding. Paula and I raced to the hospital in record time and arrived with just enough time to pray with Noah. He was awake but groggy and he was concerned with what was going on. They wheeled him away and Dr. Sindhi (transplant) arrived to explain that 1 out of 2 intestinal post-op patients have minor bleeding issues and that it was not uncommon. We waited and called the various prayer chains.

After about 1 1/2 hours, Dr. Sindhi met us in the waiting room and debriefed the surgery. It went very well. There were 2 small areas inside of his belly area (not the new intestines or liver) that were bleeding. They simply put 2 sutures in each and cleaned his cavity thoroughly. He described Noah's internal abdomen area like a warzone after the surgery. There was a strong possibility for minor bleeding during and after the procedure. He said it looks calmer now and Noah would have a good night. They gave him a few units of blood since he lost about 750cc. His face had color afterward and his cheeks were rosy. Whew! Now we know what they mean when they said that Noah's post-op recovery would have many setbacks and that we have the rest of his life to deal with issues. But, we know that he has a chance now. A chance to live and boldly go where he has not been in a long time. The next few months will be very challenging and difficult, but Paula and I are leaning on Christ and are here together for this time.

Paula and the kids are leaving Pittsburgh tomorrow. This will be the first time she has been back to California in months and she wanted to be home for a nice break. After this episode yesterday, Paula has decided to return as soon as possible. Thank you for all of your thoughts, prayers, and messages of encouragement. Please also pray for the donor's family. What an incredibly difficult time this is for them.

Oh, before I forget. Yesterday afternoon, Noah was in and out of sedation and when he heard our voice, he turned to find us. His eyes were half open, but we could see the whites of his eyes were much clearer and the yellow was literally seeping out from the corners. Paula bent down to his face and he asked her for a kiss by puckering his lips around the vent tube. It was the cutest moment. She told him that he has new organs and his smile appeared. This was the first time he heard those powerful words spoken.

God bless you.
Roger, Paula, and Noah

Aug 26, 2004 1:12pm

Hello all. Post-op 4 days and Noah is making steady gains. This morning they extubated him (pulled the ventilator tube) and he is breathing on his own. He also was visited by infectious disease doctors who reported that the bacteria he had before has been wiped out. A scope will be placed in Noah's stoma to see how the new intestines look. Noah has been asking for his favorite Popsicle about every 30 minutes. I asked Dr. Sindhi approximately how long until Noah could have something (even as small as a lollipop) and he said maybe 2 days. Noah's very large "cross-shaped" incision looks wonderful and is healing well. Noah remains on fentanyl for post-op soreness.

What an amazing kid he is.

God bless you,
Roger, Paula, and Noah

Aug 30, 2004 4:55pm

Good afternoon everyone. Noah had a pretty good weekend with no major complications at all. His progress has been slow and steady, but to mom and dad, the gains seem huge. The first scope and biopsy of his intestine was done last Thursday and was wonderful. He will have them done twice a week to monitor tissue changes. Since Noah's incisions were so very large, he is still on heavy pain meds. He was just transitioned down to morphine yesterday. He is still not his old self yet due to the pain meds. He chooses to spend his days watching movies rather than interacting with us.

Today has been Noah's most difficult day so far post-op. He is having long bouts of nausea on and off for the past few days but experiencing it all day since this morning. An hour ago, his blood pressure spiked pretty high and the docs had to give him a few doses of meds to bring it way down. He also has shortness of breath and vomiting. He is somewhat relaxed now, but they put him on an oxygen mask for additional support. Dr. Mazariegos reminded us Noah's stomach has not been used for over three months now. Coupled together with the type of surgery he had and his "lazy" stomach, his vomiting and nausea are understandable. We'll get there. He has not been able to get out of bed since the transplant, but today we were going to try and get him into a chair. That was until his pressures increased and breathing decreased. We'll try tomorrow. We must try to get his lungs expanding.

Please pray for Noah to get transferred up to the 7th floor soon for the duration of his recovery. We should be in the ICU for about another week. Also, continue to pray for his nausea. Thank you all so much.

God bless you,
Roger, Paula, and Noah

Sept 1, 2004 3:40pm

Hey there y'all. Noah had a much better day yesterday (Tuesday) than he had on Monday. Noah's eyes sparkled and he was grinning big. He was more talkative and even told mom that he felt like doing push-ups. His nausea episodes were few and minimal and his pain medication was only used slightly. His breathing is much better and he is doing so without assistance. He is gearing up for a trip to the 7th floor, which will be just around the corner.

As of today (Wednesday), Noah is able to have clear liquids. This morning he had an upper GI contrast study which looks good so far. It is taking time for the contrast liquid to get through the small intestine, so x-rays are being taken every hour or so. His spirits are way up and he is dreaming about the day he will be back home. His scope and biopsy taken earlier this week looked fantastic. The docs are making the transition of his meds from IV to pill form (now that he has a small intestine to absorb with). Soon I'll be posting some new pics taken this week.

Your prayers are being answered...Noah's recovery is going well. Most of all, we sense a peace that only God can provide. Thank you all!

God bless you,
Roger, Paula, and Noah (the kid in the ICU drinking grape punch)

Sept 7, 2004 4:58pm

Hello everyone. Post-transplant now 17 days and Noah is doing well. He is still in the ICU and hopefully will be up on the regular recovery floor by tomorrow. A very bright spot is that his pain meds were discontinued about 5 days ago. His breathing is fabulous (we are trying to make him inflate balloons for the gift shop to sell) and his lungs are stronger (we will be putting out the long-awaited: Lungs of Steel DVD). For the past five days or so, Noah has been getting into a chair for about an hour a day. He is getting stronger with each day and he should be taking a few steps very soon. Noah has been cleared for a regular diet (as in Fatburger or In-N-Out) when he can tolerate it. So far he is struggling to keep small amounts of clear liquids down. Today they put him on a clear tray of food (stuff like Jell-O, Sprite, a Popsicle, and broth) and he only had a few nibbles/sips of each item. He is very apprehensive about throwing up, so he is taking it very slowly. Mom and dad are even trying to sneak in a Chips Ahoy cookie but to no avail...Noah has no desire.

His spirits are very good for the most part. He still has moments where he gazes into the distance and will not talk. Sometimes I think the meds are affecting him, but he is off of the heavy-duty meds that would cause this type of behavior. Still, if I say something or do something funny, he will crack up at me. I know his mind must be going through many things. I bet he thought by now he would be doing better than what he is. To us, he is absolutely a different kid. I feel that once he is able to walk the halls of the seventh floor and interact with other kids at his leisure, he will do much better mentally. He is still fighting through this. We remind him of where he was only weeks ago and how close he was to not making it. The doctors are so amazed that is here with us. The transplant literally could not have taken place any longer than when it did. Thank God for His timing and His grace on Noah.

Talk to you soon.

God bless you,
Roger, Paula, and Noah.

Sept 9, 2004 8:35am

Good Thursday to all. When someone told us a few months ago that we would be trading Noah's advanced liver disease and its complications for another set of difficulties and circumstances (associated with bowel transplantation), we understood and were ready for the challenge. Yesterday, at 4:30 PM, doctors from the transplant team approached us and told us that Noah was rejecting his new small intestine. Our jaws dropped with the shocking news. The doctor went on to explain that Noah's low-grade fevers over the last week and his vomiting were signs, but was confirmed with Tuesday's bowel tissue biopsy. The doc said, "I would be vomiting too based on what I saw under the microscope." They immediately (literally minutes later) gave Noah a bolus (a dose administered rapidly) of a very potent steroid to combat the effects of what his body was naturally doing...fighting the new organ (we already know that Noah is a fighter). He would be getting another dose today and will be watched closely. Yesterday, he was cleared to move up to the 7th floor sometime today. Although, they may keep him in the ICU because of his rejection and it depends on how Noah does. We had to explain to him what was going on inside of his body because he really didn't know. When the explanation was over, he was okay with everything.

He looks wonderful. As each day passes he looks better. We learned last night that his FK (anti-rejection med as it's called) levels are a little high and could be the reason why he is so quiet and a little drowsy all day. The FK levels must be kept within a certain range in order to be most effective, but these bouts of rejection still occur. The good thing with having slightly elevated FK levels is that it could assist the steroid and we could possibly be better by the weekend. Like I said before, better to reject now rather than a year later when the chances are higher for losing this new bowel.

He started a "soft" diet yesterday and so far has been doing well with it. So, Uncle David can hold the chorizo burritos until Noah is better. Let's see how he does today and possibly could move up to solids soon. Noah is only taking very small bites in fear of not keeping it down. He did make one of his typical comments the other day when he saw a TV commercial with children drinking lots of chocolate milk. It may have been a Nestlé's Quik commercial (he loves chocolate milk).

Noah said, "Dad. I know why they have chocolate milk. Because it makes the kids drink it."

"Alright," I said.

Noah continued, "Well, it said that it helps build strong bones. The chocolate doesn't help do that, the milk does. So, they put chocolate in the milk to make kids drink it." I laughed. He chuckled. It was great!

Scary? Absolutely. Concerned? Of course. Rejection can take a couple of different paths, some being very bad for Noah. But, we know in whom we believe. A God who is eternal, all-knowing, and full of love. Because we have a relationship with Christ personally, it gives us the strength to go on with hope. He has rescued Noah from certain death twice. His miracles are provided for many reasons, including to show you that He is real and that you can have that assurance of faith as well in your life. Life is not fair, we all know that. But, in Christ, we have eternal life...guaranteed when this life passes away.

Thank you for your prayers and support. We cherish them. Keep the other kids in prayer for their adventures at their new San Diego schools they started this week.

God bless you,
Roger, Paula, and Noah

Sept 13, 2004 3:17pm

Hey everyone! Let me bring you up to speed...On Friday, at approx. 4:30 PM, transplant docs explained to us that Noah's biopsy (performed earlier that morning) had revealed no change in the cellular structure, as compared to what they saw on the previous Tuesday. He went on to say that Noah's body continued to make the specific cells that were armed and dangerous and ready to take out his new intestine. Noah is so healthy that his body was only doing what it thinks it should. By the way, the liver is not being rejected at all and continues to work perfectly. So the docs had to bring out the next stage in rejection warfare – a lethal steroid unlike what he was taking for the previous two days. This stuff is so strong, that the surgeon himself must inject it into Noah's bloodstream over about 30 seconds while watching Noah's vital signs. The steroid is called OKT3 and it's designed to attack the cells in his body that are rejecting the intestine. The steroid literally focuses on those particular cells and bursts them. The fluid inside of these destroyed cells then flow into Noah's bloodstream and may cause flu-like symptoms (fever, aches, vomiting, etc.). Unfortunately, OKT3 may also disrupt the lung function by allowing fluid to gather and affect breathing. Or, heart conditions may also resurface (like Noah's congestive heart failure). The steroid is only administered once a day and only until the biopsy hopefully reveals a positive change. If so, then he will probably get another day of it. If not, and there is no change in the biopsy, then he will remain on it for perhaps another week.

Noah was feverish and vomiting on Saturday, but since then he has been feeling a lot better. His face has swelled but should reduce when the steroids are discontinued. Through the weekend, Noah has been out of bed and into a chair to strengthen his body. He is doing much better and is taking very small steps. It's amazing to know that transplant doctors consider Noah to be one of the worst kids they have transplanted (in terms of the odds stacked against him and in utter physical despair), but he is doing well overall. Keep in mind that if Noah was not as sick as he was before the transplant, he would have stayed in the ICU for only 3-5 days after the surgery (which is common for kids his age receiving small bowels).

Paula and I also agreed to be interviewed and taped for the Public Relations Dept. here at Children's Hospital. They asked us after consulting with transplant doctors and our family was considered to be used for the taping. Once a year the hospital (being a non-profit entity) organizes a gala fundraiser dinner with Jamie Lee Curtis and Dan Marino as hosts. The guests are usually people that are wealthy and last year over 7 million dollars was donated.

Well, the camera crew arrived at Noah's bedside last Thursday and filmed him doing jumping jacks and...I'm just kidding! They took quite a few shots of us reading an I Spy book and being very engaged. You should have seen the look Noah and I gave each other during the video recording. It was a cool moment. Then, Paula and I were asked to join them in a conference room later for an in-depth interview. We talked about Noah's life from the beginning and all of the many trials we've been through with his health. Hopefully, our story will move people at the dinner event and help the hospital with donations.

Well, I'm headed back to see Noah and find out the results of his biopsy. Thank you for your love and prayers, everyone. You are all very awesome!

God bless,
Roger, Paula, and Noah

Sept 17, 2004 11:43am

Hello everyone. Sorry for the delay. Well, the results are in and Noah's rejection is on the low end. The OKT3 did its job and Noah's last dose was given this past Monday. The docs say that there is a chance the rejection could resurface to the level it was before, so they are watching him closely and are still giving Noah a lesser strength steroid. Tuesday evening Noah was released from the ICU (after 111 days) and sent to the 7th floor (transplant floor) for recovery. What an amazing night that was! Noah now enjoys the peace of his own room and the pleasures of a regular diet (just like he had two years ago).

He is responding very well so far. In fact, Wednesday morning, Paula and I had arrived at his room to find it empty. Did he check out already, we asked each other? Perhaps he took the red-eye flight late Tuesday night and was already back in California enjoying fresh mango smoothies. We were a little perplexed, to say the least. We walked through the hallway of the 7th floor and found Noah in the playroom, sitting in front of a computer flying a helicopter (it was a flight simulator game). What a sight that was! "Hey, dad!" He sounded like he had not been in the ICU for nearly four months. Noah was just so ready to leave that place. The nurse said that she walked him there and we walked him back to his room.

Since then, he has been walking daily and sits in a chair for about half of the day. His face is still puffy from the steroids, but it should shrink soon. Medically, he is low on things like potassium and magnesium, which they infuse as needed. His tube feeds (formula based) are increased daily...today they are at 55ml per hour and are increased daily by 5 until he reaches 80ml per hour. He will be getting another central line put in his chest next Wednesday and will be sent back to California with it in place. It will be used for meds in the treatment of future infections and rejections.

His once extremely low platelet count is now too high and he will be having an aspirin a day. The new liver is working wonders. His intestines are adapting well to the feeds, but they are still not absorbing quite the way they should. It's just a matter a fine-tuning everything and waiting. The docs are also trying to keep his anti-rejection med (FK – which he gets twice a day) at an acceptable level. The trick is trying to give him the right amount orally when the gut is not absorbing at 100%. It will get there soon. His spirits are soaring! He giggles throughout the day and his face lights up. Oh, what a joy!

We also got word yesterday from the docs that they expect Noah to be released from the hospital (no longer inpatient status) in a couple of weeks. Wow! That means he'll be staying at the hotel and coming to his appointments for maintenance and treatment. We are still expecting him to be here in Pittsburgh until February. God is truly working miracles with Noah! I promised updated pictures, and I will post them.

God bless,
Roger, Paula, and Noah

Sept 20, 2004 12:27pm

Happy Monday all! I just posted new pics in the photo gallery...check 'em out. Noah looks wonderful as you can see. He is doing great. He spent the weekend roaming the hospital. We walked to the 9th-floor playroom and down to the 2nd-floor gift shop. His strength is slowing returning and his wit is sharp!

This morning during the visit to gastroenterology (for his scope), he reminded Dr. Squires (Noah's G.I. doc) that he needed to do 7 push-ups today. This started back a couple of weeks in the ICU when I told Dr. Squires that Noah was saving his energy to do push-ups...well, the doc opened his mouth and said he would do a push-up for every time he scopes Noah. That's it. You can believe that Noah will never let the Dr. forget his promise...even now or a decade from now. That's just how Noah is...he remembers so well. Well, Noah said to Dr. Squires, "Drop and give me 7!" The nurses and the other doctor present were laughing. Sure enough, the doctor stretched out his arms and bent down over Noah's bed and performed his exercises (Noah allows him the courtesy of using a modified form where his feet are on the floor but his hands are on the bed rail). It was a good moment.

The scope went well and we are currently waiting for the results of the biopsy. Today, we will be heading to the playroom twice and walk outside on the patio. We're expecting a great week. God is moving powerfully here! Keep your prayers going, as you have been so faithfully doing. They rise up to God as a sweet aroma and He delights in them.

God bless,
Roger, Paula, and Noah

Sept 30, 2004 11:42am

Yes! We are rejoicing, BIG TIME! Our Noah, formerly resident of Children's Hospital Pittsburgh, has been evicted as of Wednesday. He now resides with mom at the Residence Inn for the duration of his recovery and observation period (probably 5 months). Isn't that awesome? He really thinks so. Paula said that the hotel room has been converted to a makeshift hospital room with medical equipment, supplies, and meds. She said the hotel staff will be removing some small pieces of furniture (no, not for Noah to do some old school breakdancing). They have a feverish schedule to keep: taking several meds at certain times, some twice a day, some three times a week instead of daily, and some taken when the earth's moon reaches its second orbit aligned with Mars...(so much to remember). Paula will be investing in a huge calendar for the various daily appointments and med schedule. Noah has become quite the pill popper.

He spent yesterday playing with his many toys and games he received for his birthday. He was as peaceful as he could be. So far, they have the weekends and Tuesdays free from appointments. I think Paula is taking him to go see the new movie "A Shark's Tale" this weekend. I know he will enjoy the experience.

Have a wonderful day everyone.

May God richly bless you.
Roger, Paula, and Noah

"How many cups of Rice Krispy's do I use, mom?" Noah asked curiously as he donned his new chef's hat while standing in the kitchen of the Residence Inn. He was about to embark on a new batch of Rice Krispy treats. Oh yeah, marshmallows and all. Paula stood by his side with the box of cereal in her hands as she read the recipe. It was a moment that marked a championship outcome. Here was our hero, Noah, performing in a scene – hotel kitchen – in his best role to date. He was upbeat, he was outpatient, and he was hungry.

His recovery was on schedule and he made winter of 2004 his grand finale in the great city of Pittsburgh. He was expected to return home after a full recovery by January – just short, several weeks away. Yup, he had sunny Southern California on his mind. No, it wasn't Georgia, as the famous song, but rather warm beaches where the palm trees sway and the sun sets on the wild Pacific Ocean.

He made friends while at the chateau Residence Inn. No, none his age, but instead the team of employees that worked the front desk served snacks and meals, drove shuttle vans, and everyone in between. You see, Noah's personality made it so easy to get along with. His infectious laughter and blinding wit offered anyone around a moment of fun and some chuckling too.

His late evening walks down to the front lobby provided him with a self-served cup of fresh hot chocolate. One pouch was usually sufficient and the disposable cups had sleeves to help keep his hands comfortable and a lid for extended warmth. It was a simple joy that most folks could easily take for granted. Nope, not our superhero. It was not too long ago when he was kept from enjoying such treats. If he had some pocket change, he would make his way down the hall towards the vending machines. If he could pair his delicious hot drink with a squishy cinnamon roll, oh boy. Watch out! Now that was a match made in heaven.

Although Noah was in outpatient status, he was very closely monitored by the transplant team and he was assigned a coordinator who also acted as a liaison between the patient and the medical team. She was an amazing asset to our family. Constant calls to Paula concerning his medications, test results, and very important blood levels were just a few of the vital details she helped to manage.

A rather large addition to Noah's life was his dependency on so many medications. There were at least fifteen various pills that all had a very specific task. Some were taken early morning when he woke up and others were taken at bedtime; then some spread throughout the day and at an appointed time. It was an exercise in time management and one that all three of us shared the responsibility for.

His motor skills were returning with all of the physical therapy sessions he attended. From lifting very light dumbbells to steady muscular stretches of his core to a regular diet of light cardiovascular movements. Our little guy was on his way to a full recovery. There was nothing that could stop his progress if it was left in his control. He decided to put in the work and to set his mind on doing what was necessary each day in order to fulfill every doctor's check-list item. His goal was to reach Southern California soil as soon as humanly possible.

He still had the ostomy bag he was so accustomed to wearing, only it was lower near his hip bone on his right side. His previous jejunostomy was just under his rib cage. This new location at his belt line made for a difficult seal between the square base and the area of his body that tended to bend almost always. The best part was how he could position the bag in such a way that it would be tucked under his pants and conceal the goods. Wink, wink.

Yup. It was Rice Krispy treat delight time! What better tasty morsel could you enjoy during a bitter cold Pittsburgh fall day? Well, maybe a S'mores feast. Noah was able to enjoy all of these wonderful flavors once again. It was a long time without many special foods or ordinary ones for that matter since his narrow restricted diet was prescribed…going on now for two long years. To a kid, that's eternal. To a kid who also was a foodie, that was a never ending eternal extension beyond any possible forever-ness. So, naturally, it became apparent to our little master of cuisine (in the making) that he adopt so passionately the longing to become a chef. Why not? He loved the idea of working in the kitchen and creating delicacies that made taste buds want to ask him for an autograph. Okay, that's a little weird. Perhaps they only wanted to buy his next DVD: *A Feast of Amazing Sizzle*, starring your very own Noah St. Pierre.

Nov 6, 2004 1:03pm
Post operation: 77 days.

Hello everyone. In speaking with Paula yesterday, I learned that Noah was admitted to Children's Hospital for treatment of a virus. His blood work this week revealed an increased white blood count (from the 40,000 to the millions) and testing confirmed that Noah has EBV - a virus that commonly attacks post-transplant patients. He doesn't have symptoms yet and it's a very good thing that they have begun treatment in its early stages. Since it's a virus, the docs can't really treat it directly, so they must reduce his anti-rejection med in order to allow his immune system to function more. This greatly increases the risk of organ rejection. The docs will perform a scope and biopsy of his intestines on Monday to monitor any rejection. Noah will be kept for at least a few days or for a lot longer, depending on his progress.

Please continue to pray for his recovery and a quick release. He is eagerly anticipating his best friend's arrival (Isaac) on Tuesday. Thank you all.

God bless.
Roger, Paula, and Noah

Nov 10, 2004 2:06am
Post operation: 80 days.

Well, Noah was released from the hospital yesterday (Monday) as the doctors had no reason to keep him there during his treatment of EBV. He feels very good and looks swell. He was sent home with a couple of extra meds and additional IV fluid to balance his ins and outs. Praise God! The doctors wanted to scope and biopsy Noah's intestine yesterday, but his blood count was a little low and he received a unit before he was sent home. They are very confident that his body is not rejecting at this time. Noah's anti-rejection med still remains at an acceptable level in his bloodstream, even though they have lowered the dose this weekend...his absorption is just great. Based on that, they don't see any reason to believe he is in rejection. Let's continue to pray that he won't. Also, Noah noticed this morning that he had a walnut-sized lump in his groin area. Paula called the transplant dept. and explained what was discovered. They told Paula that Noah's lymph nodes are a breeding ground for the EBV virus and the lump was an enlarged node. They have scheduled to remove it on Friday.

On a lighter note, Noah's best buddy arrived today. Isaac was excited to see pal when Paula and Noah met him at the arriving gate. Isaac brought Noah a paper placemat with other passenger's handwritten greetings and best wishes for his friend. Paula said it was neat! Together they will ride the storms of life and eat from the gardens of everlasting chocolate chip cookies.

Until next time,

God bless you.
Roger, Paula, and Noah

How do you keep an eleven-year-old transplant patient motivated to be discharged from care over 2,600 miles away and return to his home? Return to his brother and sisters? To his dad? Well, you don't have to. You see, he was ready to resume his normal and regular life that was paused back in October of 2002. He was ready to walk over to his buddy's house nearby and ask if he wanted to go to the park. He was looking forward to that car ride with Brooke, Luke, & Shelby to see the latest spectacular movie on the silver screen. He was ready to hold his hand up in the air, while in class, hoping for his teacher to choose him to deliver that answer he knew. He was ready to rest his head on his pillow – not a hotel fake that just didn't have the right combination of fluff and stiffness – no, HIS pillow. There's nothing like having your own pillow, for with that comes all of that incredible bonus material: your bed, your room, and your home. That was his best source of motivation. That was his WHY.

Yes, he was ready to embark on all of those wonderful things that life brings; all too many of which we take for granted. Not anymore. No, this was our wakeup call and it was Noah's opportunity to shine. Not that he wasn't shining brightly before, but rather this was his opportunity to take a hold of his circumstances and run forward. Not to let himself become just a victim of his circumstances, but become a student of them.

Until you taste the ripe fruit picked from the tree of such despair and misery, it simply is difficult to fully imagine life suddenly rippled with uncertainty and understand how well we have it. Have what? How well we really have life in our busy and sometimes insane lives, from Monday through Sunday. Yeah, even those upside down, twenty-four hour segments that begin with a headache and a hard drive to work. Because once you see your child laying helplessly in a distant hospital room and he's holding onto the hope that fuels his will to survive – until that very moment – you just don't see clearly through all of the haze. Or, until you witness those times when you can't stop your wife from crying profusely because of her broken heart and there's nothing humanly possible she can do to save her little boy. Sometimes it takes that smack in the face to appreciate the 5:45 PM mundane drive home. No, not always. Some are blessed with that understanding and that sense of vision without such terrible strains. Bless you, for that gift if you possess such a wonderful thing. Be sure to share that with others.

And we were welcomed by the melody of this tragedy. A haunting yet enticing melody that beckoned us. With its open arms, it gathered and embraced us as if to keep us warm from the cold world. In the end, it was such betrayal; like a tale of the big bad wolf that actually blew that house down, as the story goes.

Except, we didn't fall for any of tragedy's false promises. Instead, we allowed our captivity only to succumb to the prison walls that kept him for a season, so that one day we would be there when he would be set free. It was our future victory when we would be partakers of his release, of his life being set free. But not by his death – rather, by his new life.

If nothing else, please remember that God is completely unstoppable. No matter what happens, no matter how bleak the circumstances are. Now let that marinade in your heart for a while.

13
WE GIVE THANKS

THE COMMERCIAL JET BURST THROUGH the wide open skies on its way from San Diego, CA en route to the Pittsburgh International Airport. Luke was restless in his seat and I tried to keep him occupied with his 8" tall action figures and some coloring books. Brooke and Shelby sat near the window. They were very excited to see mom and brother. My dad and Peggy were on this flight as well. This was a Thanksgiving trip we all so desperately needed to spend together. The time apart was wearing down the kids. I could see it in each one – especially Shelby. The oldest often bear the burden for the younger siblings and this situation was no different. Luke had been missing his mom so much. She would call him often and he just couldn't understand the concept of time.

"Luke, can you take a look at grandpa's calendar?" Paula would say to Luke over the phone. "Do you see today – Tuesday the 5th on the calendar?"

"Yes mom," Luke replied.

"Okay. I will talk to you again in two more days. Look at Thursday the 7th. Do you see it?"

"I see it, mom," Luke sounded like he finally understood.

"I will talk to you again on that day," she said.

"Okay, but when will I talk to you again?" He just didn't comprehend days and time. Paula's heart was crushed and she cried tears of longing to be with our children. She eagerly wanted to hold them, each one, and reassure them that they would be alright. She desired to have them stay with her and Noah in Pittsburgh, but they needed to attend school.

This Thanksgiving visit was going to be a huge blessing for us all. Looking ahead, I knew it would be so difficult to leave Paula and Noah behind at the end of our stay. But, it would be well worth the heartache and separation. I would give the world to be by my wife's side and hold Noah on top of the world, upon my shoulders, for just a few minutes these days. I would do so in a heartbeat.

Our jetliner flew Mach speed across the vast heavens. Well, not necessarily Mach speed per se. Maybe just supersonic, sound-barrier-breaking type speed or close to it. We suppressed the tingling feeling in our bones and studied the minutes passing slowly on our watches. My heart was dancing already. I couldn't wait to see them. Luke was pretty much bouncing around in his seat and would have me race him to the restroom every so often. His warning system was not fully matured and he would rather wait until the sense of urgency to pee was paramount. Like, I've gotta go now! Classic baby boy Luke.

The hours passed quickly and soon we were hearing the announcement from the pilot to prepare for our descent into Pittsburgh. We collected our books, toys, and snacks and placed our seats in the upright position. I checked with the girls – they were eager and ready to see mom and Noah.

Our landing was smooth, then we taxied to the terminal and exited the plane. After we gathered our luggage and checked into the car rental desk, we finally walked to the parking structure to locate our minivan. The air smacked us like a whip on the cheeks. Yup, a chilly thirty-five degrees. Quite a difference from the balmy seventy-two San Diego November air we left behind. We packed the kid's gloves and beanies for the cold-weather beating we knew was ahead. We found our ride and mounted up. After a few minutes, we called Paula to let her know we were on the parkway eastbound.

We pulled into the Residence Inn hotel parking lot after a half-hour drive and parked near the main entrance. The kids couldn't contain themselves. We managed to leave most of the luggage in the minivan as we raced into the elevator from the ground floor. We piled into the narrow elevator room and it slowly climbed upward. We felt the immediate heat blasting into the hotel building to help counter the effects of wintery weather conditions. After a long pause, the doors opened and our eyes screamed with delight. The sight of Paula and Noah, well, there was nothing more perfect. Noah did his best impression of an Olympic athlete and rushed to embrace us. Paula was right behind. Tears and smiles – that summed up the moment perfectly. The grin on Noah's face had instantly erased all sorrow bottled up over the last several weeks within the chambers of my heart. Our champ was looking great and he couldn't wait to spend some quality time telling his siblings all about the interesting life of a multi-visceral transplant patient in great detail. Paula's embrace was deep and heartfelt. It killed me to be away from her. I knew for at least several days I would be in a state of bliss having her warm touch and loving encouragement.

It was hot chocolate served all around the room and our kids made themselves at home in the almost cozy hotel room. They were home in their minds. Who cares about the address, location, or latitude and longitude? That stuff didn't matter at all. Because when you have each other, you have it all. You have your mother's nurturing and her caring words to dispel all of the nightmares that plague the mind. The disaster of tragedy seemed to be all but gone. They immediately resumed those tender moments they shared with her last time they were in Pittsburgh, last summer. Without a hitch, Shelby, Brooke, and Luke nestled right up against their tender mother, ready to ride off into the sunset and put an end to this journey. Yeah, it was a priceless Hallmark moment.

Our dear friends from the local church graciously allowed us the use of their beautiful home for the Thanksgiving weekend. They were heading out of town with their family and told Paula it would mean the world to them if we would enjoy our family time there instead of the hotel. Are you kidding me? We willingly accepted and couldn't believe the generosity and hospitable gesture of folks we barely knew. The love of our brothers and sisters in Christ was powerful and was a common theme in the hearts of those who came and visited Paula and Noah during the last several months. No agenda and no motive other than to love them and be a shoulder to cry on for Paula.

We packed our things and drove to the Green's house on Thanksgiving morning. We planned to buy a turkey dinner at The Boston Market for convenience and find a local market for any goods we would need. It was a good plan. We had a map and an address, but it was like a journey in a new land. The terrain and surroundings were not familiar. Although, it was a very nice community and neighborhood. As we turned down a side street, sensing we were nearby, we noticed a large grass field and a playground tucked away off the street. We slowed a bit and looked carefully for their address.

"There it is," Paula declared. "Yay! Here we are, kids."

"Oooh, they have a nice house, mom." Shelby enjoyed the neighborhood and the cute style of their home. It had that warm curb appeal and we felt so welcomed.

We piled out of the minivan and carried our things into our temporary place of lodging. My dad and Peggy made local reservations at a nearby hotel. The home had three bedrooms, a den, a family room, and a very comfortable décor. But, it would be a little tight with our six and two more.

Our first order of business was a walk down the street to that playground we passed earlier. It was only a few blocks away, so we figured we would have a nice brisk walk and enjoy some the chilly air we never see in Southern California. Luke and Noah were out in front with grandpa. Then, as the playground was in sight, Luke and Noah burst out in a fierce race. It was a blessing to see Noah, now three months post-transplant, begin to run and explore his new life. I burned the images in my mind so that later on I could replay them – one at a time. They were fuel for later encouragement.

The girls ran after the boys and they climbed the large wood and steel forts. The slides and swings were no match for the Ziegler kids. No, they explored and conquered every bit of entertainment this playground offered them. More smiles and laughter filled the cold air. We had the place to ourselves.

This is what life is made of. This is the stuff that makes memories stay for a lifetime. We had each other. In a state far, far away – we just had each other. There was nothing or no one that could take this away from us. I didn't want this day to end. It was perfect.

As we spent some awesome time together, something made us pause and stare at each other. Was it snowing? Now, we knew what an ocean breeze felt like. Or how a ray of pure sunshine grazing our foreheads can bring a sense of warmth. No, this was something different. Snowflakes? Really? Yeah, it's called Fall in Pittsburgh, Pennsylvania. Wow! I was amazed. The kids began to giggle and race around trying to collect as many as they could with their wide-open mouths. Then, we decided to start walking back to the comfort of a heated home. The threat of getting pounded by a Nor'easter nearly an eighth of a mile from safety was enough motivation. Do you sense the intense drama? We couldn't bear the "sub-zero" 30 degrees that surrounded every pore. To us, it felt like certain doom. To the average local, it was like springtime.

We drew sticks to see who would be the one to sacrifice themselves for the group and run back to the house ahead of the clan and drive the minivan back. Yeah, it was me. I trotted carefully but quickly uphill, in the snow (light trickle at best), against the piercing winds (maybe four knots out of the east), and braved starvation (my last meal was consumed about three hours earlier) and climbed into the vehicle. Nailed it!

Okay, so once we were officially safe from harm's way and sweating bullets amidst a furnace-induced heat stroke, we enjoyed a terrific night of Thanksgiving joy. The turkey dinner was subpar but seemed like the best meal ever. The surroundings were unfamiliar (although wonderful accommodations), but we felt like we were at home. I gazed around the room continuously throughout the evening and marveled at how much fun each and every person was having. Noah was in absolute peace laughing with his siblings. His jokes were bright and funny. Luke was eating up special time with Paula and wore a permanent smile. Yes, if Hallmark moments do exist then this was definitely one for the ages.

Then, another setback hit our home front.

Nov 29, 2004 3:33pm

Wow! What an amazing visit we had in Pittsburgh. It was the best Thanksgiving ever! All of the children were together and Noah had a blast. Paula was very happy to see her babies. We even had the pleasure of spending the holiday in a real home in a suburb of Pitt. The youth pastor at Calvary Pittsburgh took his family to a cabin and he offered his home to us for half of the week. It was great. There were even snow flurries on Thanksgiving. It was very difficult to leave on Saturday.

Today, Paula called to let me know that Noah's lab work has revealed a possible bout with rejection for his liver. The enzyme levels are wacky as well as other things. He will be admitted today and have a liver biopsy tomorrow. It will confirm what they believe is going on. Please pray for Noah, he is upset and will likely be in for a while to receive treatment. He is also worried about the long needle used for the liver tissue sample.

We'll keep praying. Thank you for your ongoing prayers.

God bless,
Roger, Paula, and Noah

Dec 3, 2004 11:04am

Hello all. The liver biopsy returned positive for liver rejection in its early stages. He was given a large dose of a new steroid and will be hospitalized at least through Monday. The docs say that the process is much easier to reverse than small bowel rejection (like Noah had in September). He sounds wonderful over the phone and spends his days on the 7th floor with a buddy who has been there for quite a while (Ali - had a multi-organ transplant 2 years ago). In fact, they share a room so you can imagine the havoc they cause in the transplant ward. The other night they were both up until 4 in the morning.

Noah and Paula went to a Christmas party there at the hospital and there were a few Pittsburgh Steelers there to greet the kids. I think I was more excited than Noah was (he is a true Dallas Cowboy fan). Anyway, it was fun and Paula has a Polaroid photo from the event.

I'll keep everyone posted. We don't know if this will affect Noah's January target discharge; it's still too early to tell. I do know that his maintenance fluids have been increased this week and they were trying to discontinue them by mid-December for an early January release. We'll know more about that next week.

God bless,
Roger, Paula, and Noah

Dec 6, 2004 4:50pm
Monday briefing:

The liver numbers have doubled since Friday. The liver rejection is not reversing as of yet. This weekend, there were hopes that Noah would be released today, but what we learned this morning will not support that. When Noah learned of the news as the doctors made their rounds, his eyes swelled with tears and he tried to hold back his disappointment. Paula said that the team of doctors and nurses making rounds were crushed to see him like that. Noah is usually so upbeat, but this is such a difficult path he is on...it's hard to imagine what goes on inside his head. Later this week he will undergo a scope and biopsy to see where the liver tissue stands. We also learned that EBV levels have increased as a result of this recent treatment.
I'll keep you posted.

God bless,
Roger, Paula, and Noah

Dec 9, 2004 7:04pm

Hello everyone. Based on the liver samples from the second biopsy, Noah is still rejecting his liver. He's been getting a strong steroid and increasing his anti-rejection medication. His absorption is on the low side for his anti-rejection medication. Even though it has been increased steadily over the weekend, his numbers keep dropping. This can be a precursor to small intestine rejection, so they are watching his output and other signs closely. We're reminded again of how delicate Noah's body is concerning his rejection possibilities. But, he's hanging in there and the day passes they receive for temporary outside excursions help keep his mind off of it just a little.
Please continue to lift him up in prayer.

Thank you!
Roger, Paula, and Noah

Dec 13, 2004 2:42pm

Greetings all. Noah's weekend was fair. Saturday brought results showing a reversal in the liver rejection. Sunday showed an increase in his liver numbers (wrong direction) and being stubborn. He was given day passes to leave the hospital but had to be confined to areas where there are hardly any people (due to his suppressed immune system). He is on his last dose of the 5-day Solumedrol and we shall see where he is today.

On Saturday, Paula left the 7th floor (where Noah is) to see a friend in the ICU (a mother with a daughter who is fighting for her life). When she returned, she saw Noah pushing another child around the transplant unit. The friend is 5 years old and he doesn't have use of his legs. He uses a walker to stand and needs to be wheeled around by others. The boy has taken to Noah after they met during a clinic appointment. Paula said it was very touching to see our Noah, who is fighting liver rejection, bless another child. She said that the boy's legs hung limp as Noah carefully pushed him through the halls with the walker. A nurse approached Paula with tears in her eyes and told her how special Noah is. She went on to say that the child's mom was not there that day and Noah was pushing him throughout the transplant floor and hanging out with him. Paula walked over to the room and peeked around the corner to see Noah picking up his friend from the walker to help him sit in a chair. He struggled but managed to bring him alongside himself. Noah gently adjusted the boy's limp legs and they sat watching TV. God is even using Noah to touch other kids!

What amazing love our God supplies.

God bless,
Roger, Paula, and Noah

Dec 20, 2004 12:03pm

Yaaaahooo! We made it to Pittsburgh for the Christmas holiday! Luke, Shelby, Brooke, and I flew from San Diego (thanks to Calvary Chapel Pacific Coast) to Atlanta and changed flights to arrive in snowy Pittsburgh last night at 7:00 pm. It was a very smooth flight and Paula met us at the airport. It has been a fabulous reunion and we will be staying until Dec. 30. It's cold today (19 degrees), but we're bundling up the kids with blankets, sofa cushions, buffalo skins, and nuclear thermal underwear. Noah looks fantastic. He was kicked out of the hospital on Friday in preparation for our arrival. The doctors were going to keep him in through the weekend but were persuaded otherwise by Paula, Noah, and a nurse practitioner. He's at his appointment now and will be taking his 4-month post-transplant picture with the doctor. Can you believe it has been 4 months already? With this recent bout of liver rejection, we are looking at February for Noah and Paula to come home. Let us continue to pray for no more delays.

Last week, our good friend Jessica lost her 20-month-old daughter to a long fight with end-stage liver disease. She passed away before she could receive a transplant. She was waiting for a small bowel and liver along with Noah this past summer in the ICU. We met her mom here at the Residence Inn and Paula has been a great friend to her ever since. The Lord put Paula and Jessica together for a special reason. Paula could identify exactly with the struggles Jessica faced and was an incredible blessing as she drove her around Pitt and brought her to church. They were very good company for each other as well. Noah took it pretty hard as he loved his little friend so very much and felt compassion for her as she fought long through the very things he did. Jessica flew back to her home and will have a service today for her daughter. Our hearts are very heavy for her. Please pray for comfort.

We know that God has Noah in the palm of His hand and whatever He has for Noah, it's perfect. Today, we will live for Christ and enjoy the very breath He gives.

From snowy Pittsburgh,

God bless.
Roger and family

January 2005. Whew! Made it. Noah was firing on all seventy-two cylinders and he dripped with anticipation for his release from outpatient care. The months of treatment supported his healing and his return to Olympian form. His appetite was stellar and he enjoyed everything from hearty beef sandwiches, to french fries smothered in french fries, to triple-thick chocolate milkshakes, to all of the fruit under the sun (or whatever decent varieties Paula could find in the gloomy part of the world they were in). His taste buds never felt so good.

Paula helped him maintain his rigorous and extremely detailed medication regimen. Most of the time Noah was pleasant and had a great time bouncing around in da 'Burgh with Paula. We had leased a vehicle for her thanks to brother-in-law David (the most decorated Toyota salesman this side of Pluto) and Paula was able to get around to medical appointments freely as well as enjoy their mobility. We needed a second vehicle, so it turned out to be an awesome idea. Noah was her co-pilot and they explored the city and all of its splendors.

During the first follow up appointment of the year, Noah harassed Dr. Squires yet again during the scope of his small bowel. Noah never forgets.

"So, doctor Squires. I think you are up to eight push-ups today. Yup, this is scope number eight today," Noah said with a smile and a certain amount of confidence.

"Are you sure Noah?" The kind doctor replied with sarcasm in his tone. "I thought we were not doing that anymore."

"Oh yes we are. You owe me eight big ones doc!" Noah was like a bill collector for a large financial institution – gritty and persistent.

"Oh, okay. Here we go. One. Two." Doctor Squires was trying to cheat a bit.

"No you don't. Go all the way down, cheater!" Noah was unforgiving.

"…seven…eight," the doctor exhaled as he recovered from his modified push-up position. Smiling doctors can make young patients a whole lot better with the power of upbeat influence. Dr. Squires was no different.

Noah had such an incredible effect on those treating him – doctors, nurses and all practitioners alike. Even those whom he came across while hospitalized; those who tended to his food service and room cleanings. He charmed them all with kindness - genuine and sincere. He made a lasting impression on many whom he met and they were an important part of his world.

Then there were days where the sun didn't shine so much in his heart. You know, those days when pity parties seem like the right thing to throw – more like tantrums. Paula had some difficult times when Noah was not at his best. It was in those times I beat myself up and wish I were there. How could she do this alone? There was so much on her shoulders. The burden was intense caring for and being a superhero mother to a child recovering from a huge medical ordeal. We began to see the need for emotional support for these transplant patients and all of the trauma they endured – their families as well.

Noah began to adopt a "why me" mentality. He would say that all he wanted was to be normal. It wouldn't show itself often, but this type of thinking began to carve out a niche in his mindset. Little did he know, this would begin to take on life and grow into a daunting menace he would struggle with for a long time.

14
HOMECOMING

"DID YOU CHECK THE RETURNING FLIGHT info, Roger?" my mother asked while we waited nervously in the terminal.

"Yeah, mom. Arrival is at 11:25 and the panel says it's on time," I replied anxiously.

The Los Angeles International Airport was strangely empty. Probably because it was Tuesday morning. I had way too much energy running through my body. It was tough to remain calm and so it was for Shelby, Brooke, and Luke.

We waited for this moment for so long and it became our day of victory – Noah's day, really. We were like electrified fans holding our collective breath for our favorite world-famous rock band to descend down that narrow escalator. We felt giddy and ridiculously silly, but it was everything we ever wanted. At any moment our favorite superhero & transplant patient would be stepping off of that escalator and step back into our reality – and his new one.

Our very long banner was raised as we held it for all to see. It read in bold, loud letters: Welcome Home Noah! With our eyes trained on every person coming out of that corridor like a panther focused on its prey, suddenly the air escaped from the entire luggage area where we stood. It was like all sound immediately reset to zero decibels and time stood still. And there he was. We cheered. We laughed. We cried. I can't describe how big his grin was, especially with the huge amounts of steroid medication he was taking that caused his cheeks to grow six and a half times their normal size – but he smiled like you wouldn't believe. He ran to us and we ran to him and to Paula. She was also so radiant and wore a huge expression of relief. She made it too. This was for her as well. Her celebration and his.

We all hugged Noah tightly, but not too much because we didn't want to squeeze the jelly out of him. We embraced until the cows came in... well, maybe not that long (being there's not a farm animal in sight at LAX), but we cherished every second. The kids handed Paula a bouquet of colorful flowers, they kissed, held onto her and would not let go... not ever.

"Guess what we have Noah?" my words were filled with enthusiasm.

"What dad?" Noah answered like he expected to hear me say we had all of the Dallas Cowboys hidden inside compartments and would suddenly make their grand entrance to see him too.

"We have a limo outside waiting for you," I said. "And it's all yours."

"Yeah! Let's go!" he said as he started making his way towards the exit doors while pulling his medication bag on its two wheels.

I walked him and our kids outside to the curb where an ultra-long white pearl limousine was parked waiting for his majesty. Noah's eyes bulged out and his jaw dropped.

"It's like the one we took when we went on my Make-A-Wish trip, dad. Wow!" He was ready to take it for a spin.

He jumped in and made himself at home along with his siblings. There was Luke hopping around like he owned the place. I counted four huge smiles and told them to sit tight as I closed the passenger door. I turned to the driver and asked him if he could take them for a spin around the airport grounds (this place was huge). He gladly obliged. The black-hole tinted windows rolled down and revealed a party in the making with Noah being the ring leader. They pulled away and I could not ask for a better moment. No, this one was definitely hard to beat.

Shortly after our reunion, we rode down to Long Beach on our way home and stopped for lunch. Yup, it was Bubba Gump Restaurant. Where else would we take Noah? Of course, he ordered a huge, triple-thick milkshake, double milk and extra ice cream – no shrimp, please. Magical. We had a large table that accommodated all of us; my mom, my stepfather Lionel and a few dear friends included. I took constant inventory of our family members and just couldn't believe the blessings we were enjoying at that moment. I was the proud father to such amazing daughters and sons and a blessed husband to the greatest wife that ever lived. We all enjoyed our lunch and told stories of what the last year brought us and how the future had so many more adventures in store. Noah had a lot to do and time was wasting.

Later that evening we marveled at the new Noah. Yeah, he was Noah 2.0 and had many improvements over the previous model. In fact, he had some new hardware installed! Wow. Even from another manufacturer that worked in harmony with his framework. I couldn't believe it. Oh, but it was so true!

We celebrated many things that night. This included not having to rely on running twenty hours of TPN and lipid fluids to keep his body going. Nope, not a drop of the stuff in sight. Only a much shorter infusion of standard-issue hydration fluids over eight hours and infused via a miniature pump that was portable. Ta-da! He was able to wander the halls of his townhome in style, minus the IV pole he once used to drag along and with it attached two heavy medical devices. Can you say: top heavy? Not many people get to experience the thrill of manipulating a five-foot tall, chrome metal pipe on wheels with two massive, metal boxes connected all throughout the house. Yeah, it was a pain and a half. Although Noah did it as gracefully as anyone could. In typical Noah fashion, he seemed to make it a normal part of his daily life. After all, that was probably the easiest thing he previously dealt with. Let's see, end-stage liver disease versus hauling an IV pole around for most of the day – Yup, metal pipe on wheels wins…every time!

We had a lot to restore. There was heartache, sorrow, and disappointment throughout the last year and now it was time to get back into our groove. It almost felt like we all just completed mental boot camp, seven Ironman Triathlons, two full marathons, and survived a nuclear holocaust. We were emotionally spent and physically trying to pick up the pieces – and heal. But today was day one. Wipe the slate clean and start fresh. We sensed a newness about our future and maybe, just maybe, we could begin to live outside of the constant crisis mode we so often encountered. It was like that post-traumatic moment when the adrenaline bursts subsided and all that was left was a lethargic mess.

Paula and I tucked each of our children into bed and gave big hugs and kisses. They were relieved. The nightmare was over for them too. Luke thoroughly enjoyed having his roommate and big brother back. He hopped up on his bed with a bright smile. The boys were back.

The evening was serene in our home. I could hear the faint sound of a mechanical pump that was cycling Noah's evening hydration fluids. It was a much quieter and less imposing sound than his previous medical pump rhythmic racket. It reminded me how far he had come, but also that he still required support. I counted the seconds between the new rate of dosage the pumped was now synced to. It calmed me like counting sheep does for some. The life of a parent with a chronic-illness child – I guess only some could really understand.

**

March 2, 2005

It was time. Noah had to return to Pittsburgh for a scope and a biopsy. It was a scheduled visit and procedure that would help the doctors keep a close eye on his bowel tissue. Of course, Noah showed up with his tricks up his sleeve in a typical fun fashion. The transplant team always enjoys his laughter and sense of humor. And yes, Dr. Squires had to perform his duty in honor of our star patient. Front leaning rest position…move! Push-ups were done and one additional up/down was added from the last scope. Noah approved.

After a round of hellos to the staff, they took a shuttle to the famous Residence Inn hotel. Thank you insurance company. This time the visit was under much better circumstances and no dark cloud of stress was visible.

These scopes were expected to be performed every month for at least three or four months until the team felt comfortable with his progress. But there was great news – no scope was required until his one-year post-transplant examination in August. Yesss! This was great news indeed. Noah and Paula were back home in a flash two days later.

Noah seemed to struggle with the climate at home, which was dry and warm. The plentiful sunshine did wonders for emotional lifts, but also put a hitch in Noah's giddy-up. Dehydration episodes began to take the shape of a consistent bully and were beasts to contend with. Since his return in February, he was rushed to the ER for severe dehydration. This episode happened in spite of the daily infusion of saline – usually one-and-a-half liters of the stuff over eight to twelve hours. Even though he received this additional support every day, the fact that he didn't have a large intestine kept him from completely absorbing the three liters of water he drank every day. We would chant, "Drink, Noah, drink!"

We monitored his ins and outs every day with accurate charting notations. Still, his kidneys have taken a big blow from his anti-rejection meds and other medication combined with his frequent dehydration. A renal test was scheduled in order to determine the health of his kidneys. Until Noah can develop a pattern of being hydrated, he is not able to attend school or play any sports.

I know it rubbed him the wrong way. Our son's ongoing pursuit of being a normal kid was never-ending. He longed for this state of normalcy just like his buddies easily enjoyed. At this point in his life, he endured a torturous battle with end-stage liver disease and a survived against all odds last summer. When will the reminders go away? When will the voices of his recent past stop haunting his mind, with the nonsense of how sick he used to be? He was not about to let something else take over his life – not on his watch.

Apr 19, 2005 1:49am

Here we are in April, enjoying the beautiful So. California weather.

Noah is doing well these days. He has been enjoying bike riding, crackin' baseballs, throwing touchdowns, laughing with his buddies, and rollin' on his Heelys. I guess you could say he is back to where he was about three years ago...in a way. You see, Noah must be homeschooled by the school district because of his dehydration issues and compromised immune system. He probably won't return until the fall (where he will begin middle school). Noah is fine with that, but when you really see him day in and day out, he longs to be like everyone else. To him, it means being in a regular school where all of his other friends attend. It means being able to ride his bike without wearing a portable CAD pump/backpack to keep him hydrated. It also means being able to play ball outside when it's 78 degrees on a mildly warm day - and not pay for it over the next few days in the hospital. Yeah, and it's not even summer yet. What I'm trying to say is please understand that Noah still needs your prayers. He has a long road ahead and I'll be the first one to say what a blessing we have in his new life! Don't get me wrong. I'll take this post-transplant care any day versus where we were a year ago.

Our goal as of now is to learn Noah's limitations in regards to weather/activity and how to maintain positive hydration levels in him. We know that because he is missing his entire large intestine (which absorbs water into the system) and his ostomy output seems to "dump" excess fluids that should be retained, his oral intake of even up to 3 liters is not enough. We daily chart his ins and outs to get a snapshot of where he is and where he could be heading (i.e. severe dehydration). He is also connected to his CAD pump daily to infuse a minimum of 1500cc of saline over long periods of time into his bloodstream, sometimes more. Thank God for that thing!

We also know that his kidneys take a hit each time his fluid levels are low and toxins are present rather than being flushed out. Dr. Nanjundiah is doing an exceptional job of watching him intently and dedicating moments each day to Noah. She works behind the scenes sometimes with surgeons in Pittsburgh and she will see something develop in Noah's blood work. She calls any time of the day to let us know and how to address it early. She is awesome! She loves Noah dearly and often jokes with him about having him move in with her family. She is a vegetarian but will have a pizza party for Noah if he were to live there. Please continue to pray for God to give her wisdom and insight into his care.

Paula is extremely busy these days with Noah as well. God knew that she was going to be a stay home mom for Noah's medical care and has given her more than just a lovely mother's heart. She has been the greatest caregiver to Noah than we could expect. Paula has this stuff down incredibly well and I'm not just saying that because we're going steady or anything. I've got big shoes to fill when she gets out for a day or stays overnight with her sister. Yes, please continue to lift her up as well.

Our fundraising efforts are just now beginning to take shape. Pete has dug into a campaign for us that will involve restaurant discount cards and we are waiting for our order of green wristbands (like the yellow ones Lance Armstrong has launched) to arrive. Brother David is heading up a campaign with dealerships as well. Suzanne has brought Noah's fundraising awareness to the school's PTA board and we will be having a "Noah Z" booth at Sequoia Elementary carnival in June. We plan on doing a silent auction and raffle of some sort. Every bit counts! If you haven't already, log on to cota.org and look at Noah's campaign info. If you can be of any help with these or other campaigns, don't hesitate to call. We are in need of "hands and feet."
Thank you, everyone!!

May God richly bless you.
Team Z.

Camp Chihopi

Every year the transplant team at Children's Hospital of Pittsburgh host a wonderful excursion for those kids who have dealt with transplants, both liver and intestines, and a combination of those combined with other organs. The camp is called Camp Chihopi and it's held in West Virginia at a secluded lake amongst rolling hills and extra tall trees. The goal is to have as many children attend, but their health must be strong enough to endure the four-day adventure and not have any existing illness (infections, rejections, etc.).

Here's the stinger: no parents are allowed. What?! Who will be there to care, to monitor, to protect, to shelter, to feed, to administer meds? Yup, you guessed correctly – the transplant doctors, clinicians, and nurses themselves! Outstanding idea, right? The kids get to be kids and enjoy life outside of their home life, in addition to build relationships with others just like them. Brilliant.

The camp offers the typical fun that summer getaways provide: boating, canoes, fishing, campfires, silly songs, average food, and a whole lot of laughter. They will don the latest t-shirts that are designed and printed with the current year's logo. This will be something they can wear back home and remember the good times.

Older more seasoned campers often return to be camp counselors. The mentors could provide guidance around the camp activities, but also shed some light on younger patients and share how they were able to live life with chronic illness. This is a powerful way to build that sense of belonging amongst them, in a world that may look at these precious few and label them as misfits or outcasts.

Noah was thrilled and could not wait until the first week of August to attend. It would mark his first year as a transplant patient and also his first annual complete physical. Kids from all around the country (some from overseas) arrived the week before to camp. Each one received a physical during the clinic appointment and were cleared for the long weekend at camp, which began on Friday.

Paula and I figured that since the staff would not allow us to visit, attend, drop-in, fly over, or parachute in while he was at camp, we would make it a long overdue mini-vacation. It was perfect! We would be able to have our other kiddos stay with family and be completely sure that Noah was in the best hands. Think about it, if any of the campers required medical attention, the actual transplant surgeons were there to perform any needed procedure. Well, maybe not actual vascular surgery, but perhaps yank out a stubborn kidney if required.

I could see it now, "Hey Noah. Put down that canoe paddle and hold this IV bag up over your head while I start your midline incision," the doc would say with confidence. "Oh no doc," he would reply, "Not until you give me some strong pain meds and get me off of this boat first." That cracks me up to visualize such a moment.

So Pittsburgh, here we come. Our insurance company scheduled the flights for Noah and Paula since the camp was held just after his post-transplant exam and tests. The flight was covered along with hotel accommodations for those days. The trip was exciting for both of us and for Noah, the star patient.

**

Dr. Nanjundiah, his gastroenterologist, took very good care of Noah while we enjoyed life at our Southern California home. Being such a long way from our security blanket (the surgeons and the medical team at Children's Hospital of Pittsburgh) made it an important part of her treatment and philosophy to deliver the very best care our son required. She was second to none in her pursuit of knowledge surrounding intestinal and liver transplant medical care. She was intensely driven and felt the obligation to our family was square upon her talented shoulders. Dr. Nanjundiah was one of our heroes, especially for Noah. He really liked her and trusted her word concerning his meticulous treatment. She also admired him as well.

She referred to Noah as her star patient. Noah giggled every time she addressed him with that title. He would smile with endearment and put his head on her shoulder. It was an incredible bond that had developed.

Our doctor met with Noah one last time before his trip to Pittsburgh. She made sure his labs returned with no surprises that would prevent him from attending his very first camp. She also made sure that his transplant coordinator had traveling details and documentation for medication clearance on the commercial flights.

The trip required an entire military arsenal of gear and medications. The carry-on bag needed to contain every single medication he took daily, ostomy care (appliances and gear), a CAD pump with appropriate tubing packages, disinfectant and cleaning supplies (skin prep and such), at least one extra one liter bag of saline fluids (in addition to one for each day), and the kitchen sink. Everything a transplant patient needs to keep going.

**

"Good morning Noah. Time to get up," Paula gently said to our sack of potatoes who was fast asleep. "Let's get you to camp." She was enthusiastic and filled with excitement. It wasn't so long ago that she was by his side daily while he was fighting for his life. Now, it was a time for building memories with new adventures.

Noah sprang up like a rocket. He was wiping the sleep from his beet, red eyes. The time change didn't help; three hours difference and not in our favor.

"I'm up mom," he said with frogs stuck in his throat, but eager to get on with the day.

We quickly got him dressed and with bags in tow, we were off to the races. It was a very quick drive to the hotel meeting point or launching pad of sorts. As we parked we could see families file into the hotel lobby and a monstrous pile of luggage and sleeping bags lined up against a large rental moving truck. We followed the rest of the campers through the lobby and approached the check-in desk. A nurse from the transplant floor looked over Noah's paperwork and examined his meds for accuracy. She also had a list of times and dates for med administration – everything was on a tight schedule.

After a few more questions, she handed Noah a camper t-shirt that read: Camp Chihopi on the front. Bright colors made the transplant kids stand out from the rest. We walked back outside where the rest of the parents and kids were huddled. After a few minutes, we gave Noah our tightest hugs and Paula's loudest kisses then sent him off to start his day, his day one of transplant camp morning. He waved and grinned from ear to ear as he marched over to a large area for breakfast – campers only.

We watched him sit at a table and connect with other patients – other preteens and teens. Paula and I slowly stepped around the outside of the building just to catch a glance of our son. We stood behind a few bushes (big time creepers) so that he wouldn't see us. I grabbed my camera and snapped a quick picture or two because this moment was fantastic. You see, we hadn't been away from Noah at all since his big episode in October 2002. Almost three full years. We didn't have the luxury of relying on a sitter. Yeah, he was eleven and twelve during those years – not a kid anymore. But, the reality was he required so much constant help managing all of those medical necessities and we just couldn't bring a family member up to speed. The learning curve was too huge and we really didn't want to put that pressure on someone else's shoulders.

We paused there for several moments enjoying the blessing of what our eyes beheld. I wished the rest of the world could understand our victory. It was something only a few would deeply appreciate. Before our position was compromised, Paula and I scurried away. We were young kids again, giggling and laughing at our little secret. I loved sharing these moments with my favorite person.

All parents of the transplant campers were invited to attend a buffet breakfast across the street from the send-off point. The event was a tradition and each year a few speakers delivered the state of the transplant department. New research discoveries were announced and the pioneer himself, Dr. Starzl, gave his wonderful speech about his passion in this field. It was uplifting and encouraging. Our minds were occupied with food, new friends, and great speakers – until...

"Greetings parents," Bev said from the podium. She was instrumental in teaching us how to live with the challenges our kids had to face. "I would like to let you know your children are in the best hands for the entire duration of this camp. Do not worry." We all chuckled.

As parents of children with chronic illness, that was the elephant in the room. We were on pins and needles waiting for that phone call or that staff member racing into the dining hall with the news that our son was suddenly sick, or worse. It was what we all expected. But, we hoped for the best. Welcome to our world.

My beauty queen and I spent the weekend enjoying each other with no medical distractions. It was refreshing, to say the least. Every sixteen minutes Noah's name came up in our conversation, no matter where we were.

"Did you want an appetizer before our dinner, babe? I wonder how Noah is doing." Or "Did you see that large deer over there in the trees? Do you think Noah is seeing any deer at camp? I hope he's having fun. I hope he doesn't get any deer ticks. Those things can be dangerous. You know,

Lyme disease and all. What if he has a fever right now, would they call us? Maybe we should drive over there to check on him." It went on and on just like that for those seventy-six hours he was away from us – but who's counting?

Yeah, the life of a parent is tremendous. Add the spice of life, crisis, and medical dangers, and you have yourself very non-boring, child-rearing years. It made for a life chock full of thrilling adventures, most of which were not expected or invited. Like I said, spice.

You learn to adapt in whatever capacity to stretch yourself – or the moments themselves stretch you – stretch, pull, and tug. Helpless and wounded, but you do what is necessary to push your family through the storm. Sometimes pulling them through it and using a beat up, broken down umbrella in the process. That's where God was our anchor, through the storms that seemed endless. Yeah, never-ending pounding waves. They crashed against the walls of our lives and sometimes the blows were so severe they took our legs out from right beneath us. God was our lighthouse guiding our way through pitch black and dark gray surroundings. He was our constant beam of security. His light illuminated our path. No matter what severity the storms would punish our lives, we could always see Him and set our course back to safety.

How far would a parent go to save their son or daughter? The answer: yes. Simply, yes! You will go as far as you needed to go. To reach the ends of the continent or the edges of the universe. You just do it. They depend on you as parents. A mother and a father will dance with the devil in the pale moonlight (Batman reference) before taking a bullet for their child. You just do.

Noah didn't verbalize his dependency upon us, but we knew in his actions that he was secure with us at the helm. We structured his daily regimen in such a way that created a sense of support in his life. We did it in love, of course. He accepted, in love. It was a win-win.

As much as Paula and I had a terrific time looking into each other's eyes and laughing the night away, we couldn't wait for the return of the camp bus. Monday at 3:00 PM couldn't arrive fast enough. How would our son look? Would he have mountain rash or antler wounds? Would he be limping from a bear attack or have large boils from vicious lake leeches? I sure hope not. Maybe, just maybe, he would be just like he was when we had left him. Okay, I'll buy that.

Monday afternoon arrived and we stood eagerly with other parents by the curbside. We were on bus lookout duty and we all shared the nervous twitches in our faces as we mumbled our child's name frantically. Okay, not to that degree but we were not holding back the excitement for our kids. The bus turned the corner and made its way towards us. We peered over each other and squinted to see our child in the moving vehicle. We were impossible.

Poooooosssssshhhh! The hydraulic brakes engaged as the door opened to let out the tired passengers. One by one each child, each transplant patient, stepped out of the yellow school bus and turned their eyes to our group of parents. They were just as eager to see us and share their tales of camp life. You could see the wear and tear in their body language. And then Noah set foot on the ground, like Neil Armstrong taking "one small step for man."

We hurried over to hug him and ask how he was doing. Did he come down with any illness? Yellow Fever? Anything? Nope. Just a heavy dose of fun and a side of exhaustion. He was filled with chatter as he tried to tell us every special moment, one right after another. He would interrupt himself and say goodbye to a new camp buddy that would walk by us. He didn't have ADHD, but he sure displayed the signs and symptoms all within that ten minute period. It was classic and it was awesome!

That moment defined the champion. The pure will to push through so much opposition, wall after wall, crashing wave after crashing wave, yet he preserved. I'm going to live, he thought. I'm going to make it and show the world I am here. I will live to see another day and explore brave new adventures. I will soar to new heights that my physical calamity so desperately tried to keep me from. Champion.

Our main concern was that underlying and hidden danger: dehydration. In fact, most of the campers had to be hospitalized within twenty-four hours after they had returned. We also learned that it was normal to see over half of all campers be admitted to treat a variety of illness and conditions. If you could ask any one of those precious kids if their immediate stay in the hospital was worth it, they would emphatically say, "Yes!". How do I know this? Well, one of those happened to be our very own superstar patient, Noah Ziegler. It was dehydration, but if not cared for quickly it could erupt into further complications. We've seen it before.

So a few night stay at the Renaissance Children's Hospital would be enough to get him back to the streets. We heard tall tales of heroes and thrill-seekers from the very nurses that worked at the camp. One of their favorites was how much fun the campers had at the talent show. The costumes were usually makeshift and wonderful. We told Noah we have to plan ahead for next year's camp and be sure to come up with a great disguise.

We laughed with Noah about the many memories he gained from the greatest camp he's ever been to. He was able to meet others like him and compare their scars. It was like a meeting of the local biker gang - choppers and black shades. Except, this event had no tattoos on tanned skin, no

Harleys or leather vests. No, instead it was fourteen inch long incisions, ostomy bags worn openly on display, and medical CADD pumps tucked away in backpacks. Membership required: intestinal transplantation at minimum. It was an exclusive club, to say the least.

Now as the gang rested up at Children's Hospital, each of them in their private rooms, the seventh floor was hopping. You could hear some of the conversations between kids from the hallway outside of Noah's room. It was great to hear such chatter. Parents often get overwhelmed with grief and depressing news while staying with their kids. Any laughter or upbeat conversation was very much welcomed.

I left Noah and Paula for Southern California. I had to return to work. Noah was later restored to health and he was able to catch the plane with mom by the twelfth as scheduled. It was a very nice chapter in our son's life now put to rest.

We were thankful that such a wonderful organization had created a getaway for our precious kids with chronic illness. Thank you, selfless transplant nurses, for your tireless efforts in keeping our kids safe. Thank you, kind physicians and surgeons, for making sure our kids got to know a side of you that creates smiles. Thank you to our special children for sharing with us so many priceless moments. They will always be burned in our hearts and in our minds so that years later we can replay the happiness. Sometimes, there won't be any smiles and we will need those very moments to help us fight through tough days. There were certainly more of those days ahead.

15
PURSUED BY PTLD

"WHAT'S WRONG SWEETHEART?" Paula asked Noah as she gently touched his forehead. She frowned the moment she realized a fever was present. He looked tired and had been quiet the entire day.

"I feel sick, mom." Noah's little voice was weak as he turned his eyes to her face.

Paula took his temperature and confirmed her suspicion. It was a high fever and we acted quickly.

We rolled the family into the van and hurried to the emergency room. Shelby, Brooke, and Luke were confused with the sudden exit from our home. Paula called ahead to Dr. Nanjundiah so that she could make arrangements in advance of her arrival to meet us. We didn't see this coming and it was on the heels of such a great adventure to his Pittsburgh Camp Chihopi excursion.

Once we got to the hospital, about twenty minutes later, we checked Noah into the unit. A quick triage assessment led to a bed and Noah was tended to quickly. It wasn't long before Dr. Nanjundiah arrived to oversee the details and make any necessary calls to the Pittsburgh doctors. Here we were again.

A very long two days later and Noah was scheduled for an ambulance ride...to Pittsburgh. He just couldn't shake whatever it was that hit him like a ton of bricks. He was stable enough to fly, but his doctor felt that it was necessary to get him to Children's Hospital as soon as possible. The transplant doctors agreed because of how sensitive these patients are with anything that could jeopardize the organs. So, once again Noah needed an air ambulance. And once again, Paula left with him to be by his side.

This just didn't seem right. Not at all. After a tragic 2004 summer waiting at death's door for months and finally getting that wonderful call for organs, I couldn't see our son go through another blow like this. How much can a child take? This sent chills up and down my spine, like the most unreal horror movie. But, this was no movie and we were not actors. No, this was a reality and happened to be just as tangible as I could imagine.

I remembered how strenuous it was for us last year. I pictured Noah in that hospital bed, fighting inside the walls of the intensive care unit. It easily overwhelmed my mind and consumed my thoughts. Picture a World War II propeller-engine fighter plane soaring above the earth like a rocket. Now, the plane gets riddled with large caliber bullets – BAP, BAP, BAP, BAP! The attack sends our small plane into a spiral tailspin. You can hear the screaming engine whine as it builds up speed in its descent back towards earth…screaming and smoking! That's how my life looked – at least from my perspective.

Aug 31, 2005 3:17pm

Hello everyone, I'm here writing to you from good old Pittsburgh! I'm sorry it has taken so long to update Noah's Carepages, but we have been incredibly busy. As some of you may know Noah became very ill with septic shock due to a central line infection. Once again my world was turned upside down. To see my baby so sick again was like pulling my heart out of my chest and stomping on it a million times. My children have been so patient through all of this and are so very sad to see their brother in so much pain. Please pray for them. Noah is improving overall. We got all the infection under control and pulled his central line out. His mouth sores are finally drying up and his thrush in his mouth has gotten a lot less sore. He's eating again like a horse and able to talk and laugh without his mouth bleeding. We talked to the docs and they think he will most likely be released on Saturday if everything continues to run smoothly. We should have a renal visit while we're here to discuss Noah's dehydration issues. We need an end to this real soon so we don't have to have a central line anymore.

Please pray for all of us and I will continue to update you the best I can.

Lots of love,
Paula & Noah

Sep 6, 2005 3:13pm

Hello, all of my dear friends and family. We miss you all in Cali! Things here are getting much better. Noah is healing well and is scheduled to be discharged tomorrow (Wed). He is excited to start school next week and get back to being a kid instead of a patient. We are still having dehydration issues and have increased his IV fluids to 10 hours overnight. The docs are just confused with Noah's situation. He should be off of fluids by now and should be able to run around like a normal kid without dehydrating. But of course, Noah never does anything like any other kid! We need lots of prayer in this area! We want so badly to have a little rest and be as normal as we can. We want Noah to have sleepovers at his friend's house, play sports, attend school without worrying about him passing out on the playground from dehydration and most of all feel like a normal 12-year-old boy!! We know God can do all this and more. He is the healer and He is the Father of peace. So, all those brothers and sisters out there please pray for peace on our family and healing. Our God is an awesome God!

We are scheduled to fly home on Sat the 10th if all continues to go well. Noah is still continuing to have mouth pain and new ulcers keep creeping up on his throat and tongue. They said if Noah can handle going home on pain meds they will still discharge him tomorrow. Well, all my faithful friends and family, that's all for now.

Thank you for all your love and support!

Lots of love.
PZ

Back home, we remained on alert for any latest news on Noah and Paula's homecoming. We all missed him and his chuckling laughter. All we wanted was to forget how much he suffered last year, but it was so difficult when the current events were so abrasive. The family's wounds were trying to heal, but it felt like a scab that kept being tugged to reveal the raw flesh beneath. Our hearts wanted our daughters and our youngest son, Luke, to rise above the trauma they had also endured. *Lord bring them continual healing,* we prayed.

So, the sudden and unexpected treatment Noah required in Pennsylvania was a tough pill to swallow. When he seemed to get over that hump and his health improved, more was piled on.

Sept 9, 2005 6:29pm

Hello everyone. Paula just phoned me to give me the bad news. The docs have discovered EBV in Noah's lymphatic tissue, inside of his intestines. The trip home to California has been delayed. The best we have right now is maybe a week or so until he can return home. Pray for healing for Noah and this nasty bout with EBV that has been going on now for one year. The potential for it to settle in an organ and compromise it is real. At this point, the last thing we need is to require another intestinal transplant. Needless to say, we are crushed. We are exhausted in all ways and desperately need peace. Noah has yet to learn of this news as he is at a friend's house (Joey from Calvary Chapel Pittsburgh) and we know that he will take it the hardest.

Thank you all for your faithfulness.

Roger

Sept 13, 2005 2:49am

Monday has come and gone. Tuesday will bring Noah back to Children's Hospital for intensive testing of his bowel and lymphatic tissue throughout his body. With the use of two scopes and a complete C.T. scan, we should have the results by Thursday.

This is what we've learned: since Noah is a post-transplant patient and relies heavily upon his immunosuppressive drug (Prograf, or FK) to keep his body from rejecting his new organs, the EBV levels can increase in his body. We've seen his levels over the past year hover in the 100,000 range with daily medications used to fight it. Well, his levels as of last week were in the 3,000,000 range. We also know that EBV, an innocent virus to us non-transplant folks, can cause PTLD (post-transplant lymphoma disease), which essentially is cancer. The very drug that maintains a delicate balance of harmony in Noah can also allow this horrible disease. If his Prograf is lowered to help prevent this, he may go into rejection, which will require Prograf to be increased...then we're back to square one facing PTLD. The docs will know by this Thursday if there is evidence of PTLD in Noah, and if so, I'm afraid the stay in Pittsburgh can be lengthy and the course of treatment will include chemotherapy. Our prayers are focused on that God will heal Noah of any presence of PTLD or EBV in his system...immediately.

Noah's spirits are ok, except when he's feeling very fatigued - a side effect of EBV. Paula will be renting a car through her Marriott reward points this week and take Noah out and about. The Pittsburgh friend's we've made since last year have been phenomenal as well; taking the time to pick up Paula & Noah and including them in various activities. As you can see, God leads us through the fire, but we will not get burned.

Love in Christ,

Roger

P.S. Shelby, Luke, and Brooke are doing well here with me. They started school and are expected to win the award collectively for the "Most Patient and Awesome Kids" sometime later this year. Thank you for your prayers!!!

Sept 16, 2005 12:12pm

Hello all. Yesterday, Paula and Noah went to clinic and met with the docs. Great news - there is no evidence of PTLD in Noah's body/intestines! We were extremely relieved. Whew! Talking about dodging a bullet. However, since his EBV count is very high and concentrated in the intestines, there is a greater chance for intestinal rejection. That translates into more time in Pittsburgh for Noah. The goal is to acquire two good cultures (taken once a week) of his bowel as they continue to aggressively treat his elevated EBV count. So, they will take a sample next week and the following week. Best case scenario: they could be home as early as the first week of October. If there is a bad culture their return home will be delayed. Yeah, this could potentially develop into a much longer stay, but we are praying for them to return as early as a couple of weeks. If you could do the same, we would all appreciate it.

I spoke to Noah yesterday and he sounded remarkably well with the news. He was in the middle of ordering food (I think a triple thick milkshake was on his order), so that could be a big part of it. We talked about football a little (how 'bout them Cowboys) and he asked how Spike was doing (his little - no really - his very little dog). I told Noah that if Spike could speak, he would sing him a song.

Anyway, we'll keep you posted as the week develops. Have a great weekend!

God bless you.
Roger

Sept 22, 2005 3:47pm

Ok, folks, this just in...intestinal biopsy results show no presence of EBV and the levels are down to 500,000 in Noah's system. Awesome!! The docs told Paula that the biopsy looked excellent and another endoscopy will be performed early next week. If all looks good then Noah will be released on Oct. 1. At this point, the docs have discontinued a few things and have increased others. One goal is to achieve a daily ostomy output of 300 ml (which is crazy low for Noah). One method being used is Imodium three times a day. Can you imagine if any one of us took that much, how backed up we would be? Well, it seems like a doable solution to hopefully a reachable goal in the near future.

Since Noah has kidney dysfunction (renal functions are at about a 70% working rate), they need to decrease his output in order to get him off of maintenance fluids (given overnight through his central line for 8-10 hours for dehydration). We know that the more Noah gets dehydrated, the greater the chances for rejection occur (among other things such as dramatic increases in fever, etc.). We are trying to get Noah back to school when he returns to Cali, but at this point, it looks like he would return on a partial day schedule.

Please pray for Noah and Paula as they continue their stay in Pittsburgh. They have been getting fellowship from Calvary Chapel and some fun time here and there, but they are extremely homesick.

Thank you and have a super day!

God bless.
Roger

Sept 29, 2005 3:18pm

Thursday brings terrific news! Paula and Noah just left their clinic appointment and Noah is released from care. California or bust! Yup folks, its ticker-tape parade time. Time to churn the butter...time to gather the freshly-laid eggs...time to milk the cow once again. It's gonna take more than a hurricane to stop Noah now. He's already planning what he'll be doing the moment he arrives home..."I'm going to pick up my dog - even if he growls at me, and play video games in my room," says the young pirate. Aye matey. There be no curse to have him walk the plank. No need to shout "parlay" at the top of his lungs 'cause ain't no Black Pearl and the infamous Captain Jack Sparrow gonna capture Noah – my best pirate impersonation.

Paula and I are already talking about Christmas this year. It will be the first at home (no Pittsburgh or L.A. hospital) since 2002. It's the simple things in life that we love and celebrate. When our family is together, it's priceless. But first, we have a birthday party to plan for Noah. I think we are a little behind - his day of birth was Aug. 19. Since he's been so sick in the hospital and in Pittsburgh for treatment since 8/19, his celebration will be smashing!

Thank you for your ongoing support and prayer!

God Bless.
Roger

The house was settled once Noah, the star patient, and Paula had arrived from the unexpected treatment in Pennsylvania. If you didn't know any of the recent past year's events and examined the interaction between all of the family members, you would have no clue what was going on with each one of us. Traumatic events became commonplace and we excelled in functioning within that mode. It was an unhealthy lifestyle that caused stress layers like a seven-layer cake – very deep. Keep in mind, none of us selected the grand prize of chronic illness that was hidden behind curtain number two. If that was so, if we had a choice, we would have selected the tropical family vacation behind curtain number one instead.

I know that we all must face various trials in life. Through them, we become better individuals and can help others who happen to travel into the same pitfalls we have experienced. Sometimes you can't see beyond the next thirty minutes of the crisis. Sometimes you feel like the world views us like we are stuck in a huge maze larger than a football field and encompassed by walls of stone over fifty feet tall. As we stare dumbfounded at a crossroads without any clue, those who stand on the wall's edge looking down at us have life's answers wrapped up in a cute fortune cookie. They toss these nicely packaged words of wisdom down to us and we feel them shower down upon our lives. Once opened, the words have the best of intentions, but only seem shallow in a world that craves hope and genuine love.

We became our own family's greatest cheerleaders and therapists. We had no formal training and received no education for this field we seemed to find ourselves living in. The school of hard knocks label seemed fitting, but add to this the knowledge and wisdom of our God and now you have a family unit that can survive anything. It is by His grace we stand.

Our hugs and kisses meant the world to Luke, Shelby, Brooke, and Noah, as well as to us. We recharged our hearts during this time when we were together. The unspoken reality was that at any time Noah could require an immediate trip to somewhere. While I was away at work, Paula created a home life that surrounded our children with love and nurturing. Even when the storms of life were overwhelming, her guidance and insight to their needs were absolutely powerful. We held onto each other – tightly and securely – and made every moment count. These were the times that a twenty minute trip to the nearby city park was a healing getaway. A place where we could capture these treasures and cherish them. It's funny what this life can do to us.

After the scare of PTLD, we reached another level of concern for

Noah's health. We were not just parents of a multi-visceral transplant patient, but parents of a child who still had certain needs that branched into different areas of his life. One of the most daunting was his strict need for daily hydration infusions.

Even after a year, his body required this as a standard means to remain healthy. Most patients like Noah are off this support within a few months to a half a year at the most. The doctors hoped for Noah's body to adjust and to absorb fluids taken orally so that the IV line could be removed. This was another potential area for infection. The transplant team had no real timeline as to when he could expect this but remained hopeful.

Noah worked around the inconvenience of having an IV line in his arm, inside the bicep area. We became creative in how we "dressed" his site, as we called it. If we found an older pair of socks with SpongeBob or a crazy skateboard design, we cut and removed the toe-end and made a fancy covering several inches long to protect his site. It was clever and fun rather than a boring tan bandage wrap.

His infusions were scheduled during sleep, about ten hours long, with his portable CAD pump. When he wanted to shower, we waterproofed his upper arm with plastic wrap and several feet of tape. It was so much easier than when his central line was in his upper chest area. During those times, we had to create deep sea diving suits and brought in a closed-circuit, oxygen rebreather system so that bubbles will not give away his position to the enemy. Well, maybe not that much gear, but enough coverage to prevent moisture invasion. Because you know what that would lead to, right? Yup. Infection.

We learned that infections were the number one cause of death in these patients and not necessarily rejection. We fought hard and long to keep him out of the hospital, but maintain a balanced lifestyle that a twelve-year-old demands. One day it was fast skateboards and reckless half-pikes (not really) and another day it was aggressive video gaming that solved all of life's mysteries (also, not true). The key was as much normal as his health would allow. This was very difficult at times, especially when Noah wanted to stretch the boundaries of his life. After all – he earned it!

Oct 13, 2005 6:50pm
PTLD threatens again.

Wow. It's hard to believe that Noah and Paula returned two weeks ago. Time rushes by so quickly. Noah is enjoying his days back home and has much time on his hands. He has not been in school the past two weeks because he needed to get released from certain meds and the G.I. doctor handling his care didn't feel comfortable doing so yet. The infectious disease doctor saw him today and discontinued the acyclovir he was taking 3x a day for the herpes virus. The sores have been gone from his mouth, but you can still see the remnant of a blister under his left eye. Anyway, he will be starting school tomorrow for about 2 1/2 hours (of course including lunch). Since he is heading back into the 6th grade instead of moving on into junior high (because he missed roughly the last 3 years of school), all of his buds are not there. We know he will be making new friends and that will not be a problem for him.

Noah and I went to Disneyland last Friday (thanks for the annual passes Grandma and Grandpa Mora) and he had a blast. He was still weak from all of that hospital treatment during the last couple of months so we took it easy. We also had our liquid hand sanitizer with us. I was very careful with him and made sure he kept his hands clean from all of the times he touched a handrail.

It has been terrific having Noah and Paula back home! It's difficult to imagine the family being separated again, but we know that this can happen at any time. Given those circumstances, we have been considering moving to Pittsburgh to remain together if he requires hospitalization in Children's Hospital of Pittsburgh. The surgeons that performed his transplant will continue to follow Noah's care and make decisions best for his quality of life. Anyway, keep us in prayer as we move forward with our adventure.

God Bless,
Roger

Nov 1, 2005 6:21pm

Hello all. Well, back to Pittsburgh again after such a short stay at home. Last week, the Pittsburgh doctors called for Noah to be sent back for testing. He has a very large lymph node on the right side of his neck and they need to test it for lymphoma. This time, the docs will sample the tissue for a biopsy, as well as several other things like a colonoscopy. They are giving us a vague window of two weeks for this trip. Paula and Noah will be flying out of LAX this Thursday morning. We are praying for negative results and a return trip in time for Thanksgiving.

Noah has been feeling quite well these days and has started school part-time. It's nice to see him interact with kids at his school. His EBV count is down to 150,000 which makes us wonder why his node is enlarged. I guess we'll see soon enough. Paula will try to keep Noah occupied during their time there. She has already called our friends back east to plan some activities.

God bless.

Roger

Nov 8, 2005 5:04pm

Hi everyone. Noah and Paula report that Pittsburgh is very cold. Noah has been busy with many different tests and doctor consults. The preliminary verdict is that he could have PTLD and if so, will begin treatment right away. The med of choice in these cases is Rituximab (used in cancer patients) and will take a period of six months to complete. The docs are giving Paula the third week in November to possibly be back home. If he is positive for PTLD, he may either be sent home with weekly trips to the Oncology dept. for doses of Rituximab or they may decide to keep him in Pittsburgh for the duration of said treatment. Noah has been a bit on the tired side, but so far his spirits are up. He is very thin and continues to struggle in gaining any weight (a common side effect with fighting EBV).

In the meantime, Noah and Paula are trying to enjoy their spare time with other transplant families staying at the hotel and frequent visits to Starbucks for a hot delightful beverage. Of course, Noah is up to his antics with a new marshmallow rifle he recently acquired. It propels the small-sized mallows, one at a time, through a PVC pipe-shaped into a hand held rifle. He places one into an opening at the top and blows the mallow through the pipe. The marshes fly at a pretty good velocity into various unaware targets (surgeons, transplant doctors, and nurses) with very good accuracy. Noah continues to make his mark at Children's Hospital in Pittsburgh.

Thank you for your thoughts and prayers through this most difficult time. We appreciate it!

God bless.

Roger

Nov 14, 2005 2:11pm

Ok, everyone, we dodged another bullet. Thank you, Lord! Noah's results are negative for PTLD. The EBV is causing his lymph nodes to be wacky and the docs tweaked (lame medical terminology) his meds to compensate. He called me on the cell moments ago and of course, I was waiting eagerly, knowing they had a clinic appointment this morning. I answered and heard him say,

"Hi, dad."

"Hello, Noah," I replied.

Noah calmly asked, "So how's work?"

Now I was just about on the edge of my seat waiting for a shout of joy or a loud YEEEE-HAAAAW from him, but instead, I got a mildly interested twelve-year-old asking how my workday was going. Needless to say, I immediately asked him if he was coming home or not. I could tell he was smiling on the other end when he answered, "Yes!" Ahhh, relief. Pittsburgh wants him back December 8 for more follow up. So Paula is trying to schedule the appointments in advance to get back in time for Christmas (at home - what a concept).

Now it would not hurt if you lifted Paula and me up in a sweet little prayer concerning the stress levels we are managing. The rollercoaster of emotions and threats of lymphoma seem to be lurking around every corner these days. Not to mention Noah's fragile state of health. I can see more of my gray hair lately (what's left of it). And even though we know God's plan is being crafted, we struggle with stuff all of the time because of this crude matter we call our flesh. Thank you for your faithfulness.

God bless,

Roger

P.S. Noah better not try and take his marshmallow gun on board the airplane. Remember Ralph with his Red Rider, 200-shot, range-model, air-rifle? Well, you get the idea.

Nov 29, 2005 11:42am

Greetings everyone. I hope all of you had a wonderful Thanksgiving holiday. Needless to say, ours was fabulous as we spent the long weekend together at home with family. Noah kept eating and eating. One of his favorites was Grandma Velma's green Jell-O...oh yeah, eat up my boy. Noah has been doing terrific these past days. So much so that we've been on guard (you know, that calm before the storm), but we are very pleased with his progress recently.

Our doctor informed us yesterday that Children's Hospital in Pittsburgh needed Noah back for follow up and further studies. One change they would like to make is to lower his already low level of immunosuppressive medicine. In doing so, there is a chance he could reject his bowel and they need to have him there for intestinal tissue tests. We tried to convince the docs to keep Noah home, especially through the December fun-filled weekends just before Christmas. Well, our efforts fell short. Paula and Noah will be flying Sunday, Dec. 4 and hopefully returning two weeks later. In a mad rush to decorate our home, we will be getting a Christmas tree at the end of this week and slamming the decorations. The scene will look similar to the one portrayed in "Christmas with the Kranks."

This will be Noah's third trip to Pittsburgh since September. I'm left wondering how much longer and how many more times? You know, there's this band called Third Day and they have some great music. They recently released a new album and a song called "Tunnel." The song talks about going through trials and how there is hope through Jesus. As we are faced with conditions designed for our strengthening and increased closeness with God, we do know there is a light at the end of the tunnel for us. If you get a chance listen to it. It's awesome.

We appreciate your concern and steadfast heart of prayer. It encourages Paula and me to know that we have you behind us as we continue this fight for Noah.

God bless,
Roger

Dec 8, 2005 3:30pm

Hello all. Paula just called to let me know the CT scan performed yesterday revealed a small mass in Noah's lung. He's being admitted in the hospital for a procedure (biopsy). The mass is about the size of a dime and it was not present last month. Paula will be seen by a pulmonary specialist as well. It sounds like they will attempt the biopsy with a scope, but if not, then they will make a small 5" incision to gain access. It is possible that this is only a fungus mass - or it could be PTLD. Noah seems okay with the news. All he wants to do is play in the snow. Since he'll be in the hospital, he can walk down to the cafeteria which has an open atrium-like area and see it.

Paula was crying on the phone. It's so frustrating that she is so far away and I can't comfort her. It's too soon to know but we don't know if they will be back for Christmas. Please place him on your prayer chain wherever you are.

Thank you.

God bless.
Roger

Dec 13, 2005 4:51pm

Now I know what a cat must feel like having nine lives. The pathology report came back NEGATIVE for PTLD! Can you believe that? Talk about another HUGE close call. We do know that Noah remains in this area where he is borderline PTLD and will be monitored with extreme scrutiny. Paula is negotiating Noah's release with the hospital warden based on good behavior (well, not really - given that he loves to be mischievous while on the seventh floor) and they should be on a plane Friday. Did you hear that? Friday! In time for Shelby's 14th birthday party on Saturday. It looks like we will be spending Christmas in sunny California this year.

My goodness, I am spent. I think Paula and I need a relaxing getaway after these up and down weeks lately. And poor Noah, he is right there in the middle of it all. He did go ice skating today in downtown Pittsburgh. There is an ice rink outside in the business center and he had a blast.

The doctors are expecting him back again next month and I'm afraid frequent trips to Pittsburgh are in Noah's future. Hmmmm. Relocation seems inevitable at this point. We'll see what God opens up for us out there.

God bless.
Roger

16
GOODBYE FOR NOW

"If joy really comes in the morning time,
Then I'm gonna sit back and wait until the next sunrise.
Goodbye for now..."
-P.O.D.

MY FATHER WAS A CHIROPRACTOR in Southern California and he had a few patients whom I also knew. Shortly after graduating high school, I moved from Whittier, CA to the laid back culture of San Diego and lived with him for a couple of years. One of those summers, my dad connected me with a friend from church who operated his own landscaping business. I was looking for work and Noah, his friend, needed a hand to dig ditches and build sprinkler systems.

I worked with him for a few months and realized the meaning of hard physical work. But, it was a great time getting to know Noah, especially because he was a very talented musician. Since I played guitar and enjoyed rocking the jams myself, I appreciated his talented drum skills. He was a master on his kit!

Well, I also met his wife and children during these months. His oldest son, Noah Jr., attended high school and I would see him in the church youth group as well (I helped as a junior counselor for a season). Needless to say, I enjoyed working with Noah Sr. and also admired his close relationship with God. He was an inspiration.

So, fast forward from that summer to 1993 – about 6 years later – our son was born. Yup, we named him Noah. It was a special name indeed and one we admired as told in the biblical story about Noah and his family. Noah followed God's command, and as a result, his family was saved. We loved what that name represented – both the historical man of God in the Old Testament and in my personal experience working for Noah Sr. – it was a solid name.

In April 2006, my dad reached out to me and we talked about my son's latest health concerns; there was always something to discuss regarding his health.

"Hey Rog, do you remember Noah from church?" my dad asked.

"Oh, yeah. Noah Sr. from those days when I lived in San Diego. Yeah, why?" I replied.

"I ran into him at the office and he asked how you were doing. I explained how you've been and told him about Noah's health concerns. He was taken back and said he would pray for you all." His voice was excited about the next part. "I remembered how Noah liked the band P.O.D. and since his son is the drummer, I asked if he can get him a shirt or something."

"Wow. That would be great, dad! Thanks for thinking of Noah," I said.

"Wait," my dad interrupted. "Noah Sr. said he would hook you up with two backstage tickets to the next local P.O.D. concert."

"Oh man! That is amazing!" I was a pumped up for that exciting news. "He's going to be so surprised when he hears this. Thanks so much, dad, for the excellent news."

Now Noah Sr. had his son, Noah Jr., and taught him to become a drummer with a sick beat. Noah Jr. became pretty good and formed a band with some buds. Well, one thing led to another and they eventually hit the big time music scene. P.O.D. has released numerous albums with incredible hits. Low and behold, they happened to be Noah's favorite band. And he will be backstage rockin' out to his favorite tunes right there with the band – right there on stage! Now that was an awesome gift that God pulled out of His massive blessing bag.

Later that day, I told Noah the great news and he just about jumped out of his skin. He was elated and ready to go right that minute. I had to restrain him and hold him down before he hyperventilated. Yeah, he was pretty happy.

A month later, Noah and I drove to the House of Blues in Anaheim. We arrived at 8:30 PM, just as Noah Sr. instructed us, and he said he would meet us there. We picked up our passes at will call and walked through the busy restaurant and right back to the theater area. There was a band playing a set and it was very loud.

We waited in the aisle on the left side of the theater and then after several minutes, Noah Sr. found us. We embraced and I introduced him to my son.

"Noah, this is Mr. Noah Sr. - Wuv's father," I happily said. (Noah Sr.'s son, Noah Jr., went by his stage name WUV). Confused yet?

My son's eyes opened so wide, almost beyond capacity and his smile strained every facial muscle he had.

"Wow! Nice to meet you," Noah said politely as he shook his hand vigorously.

"Let me take you guys on back now," Senior directed us with a hand wave and turned briskly towards a side stage door.

We followed quickly behind him so we wouldn't get lost behind the stage area. He turned sharply after walking down a long flight of stairs and opened a door that let us to outside of the venue. *Wait, don't they play music IN the building?* Noah and I looked at each other as we followed close behind, but we were confused.

We followed him through the parking lot, still confused until we saw it right there. Boom! The P.O.D. tour bus, in the flesh (well, in the metal). The large letters covered the entire side of the vehicle in white against a black background finish. It was cool – very cool! And we were going to be invited in. Who cares about Air Force One, or the NASA space shuttle? No, this was incredible and it was all for Noah.

Noah Sr. opened the bus door and stepped inside. "Follow me guys," he motioned us with a nod and a smile. He didn't know it, but we felt like we were embarking on our first steps into Willy Wonka's Chocolate Factory and all of its amazement. I think I pinched myself to make sure this was really happening.

The bus looked like a cool hotel lobby inside – larger than life and displayed that famous rock-star style. We saw Noah Jr., his wife, and his son – his Noah Jr. (now this was about to get very confusing very quickly). So, I counted four people named Noah all in about a ten-foot diameter. We all had a pretty good laugh about it.

We met the other band members and couldn't believe our eyes. And my son, well...he was in a state of bliss. You could not see the previous strenuous ordeals in his eyes. Nope. Not a whisper of any pain or suffering. Instead, all you could see was a horizon filled with amazement, wonder, and dreams fulfilled. I was front seat to this special occasion and cherished each minute.

After both Noah kids ran to the back of the bus to play the latest video games, I sat around the table with the others telling of my son's life of illness and transplant travels. They couldn't believe how well he was doing. Somehow, Noah Sr. convinced the band manager that this was part of a Make-A-Wish dream for our son. Well, if that's what he wanted to think then so be it. My goal was achieved: to get Noah backstage to witness his favorite band. Well, that part didn't happen just yet.

Soon the band had to make their escape and prepare for the set. Once we gathered ourselves, including the spouses of the band members, we made our trek to the backstage area. Noah was living the good life, with whip cream and a delicious, plump cherry on top. He walked a few inches taller in those moments and he felt like he ran the place. You know, Mr. big shot band manager and producer. It was great!

Before the curtain lifted, we assembled stage-right in perfect view of Wuv's kit and simply the best view in the house. We could hear the crowd from behind the black veil and it sounded like hundreds were ready to see

P.O.D. bring the house down. I could see the massive amplifiers stacked behind the elevated drum set and they flanked both sides of the stage. Whoa! This was going to be a loud one!

Then, from behind us walked out Sonny, Wuv, Tre, and Jason, ready to get it on. They stood at their assigned places with instruments in hand, Wuv holding his massively thick Vic Firth sticks. He adjusted the hi-hat and made sure his cymbals were at the perfect location.

Suddenly, a voice over the theater sound system announced the band and the tall curtains ripped open – from the center out towards left and right evenly. Instantly, the thundering guitar chopped through the air in perfect timing with heart-pounding, bass drum thunder and crashing cymbals – it was the opening hit song: "Boom"! Sonny exploded on vocals crushing the stage with his Vans sneakers, but there was no sneaking going on. He was a man crazed dancing to the song and throwing his impressive dreadlocks in a large circular motion. He attacked the microphone: "Boom, here comes the Boom! Ready or not, here comes the boys from the south!"

In the electrifying moment, I turned my eyes down to Noah who stood right next to me. We exchanged expensive smiles that anyone would pay hundreds of dollars just to wear – but they were ours. He shouted a few words, but they were drowned out by the sounds of heavy distortion and crushing melodies. Lights moved to and from the stage like they were searching for a prison break escapee. Sometimes they pierced our eyes for a split second and caused momentary blindness. Noah was in his glory! He moved his arms like he had no worry at all. Forget the IV line tightly secured to his bicep; the tubing wasn't going anywhere. *Go for it, Noah. Have a blast*, I thought. His head moved in sync with each beat, just slightly – no concussions here. His knees shook to the tempo of Wuv's bombing drum beats. Awesome couldn't define it any better. Simply and purely awesome.

Song after hit song blazed through the air and Noah knew each one by heart. Especially when they performed his favorite song: "Goodbye for Now." It was a beautiful melody with a slower groove undertone. I read his lips as he sang the words like he was a backup to Sonny. He sang and moved passionately like he was paid to be their number one fan. Then, before the next song, Sonny asked all of the kids who were backstage to come up front at center stage. There were about seven or eight in all. Some were children of the band and others, like Noah, were just friends. They all stood on the stage just like Sonny had asked them to and he said a few words about the youth of today. Then they played their song: "Youth of the Nation." It was cool.

And there he was, Noah, the mayor of hard rock himself grooving from side to side as he faced the audience and waved one arm over his head in unison with the beat. He told the audience with every fiber of his being that he made it; that he had conquered death and made it to this once-in-a-lifetime moment. His actions spoke volumes and I knew the backstory behind his celebration. *Go, Noah! Go get 'em. Tell the world your story and show everyone that you did it, son.* I was the proud father who wanted to parade his son on my shoulders and ride off into the sunset. But, we had a killer concert to enjoy instead.

After the legendary set, the band hurried off stage and the audience went crazy with applause. We followed Noah Sr. back through the maze of hallways and corridors to the parking lot where the bus was parked. The cool fresh air was soothing as we exited the building. Noah was winding down off of his concert high and wiped beads of sweat from his forehead. After about twenty minutes, Wuv appeared and we told him how much fun we had. He smiled and thanked us for attending the show.

Wuv went to the bus and brought out one of his custom creations. It was an ice chest on little wheels with tricked out "low-rider" style handlebars. P.O.D. stickers graced both sides and it had a real motor attached. Oh man, it was a mini-scooter that you sat on. He asked Noah to hop on and he didn't hesitate. Vroom! He sped off to the other end of the lot like he owned the place. It was sweet.

After the crowds had disappeared, Wuv brought us back into the House of Blues. He led is over to the band's merchandise area and asked Noah to pick out whatever he wanted. There were T-shirts, hoodie sweatshirts, decals, drumsticks with the band logo – you name it, it was there for sale.

"Really?!" Noah's voice shrieked. "This is too awesome!"

Wuv assured him that he could pick whatever he liked and it was on him.

We thanked Noah Sr., the band, and Wuv for their generosity and hospitality. Their precious gift was exactly what Noah needed. It was a boost from living in the mundane, illness lifestyle and it was a bucket-list type of dream realized. They were happy to be a part of such a special day and said they would be praying for my son. It was brilliant; the way a kind gesture could lift spirits and help children with chronic illness feel superhuman.

The 22 Freeway was empty at 11:30 PM. All you could see beneath the staggered street lights was a streaking, silver Tundra pickup truck occupied by the most blessed fifteen-year-old, on his way back home. He gazed out of the passenger side window and his mind dreamed of his next adventure. If you looked close enough, you could see his left hand tap his leg in perfect time with the melodic sound of his favorite P.O.D. jam that boomed through the speakers. You see, this was his night and he was the mayor of hard rock. And almost as if you could read his lips in sync with the song, "Goodbye for Now," he formed a slight grin at the side of his mouth. Brilliant.

**

Early 2006 brought no surprises, really. Noah battled with the EBV virus and the threat of post-transplant lymphoma disease. The second trip to Pittsburgh during February was a very important one and I also made the jaunt with Paula and Noah.

Feb 22, 2006 11:53am

Hello everyone. Can anyone say "Whew!?" What a relief! It was that time again last week for Noah. Another trip to Pittsburgh, or Blitzburgh as they call it, for a repeat of tests to determine where Noah's EBV levels stood and how his lymphatic system was handling the virus. As you may already know, the last six months have been very difficult in that Noah has been out to Pittsburgh once a month for these strict tests. The doctors have been watching his EBV numbers closely and felt that if they did not drop significantly this month, Noah would begin chemotherapy in Pennsylvania. With every swollen lymph node that presented itself, we were faced with the almost sure decision to fight PTLD.

Well, I flew out to Pitt to be with Paula and Noah this past week and we had to wait until Thursday for the news. Dr. Sindhi explained that the EBV levels were the lowest they have ever been in Noah (incredible!) and that the lymphatic system was not showing signs of stress, which would suggest a need to biopsy another lymph node for PTLD. He went on to say that Noah's recent growth and overall wellness leads him to believe that PTLD is not present and chemotherapy is not needed. He added a complex explanation of how Noah is just one of those few cases where all of the decades of research and experience in intestinal transplantation allow for a successful recovery with the specific treatment administered there at Children's Hospital of Pittsburgh. The bottom line - what they do really works! They have trained Noah's cells, typically designed to resist a new graft (new organ), to understand that the foreign body is NOT an enemy. Noah's anti-rejection medicine is given in such a low dose today that the reading is barely measurable. This means that his immune system is able to fight common bacteria and virus strains better and allow his body to accept his new organs as time goes by.

Another point he made was if we were to decide not to follow the course of care planned by them or perhaps be under the care of a physician in California, who may want to introduce other forms of treatment based on other research, it will alter the progress Noah has made thus far and can be life-threatening. Of course, he used many big words and often had to use words I could understand, like "cheeseburger" and "ice cream," but he made his point thoroughly to us. It was clear...no PTLD and keep doing what we're doing because it's working!

Noah didn't have any gadgets or tricks to play on the doctors this time around. Although, he did borrow a large Nerf rocket launcher from his bud Ian (who was on the 7th floor for treatment) and decided to advance an air-assault on the transplant nurses. I love to hear them scream across the hospital wing, "Noah. I'm gonna get you!"

Of course, the weather was cold. In fact, it was too cold to snow. Oh yeah, that is possible I guess. One night, we decided to head over to Baskin-Robbins for a scoop of our favorite ice cream. Since it was minus seven degrees outside, Paula decided to remain in the car with the heater on "fever setting" or "heat stroke" while Noah and I braved the icy winter chill – it was a death march.

A scoop of creamy, chocolate ice cream - $2.79

A souvenir Steeler t-shirt - $10.00

You and your son staggering in minus seven-degree temperatures while licking your ice cream cone and wearing your Big Ben, Steeler t-shirt - PRICELESS.

After all of the testing was completed we flew back home. Get this, Noah doesn't have to return to Pitt for three months. What a deal! And we flew back on the same plane. What? How did that happen? Well, I bought my ticket on Expedia and selected the red-eye, non-stop round-trip out of LAX. The return flight was scheduled on Sunday evening and Noah must fly back non-stop in the event of any medical needs that may arise. When Paula spoke with Kaiser's travel agent, they had two tickets left on my flight back, so we sat in the same aisle. Not too bad, huh?

Thank you for your endless prayers.

God bless,
Roger

We were on a high note since receiving the great news from the Pittsburgh doctors. We appreciated every good word in that sense because it has not always been rainbows and butterflies. We hoped for a year of progress for Noah and his health. So far, it was shaping up this way.

Later in February a buddy at the office, Mike, gifted us with passes to enjoy our first NASCAR experience. It would be seriously fast fun. Mike gave me the rundown on what to expect, which helped us prepare for the outing.

We arrived on a warm February day under a cover of clouds. Noah was ready for the heat – he was well hydrated. We made our way beyond the entrance and walked through a trench of endless vendors. They all sold the latest apparel and novelty items from the most popular drivers and racing teams. Of course, there were food vendors galore who served mouth-watering goodies. We located the grandstand entrance and found our reserved seats in the stadium. We were early and excited to get our groove on – NASCAR style.

I noticed some folks wore ear protection; the headsets were bright yellow (not very subtle). Curiously I asked one of the employees about these and I learned they were not only ear protectors, but you could listen to many radio frequencies used by the drivers and their pit crews. Sort of like eavesdropping, but it was allowed. That's all I needed to hear. We left our seats and walked up to the official NASCAR booth for one of those awesome devices. I made sure Noah had a better than average experience. He didn't complain at all.

Now, back in our seats, we waited for the race to begin. Noah focused on conversations spoken over the various channels and he was intrigued. The headphones were huge on his wee little head and his oversized grin could not be contained. Our seats were almost dead-center in the grandstand and Noah had his binoculars glued to his eyes as if he searched for a long lost puppy.

It wasn't long before we heard those famous words over the loudspeakers…"Drivers. Start your engines!" That announcement was immediately followed by a chorus of thunder, lightning, and those muscular engines that started in almost perfect unison. Vrooooom! The noise sent chills up our spines and made Noah's smile grow by several inches. We looked at each other and each gave a loud shout, "Ooooohhhhhhh yeeeeaaaahhhhhh!"

The cars were several rows down from us, but when they approached from the west we felt the rumble in our seats and in our connective tissues. My natural response was to shout at the same decibel level those race cars delivered as they sped over 200 MPH. They raced past our eyes like flashes of blue, red, purple, and every other color you could imagine. Each vehicle was painted with color schemes that matched their sponsor's logo and would not be suitable to use in a drive-by crime; they stood out like a rhinoceros lounging in a fancy candle shop.

The race track offered nothing more than a huge oval shaped, continuous movement of cars, over and over. After about forty or fifty laps, we had decided to take a break from the physical demands of watching this competition and head over to the vendor area. He looked a little exhausted; probably from the combination of heat and strenuous shaking of body tissues (but loving every second of it).

We grabbed a refreshing drink, some hot delicious food and talked about how amazing the fun was. I made sure his level of hydration was suitable for more race enjoyment and that he was alright to continue. We stayed about thirty more minutes and then left a little early, before the last several laps. It was a nice round of good times. Definitely one for the record books!

Noah curled up on his side in the large passenger seat during the hour drive home. He was tuckered out and checked out a bit early. I was the happiest papa driving home that afternoon. I checked that empty box in my mind. One unforgettable NASCAR race for Noah: done.

**

I wish we could contain all of that happiness bliss and spread it evenly over the course of years and years. But, as we all know, life happens. March brought with it more of that very thing.

Mar 8, 2006 6:00pm
Just visiting...well, kind of.

Noah is back in the hospital, but so far so good. Late Monday evening we called Noah's doctor and explained how Noah was feeling. We gave her his blood pressure, pulse, and temp, as well as all ins and outs for the day. Her instructions were to drive him to the local ER where she would meet us. Of course, Noah was not happy about that. It took about 30 minutes to have him walk willingly to the car. He was certain that he would spend at least 3 weeks there or be transferred to Pittsburgh. We arrived close to midnight and the doctor immediately called for ambulance transport to take him to the big hospital in Hollywood. Our fear was that he had another one of those "special" bugs. You know the ones I'm talking about. The bugs that think they're Rambo and have a "never say die" mentality.

He arrived at Kaiser Sunset around 3 am and I arrived shortly after in my minivan. Paula was still home recuperating from her dry-socket, dental nightmare...but that is a whole different story that requires its own Carepages. I met Noah in the pediatric ICU and he said, "Hey dad. That was the best ambulance I've ever been in. It had a television screen and they played a movie for me." Now, if I stay up until 3 or 4 in the morning, the last thing I will do is cheerfully make remarks like, "I just saw a Bug's Life while being transported with a medical team," but Noah is built differently than I am.

As you may have guessed by now, Noah was not very critical. The slight nausea and stomach ache he had earlier were both gone. His vitals were all very good - thanks to several bolus infusions of fluid. I slept there in a small & dark room (the nurse called it the "Kaiser Hilton," but her humor was not convincing), but who cares when you need to be with your son at the hospital. By morning (no, there were no butterflies flopping in the air, or sounds of violins playing soft melodies) Noah was doing well (still). This whole business of getting him there was done because of Noah's history of losing blood pressure rather quickly. We agreed with the doctor that he needed to be there in the event he needed immediate treatment instead of being stuck somewhere that is not equipped to handle critical medical emergencies. Cultures were taken, blood was drawn, and the day was shaping up to be a waiting game. I left Noah Tuesday evening because he was doing perfectly well (I mean he was telling the doctors and nurses what meds he currently takes and advising them when their charts were wrong). I had to see how Paula was doing (can you say Percocet every 3 hours backward while holding a heating pad to your lower jaw?)

Anyway, Noah will probably be released tomorrow and we will go see him tonight. The only thing so far that was diagnosed was dehydration. I'll keep you updated.

God bless,
Roger

Apr 3, 2006 5:02pm
Just visiting...again!

Alright, Noah. You have got to stop giving us these hospital visits. On Saturday, Noah's pick line (located on the inner bend of his right arm) became swollen and red - a big sign of infection! So we got him over to Kaiser in Anaheim and the kids went with Paula's sister Lisa. Noah's doctor was there caring for three of her other patients who were also hospitalized, so it was great having her there instead of communicating through the phone. Instantly she decided to pull the central line and schedule for a new one to be placed. Noah stayed overnight and on Sunday the docs knocked him out and placed a new line in his left bicep. When the old one was pulled, they found pus on the tip, so he is on antibiotics for that infection. He didn't have any fever, so we were elated. Noah said he's happy that the new IV access is on his left arm so that he can throw the football better and swing a bat. I'm glad he's seeing the bright side of this because mom and dad cringe every time he has to set foot in the hospital or ER. I guess that's part of parenthood.

Noah will be back in Pittsburgh on April 30 for further testing of his EBV levels and biopsies. Mom's not looking forward to it. It seems we had such a long and hard March.

God bless,
Roger

It was middle April with spring in full force. The early morning dew was settling on a calm morning across the nearby grassy fields. The night was dark, still waiting for a kiss of sunlight to rise across a vast, west coast horizon. And the Nascar-like sound of our minivan racing across greater Los Angeles broke the peaceful silence. We rushed Noah to Kaiser Sunset in Hollywood for what appeared to be signs of intestinal rejection. Oh brother.

By that evening, and after a scope of his bowel tissues, his condition worsened. His ostomy emptied around 2500ml of pure watery-like output rather than 500-800ml of chunky stuff in a day. Indicators of rejection. The intestinal scope also revealed a very agitated and upset bowel. With no other recourse, the transplant doctors were notified by the attending doctor at Kaiser and Noah was transported to Pittsburgh via air-ambulance by Friday morning.

The mission was to save his precious bowel. When they landed, Paula and Noah were transported to Children's Hospital by ambulance. The transplant team was ready and waiting. At their arrival, Noah was taken straight to Dr. Squires for another scope of the bowel. But this time, there was a change.

"Well Noah, I guess you just want to spend Easter here with us. Your bowel looks fine," said Dr. Squires.

"What," Paula replied in amazement. "You're kidding right doctor?" She was more amazed than anyone else. You see, she always attends each scope and is able to view the monitor as they are performed. What was red and inflamed tissue the day before was now bright pink and calm right at that moment. Miracle. So, she thought perhaps the pathology report would reveal some sort of nasty intestinal virus outbreak (like rotavirus) or something, right? Nope, clear. That's right, C – L – E – A – R. You could write those letters across the sky over a stadium filled with Steeler fans with no hesitation that every human soul would understand that very word. Unmistakable and undeniable.

So now what? Well, our favorite patient and superstar mom attended the Easter service with a day pass at our "other church" in Pittsburgh. They were able to get picked up and enjoy the company of many who cared for them during recent years before. It was also a mini celebration of this most recent victory. God is good!

Later that day, Paula was informed that Noah would be discharged and remain on outpatient status for the rest of the week. Normal follow up procedure before sending them back home over 2,500 miles away. It was certainly amazing to see God's hand move. There was no rejection, no virus, no nothing...and his output had returned to normal by the next day. Simply amazing. But, still a scary moment for Noah. He couldn't stand hearing bad news about his health or urgent setbacks ready to take him down. It was his reality.

So far, Noah's EBV count continued to remain low. Lymphoma concerns were pushed back even further, but he continued to have his levels tested every two weeks. He remained on six to eight hours of IV replacement fluids nightly, and with the warmer weather approaching, we would have to keep a close eye on his hydration levels. Noah working in a steel factory or collecting hot, liquid lava samples for scientific research is definitely out of the question.

**

The transition into summer was mostly uneventful. Noah was able to manage through the beginning waves of hotter days. Although we lived in Southern California with nice weather year round, the townhome we lived in had a pro and a con.

First the con: no air conditioning. Even though we were only six miles from the fantastic Pacific Ocean and often felt the soothing breezes from the west, our place got a little toasty. Our bedrooms were upstairs and the heat always seemed to nestle in our rooms.

Now, the pro: because we lived within decent proximity of the beach, we were able to enjoy a quick jaunt to the shoreline and take in some beauty and cool air. There was something about having the ocean nearby

203

and it especially moved Paula. I think she expressed more than several hundred times that she would enjoy being a dolphin and have that ability to swim through the big, blue ocean. So, we enjoyed mini-getaways many times throughout the week.

Our star patient dealt pretty well with the newness of higher summer temps. Our townhome also had a community swimming pool (that would be another pro). The kids enjoyed swimming and cooling off. Noah required a stack of Tegaderm dressing to waterproof the IV site and the last thing he needed was a line infection. Minus the eight layers or so of artificial covering, he looked like a regular lifeguard. The pool was icy cold and it kept his body temp down for hours afterward.

We had one scare that put Noah in the hospital. It turned out to be a dehydration episode and not an infection after all. He was treated and released after a few days. He also had a tonsillectomy because of inflammation and infection tendencies. The procedure went very well and upon discharge, he enjoyed ice cream for days.

So far, his year was sprinkled with a few bright spots that included some very intense fun and serious good memory-making. This next adventure would be no different and it was shaping up to be the grand slam, the granddaddy of them all to date. The goal was simple: to keep Noah healthy. And healthy he was.

17
HE'S THE BIG KAHUNA

When life gives you lemons…go to Hawaii.

IT WAS TWO YEARS IN THE MAKING. Not many things take this much time. A splendid guacamole dip with all of nature's finest ingredients takes no more than ten to fifteen minutes, including prep. Luke, in a full sprint from our living room downstairs to his upstairs corner bedroom (avoiding punishment for something naughty he did – he excelled in this area), maybe took 4.3 seconds.

Well, it was two years from the middle of that 2004 grueling summer when Grandma Romie made a promise to him. As he lay there in that hospital bed, struggling and fighting against time as he waited for his organs, she told him once he was well she would take him on a trip to Hawaii.

He thought that would be the greatest time ever. Hope can be bottled up in a distant, future destination: a place, an event, or a magnificent gift – the trip to Hawaii encompassed all three. She urged Noah to hang on and to fight; to get his transplant and to heal. When he was physically ready for travel she would honor that commitment.

On a somber note, since that wonderful promise Grandma Romie made to Noah, her boyfriend unexpectedly passed away. Mike was a wonderful person who was like a grandfather to our children. During some of those terrible, urgent trips to the hospital, he would often stay at our home and tend to our other kids. They all called him Grandpa Mike and he would be dearly missed by our family.

Romie and Mike had originally planned on taking Paula along with Noah (one of us was mandatory due to his complex healthcare needs), but with Mike's passing, I took his place. We were also gifted airline tickets from a friend at our church. His family trip experienced some flight delays and the airline compensated him with four round-trip tickets. We used those passes for our travel experience to tropical Hawaii. What a blessing!

The short term goal in the summer was to prevent Noah from becoming infected with any exotic strains of rare forms of bacteria, debilitating illnesses, or anything that required his body to be within a stone's throw from the likes of a hospital or medical facility – prior to our August trip.

Of course, he received the usual warnings from us, protective parents. They included: "Remember not to lick doorknobs and handrails," or the ever popular "don't breathe, don't exhale, and don't blink when we change your central line dressing." I'm sure to him we sounded like those wonderful yet invisible parents of the Peanuts characters. You know, "Wa wah wah. Wa wah. Wahhh?" Yet, even those silly reminders were heartfelt and Noah kept and heeded each warning for years to come.

Although July managed to bring heat and perspiration, our upbeat son stayed hydrated as best as he could. But, there was one hospital visit. Yes, it only takes one to potentially destroy a fantastically planned vacation. Still, the doctors managed to address the matter head one and the team swiftly acted on his behalf. It was a short stay and he was finally kicked out. Oahu, here we come!

**

The Ontario Airport was eerily quiet at 6:30 AM in the airline terminal. Romie made sure our party arrived early to avoid any chance of missing our flight. We had a good hour or so before we could board the huge airbus and naturally as men we had to go forage for sustenance and for meat. Noah and I grabbed our spears and leathery straps that carried our few hand-made arrows. I'm kidding. The straps were made from dried-Saber tooth Tiger pelts. Geez, my feeble memory. So, we told the women we would find food and be back very soon.

After a few minutes of giddy talk with Noah, he was thrilled with excitement for this trip, we found a place that just opened for the morning rush. Fast food indeed, because when time is of the essence, slow food will just not suffice. We grabbed up mega-sized burritos filled with delicious cuts of smoked bacon, freshly laid AA-grade eggs, melted sharp & Colby cheeses, delicately browned Tennessee sausages (really?) and juice from nearby orange groves, then we headed back to the women. Well, maybe we just ordered a few number four combos with hash browns and cartons of juice. But, that definitely hit the spot and with all of Noah's giddiness going on I had him cracking up at just about anything that morning, including whatever food we ate.

So, after lift-off and with the four of us tucked into our seats, I noticed little man dozing off. We had several hours of flying to do, but it was a direct flight. Paula and Romie enjoyed colorful conversation and I had my thumping music playing through my earbuds. Hawaii, here we come.

A nice landing on Oahu brought big, huge smiles. (That is one of those Luke-isms we enjoyed – big huge.) Once outside, we breathed in deeply and exhaled the tropical atmosphere. It was humid and hot. *Oh boy, we're going to have our hands full keeping Noah hydrated*, I thought.

"Noah, start drinking your water," Paula said to him abruptly. He got the point. A few signatures later, we fled from the airport in our shiny rental car en route to the resort. I slammed on the air-conditioning and we fanned Noah swiftly with our hands like we were flying or something. Eventually, the cold air kicked in and we had icicles growing from his eyelashes. What a site!

We followed our map to our final destination: The Marriott Ko Olina Resort. It was about a twenty-five-minute drive and Noah enjoyed the surrounding view. We arrived mid-afternoon and couldn't believe our eyes. Oh, the beauty of the west side of the island was purely magnificent. We climbed out of our car and had our luggage gathered by a friendly attendant.

"Hey Noah," I said, "be sure to tip homeboy" as I motioned to the staff member hauling our bags ahead of us. He turned to me with a puzzled look.

"I don't have any money," he answered. I slipped him a ten spot and he handed it to the friendly man when we reached the check-in desk.

Eventually, we made it to our rooms and we were blown away with our new surroundings. Our accommodations were divine. I told Noah to call Grandma Romie on the phone after I gave him her room number. Again, that puzzled look appeared.

"We just saw her two minutes ago, dad. Why?" He asked.

"So we can find out what time she would like to meet for lunch," I said in a silly, matter-of-fact tone.

"Oh yeah," He agreed. "I'm starving!" So he dialed the room number and held the receiver to his ear.

"Grandma? It's me, Noah." (Like there would be anyone else in Hawaii that would call her room referring to her as grandma. You got to love his cuteness). "Do you want to eat lunch? Yeah? Okay. I'll tell my mom and dad. Bye." He sounded thrilled and ready to take his first step into this new wonderland experience. "She said to meet at her room in ten minutes."

"Alright chief. Sounds like a plan," I replied as I rubbed my belly. We quickly freshened up and made our jaunt to Romie's room. She had a magnificent view overlooking the resort's pool, the lagoon areas, and the vast Pacific Ocean. It was breathtaking!

We meandered down through the tropical courtyard lined with large palm trees throughout the winding pathway and nearby swimming pools. We saw friendly faces worn by all staff members and other guests enjoying the time of their lives. It was like a literal paradise. Or at least one that I could imagine.

We found a casual dining area with outdoor seating beneath the

Hawaiian sunbeams. We sat in our cozy chairs and exhaled the words with our physical expression: *we finally made it.* The relief was contagious.

As the warm coastal winds blew and our sunglasses kept the bright afternoon at bay, we ordered ice cold drinks and lunch in the most comfortable setting you could imagine. We enjoyed our view of the private resort's lagoons that were a mere seventy-five feet away. Noah looked bit wiped out from the jet lag but kept the lethargic waves at bay with a freshly made, ice cold pineapple smoothie – with extra lush pineapple. It was delightful and the exotic hand-crafted drink carved a smile that spoke volumes on his demeanor.

"Delicious!" He said as he pressed the chilled glass up against his steamy forehead. "This is paradise."

It was at that moment when I realized we were actually in Hawaii. I mean we finally landed in paradise with Noah, the ambassador of fun and he steered the ship. This was his trip. This was his time. Grandma Romie made a promise to him and she cashed that check two years later, so to speak. She reached her hands to him and held his face while she pressed a loving kiss on his cheek. Her smile and her eyes captured every emotion she saved up until this day because she saw Noah when he was at his worst and remembered those desperate times all too well. No, this was a different moment; a spectacular day to cherish for years to come. Her special grandson had pulled through the storms and fought to survive. Her eyes released that pain and transformed it into joyous pearls. And she cried as she held our Noah, but this time she cried in celebration of his life and to cherish his moment abundantly.

Noah made his plans – his itinerary. The highlight on his radar would be the dolphin excursion among the many wonderful events planned on his schedule. The dolphins were saved for a couple of days into the trip. First, we scheduled a trip to the North Shore, scuba time in the ocean off the catamaran, and a fun adventure into the local swap meet – Grandma's idea.

So, while at the swap meet, I grabbed up Noah and separated from the girls. I wanted to have some time with my boy doing manly things. You know, getting tattoos, shooting guns, drinking chocolate milkshakes and eating barbequed flesh. We started down the long aisles of countless vendors and food stands. We stopped at a neat coconut drink stand for Noah's first sip of the exquisite milk nectar. Our eyes were focused on the drink master as he cut the outer shell with a thick machete and dropped a long straw in the ice-chilled center. He handed it to my eager son and Noah held it with both hands, sort of like holding a bowling ball – it was that large. I built up this amazing drink of the tropical gods as if it was nature's mind-blowing syrup. Naturally, he was expecting something specific in his mind and on his palate.

"Yuck!" he blurted out after his first drink. "That's nasty!" Okay. So his palate is not yet fully developed, I get that. My goal was to have him try new things and we just checked that one off the list. I took the coconut and gladly sipped the remaining fresh nectar.

"Let's go look for another great find, Noah." I was on a mission to acclimate to this new culture.

We stumbled upon a tattoo parlor – well, not really a parlor. It was more like a swap-meet version of a face-painting stand. This one had hundreds of shapes to choose from and they could all be applied on the skin with henna ink.

"Hmmm," Noah said as he scoured the examples displayed in search of the perfect one. I hoped he picked one that revealed the power of his spirit. Maybe an image like a warlord panther hunting its prey in a dense jungle setting. Or, how about a battleship punishing a nearby hillside with its massive cannons of thunder and fire.

"There it is, dad." He pointed and grinned. "I want that one." The winner: a ferocious dragon prancing through a destroyed village – the victim of its wrath of fire. Noah was thrilled for his first tat. That's right son, you've earned it. The skilled artist applied the plastic stencil over his body part of choice: his bulging muscular calf. Okay, that's cool.

Once the black ink was transformed into this beast on his skin, I realized it was not the vicious animal I had imagined. No, instead it was just a one-dimensional shadow figure of what most reasonable adults would call a dragon-like image…if they were squinting…in the rain. But, he was tickled and wore it proudly.

Our quest continued through the collection of souvenirs, food delights, and all of that Hawaiian culture splendor. Since Noah scored his first tattoo, I figured we had to hold off from going down the rabbit hole of other treachery and villainous adventures. So, we kept it mild and ended up with the ladies waiting for our barbecue pork lunch with all of the trimmings. We left satisfied, impressed with the culture, and my main man sporting a "tough-guy" thrashing dragon tat on his limb. It was a very successful outing.

We explored the resorts fantastic attributes, one at a time. Including the remarkable lagoons located in walking distance from the main grounds. We soaked in the bath-temperature water and watched Noah enjoy every single minute of paradise. He used his scuba mask to peek down into the calm water and witness sea life in small portions. He was amazed. Small-sized jellyfish infiltrated the lagoon and sometimes we felt their tiny shocks delivered from their defense system. We kind of laughed and didn't let that stop us from wading in their habitat.

We moved from one side of the shoreline to the other, even under the cover of nightfall. As the sun set across a deep-colored horizon, we wanted to stop time and stay in the moment. Was there any way we could be here a little longer? Say, another five months?

One of Noah's list of tropical adventures included an excursion into the Pacific Ocean where he would swim with the dolphins. A large catamaran and about twenty of us, including the crew, set sail one late morning. It was remarkable to see Noah snorkel with Paula. After all, he didn't really care for water activities, but he made every effort to enjoy these once-in-a-lifetime memories.

The water was very choppy giving them both a little motion sickness. They returned to the boat, but only after seeing incredible views beneath the ocean and sea life. Large sea turtles and other wonderful creatures made the rough water worth the effort. On the way back, we were looking for dolphins. After all, it was also a dolphin excursion.

Noah blew, or made the best attempt, at blowing through a large conch shell. We were expecting a thunderous roar, but instead heard a pip-squeak sound sort of like a war cry of the mighty chipmunk. Needless to say, the whole experience was a wonderful time – except for the missing dolphins. That part was a bummer.

The next day we explored the resort's gift shop/refreshment store. Our boisterous conversation included the great time we had the day before and, even though Noah didn't see any dolphins, he had a blast. A very friendly store manager overheard our discussion as we shopped for some treats and he introduced himself.

"Hello, my name is Ray and I couldn't help but overhearing your conversation," he said politely. "Did you say you were looking for dolphins on your trip?"

"Hi there. Yes," Paula answered with a smile. "We've been having the time of our lives here and really wanted our son to see them during our trip to Hawaii." She continued to explain the nature of our trip and how Noah was a miracle child who fought to great lengths in order to survive. Not a couple of minutes into her stirring words, our new friend Ray had eyes swelled with tears. He was moved with such compassion to Noah's story and was happy to hear that he had made it through such amazing circumstances. We must have spoken for several minutes before he made a promise to us. Since the boat outing didn't go Noah's way, he was going to set up another trip for us with a different excursion and he basically guaranteed dolphins for our son. Now I don't know if he was personal friend with the mighty Titan who ruled the seas, or maybe he had connections with Aquaman, but his words were firm and we believed him.

He went on to say that their famous Luau was being held in a couple of days and we were invited as his personal special guests. Wow! What an amazing gesture. We were shocked and very thankful. Noah couldn't wait. We shook hands with Ray and went on our merry way.

The next day it all came together; there were dolphins and by the schools. They swam around our large vessel and seemed like they knew something. Almost as if they were celebrating Noah's victory in life and swam by his side of the boat in special formation or something. He was laughing and loved it! He had about thirty minutes of dolphins all to Ray's credit and efforts. What a blessing that was!

Later that day we ran into Ray at the same store. We told him about all of the many dolphins we saw and how much fun Noah had. Ray was moved with happiness and was only concerned with making sure Noah had the best experience possible. He reminded us of the Fia Fia Luau held the next day. We were thrilled.

With all of the drives we took and sights Noah took in, it was amazing how well he did physically. It was by far the most difficult climate he had experienced, with heavy humidity and around the clock heat. He stayed hydrated and he was connected to his fluids every night. We knew this would be his best aid and the difference between a calm night and a trip to the hospital. He lasted through the week and had one full day left in the tropical setting.

The final day had arrived and the highlight was Fia Fia. It was held outdoors at the west side of the resort overlooking the orange burnt sky. The layers of deep reds and amber were like curtains on display above the setting glow of the sun. There were upright, lit torches and wonderful tables decorated with flowers. A large stage ready for entertaining was positioned for all eyes to see.

We checked in at the front area and Ray was there as the main host. "Hello Noah and family!" his face lit up extra bright when his eyes met us. "We have special seating reserved for you at the center table. Please follow me." We felt like important officials or something. Noah ate up the royal treatment.

We sat and said hello to those around the large table. It was community seating with other friendly guests. After refreshments were served, Ray stepped up to the microphone at center stage to start the evening's festivities. He greeted all who attended and made sure that he announced Noah and family as his special guests. We were extremely honored.

The show began with Chief Sielu who told stories about his background and his life becoming the chief of his tribe. His story was compelling and he made the evening so much fun. Until – he walked over to our table. Like he was on cue, he began to speak with Noah and interacted with him. Then, he found me. He asked me the funniest questions and eventually urged me to drink this fantastic beverage reserved for chiefs in his culture. I couldn't refuse, but it did not taste like a root beer float by no means. It was more like swamp water with a pinch of Miracle-Gro. Yup, nice.

I was fitted with a special hand-woven headdress similar to a twig crown and was invited to join him on the stage. Along with a few other chosen ones, I graced the stage with the great Chief Sielu ready for some intense gang-initiation or something. The drum beats began and we all learned the art of Hawaiian war dancing. I saw the others goof it up and embarrass themselves, so I put all of my Hispanic heritage into my hips and focused. Boom, boom, boom – my hips kicked to the left, then chomped to the right in rhythmic sync to the drums playing in the background. Then my arms, held at the hips, swung up above my head like I was holding a large spear. I was in dance attack mode and Noah was cracking up. That's all that mattered. He absolutely thought I was hysterical. I completed my series of moves with a frozen face pose with my eyes frowned, mouth wide open, and my tongue fully extended and curled over my bottom lip. I was instantly transformed into a new person. Along with the others on stage, we had the hundred and fifty guests laughing uncontrollably. It was perfect.

When I returned to my seat, I turned to Noah and asked how I did. Of course, he said I did the best. I slipped him a five from my wallet and appreciated the gesture. But really, he was having an amazing evening. Here he was, the Big Kahuna, VIP extraordinaire on Oahu. Our star patient sat beneath a hundred-thousand stars and wished on each of them that perhaps he could stay in that moment forever. He was alive and most folks wouldn't have the appreciation for what that completely meant for us – for him. Unless you could walk in those footsteps years before, it would be impossible to know how far he has made it. Alive indeed.

He used every sensory tool available to upload each and every detail. He learned to do so because his short history repeated the same pattern and taught him the same lesson: to be ready at a moment's notice for that unexpected medical setback that lurked right around the corner. But today, no such setback existed. No, only wide smiles and fluttering hearts. Life was sweet!

The next day our commercial airliner glided at about forty-thousand feet above the Pacific Ocean and we were tucked safely into our seats. Exhausted from a wonderful Hawaiian getaway, we sat slightly lethargic. And Noah, well, he was fast asleep. I could almost make out the images that danced in his head, from all of those precious dreams that played out. They were scenarios designed with Hawaiian flair and excitement.

The trip was a huge success! There was simply no other way to describe it. No illness sidetracked his excursions on the island and no infections prevented him from witnessing all of that tropical splendor. I was honored to be there with him. I was able to secure in my heart some wonderful memories – stacks and stacks of them.

He was able to chalk up many firsts on this getaway. His first ever tattoo, his first time swimming with ocean life in the wide-open Pacific, and his first Hawaiian luau. Yeah, he was so far away from that kid who once was held hostage to illness in the hospital thousands of miles away. The one who waited on that life-saving list for precious organs. It almost seemed like several years ago, but then again it also seemed like last week. Pain has a way to make you vividly remember the memory of its fresh sting. And we were caught in its unstable wake for years to come.

PATCHWORK KID

18
MISERY IS PERSISTENT

"The road is long
With many a winding turn
That leads us to who knows where
Who knows where
But I'm strong
Strong enough to carry him
He ain't heavy, he's my brother"
-*The Hollies*

THE LAST FEW YEARS HAVE LEFT BEHIND a variety of scattered debris along our beaten path. The ravaged evidence of the furious storms of life that violently shake transplant families was all too real. Sometimes in the way you catch yourself staring out into empty space, being captured by recent episodes that consistently replayed like never-ending reruns of a horror movie. Or, perhaps in the rage of anger bottled up by our son that managed to manifest itself at the most peak times of stress. In all cases and examples, the truth was obvious – transplant children and family members most definitely required trauma therapy. Emotional support at the very least.

Often times Paula and I would revisit Noah's life in the hospital (through conversation), whether in Orange County, Hollywood, Bellflower, or in the state of Pennsylvania. He logged many stays over the course of a few years, not counting the summer months of 2004. We often joked that if we had one of those reward system punch cards and pulled that out of my wallet for each episode upon hospital admission, we would probably have one of those vacations a family only dreamed of enjoying.

We chuckled because at this junction of our lives with Noah it was all we could do except for running full sprint to the insane asylum. Why? Well, chronic illness, that's why. Unless you've tasted its poison, it's almost impossible to describe. No, laughter seemed to be one coping mechanism we had adopted, although it was not used to diminish our son's struggle or illness-caused disability. Instead, we sought out humor when appropriate to bring light to certain situations for Noah. And of course, Noah was right there in the mix as well, giggling and using silliness over something he had conquered. It was his way of saying, "You can't control me short-gut syndrome." Laughter was a fierce weapon he bravely wielded.

He learned not to take himself too seriously – sometimes. He took it all in stride. It amazed me to see such fortitude and courage. It was encouraging that he was so strong at his tender young age. This would only help him as he grew older. He definitely was a fighter and there was no denying his intense will to live.

I imagined his journey in my mind; his road within this life in a vivid, dream-like scene. Sort of mirage-like imagery that portrayed his calamity. I could see the outline of his shape as he walked along a road ahead of me. I witnessed his teenage frame, so thin and long-limbed making his way across a desert of troubling storms. He carried himself confidently taking cautious steps and pushing forward one at a time. Each step was calculated and considered. As the ferocious winds hurled waves of sand against him, he leaned in against the pressure with all that he had.

His physical outline included an IV pole with countless medical pumps attached; one hand tightly clenched to it as the object acted like an anchor and he slowly pulled it from behind. The bottom of the stand created a deep trench in the hot sand. The weight of the medical pumps that were attached caused the pole to sink deep, like a rudder on a large ship. I could see his ostomy the size of an upright, vacuum cleaner bag, attached to his lower right side. It weighed him down because it was filled with so much volume and it made each step taken with his right leg more strenuous than his left. He suffered with the heaviness of the medical equipment and with his ostomy appliance.

His movements became staggered and the uphill sand dune climbs made it more painful to endure. The beads of sweat were unreal, almost pouring from every visible pore. The dehydration was intense with nothing to drink in sight. It became obvious that the emotional stress of his medical issues was weighing on him as he grew older. The storms never ceased in his life. No, they only decreased in fury and in duration.

The scene was all too real, as though he was actually banished to this desert place. It symbolized his journey and it provided both a vivid and accurate depiction of his reality.

We taught him to pray through these situations and to lean on God for all things – for strength, for direction, and for purpose. He just didn't hear our voices, but he also saw our actions demonstrated in our lives.

There were hundreds of moments it seemed when we applied Tegaderm to his central line entry point on his skin, or cleared a line occlusion formed with air bubbles (infusion via any one of the pumps he had used), or helped him count and separate over seventeen different medications to put into his weekly pill bottles. We continuously encouraged him and reinforced each level of progress that he made up to that point. For in these moments we were able to pour into him emotionally and provide that priceless support he desperately needed. And not just because of his chronic illness, but also because of his critical stage of pubescent maturity and those extremely hard years in life we all are thankful that we never have to relive again.

We were warned from the transplant team concerning the days when he would reach puberty and enter those junior high and high school ages. The development of each child is different, but the additional stress of being a post-transplant kid often multiplied the stressors significantly. Significantly!

The stress was often louder than words. In Noah, in our children, and in us as parents. The equation became more difficult to solve and more complex with each month that would pass. The stress fractures were not really visible, but we felt tremors every now and again.

We grew wiser to a level that helped each new encounter become almost standard-issued situations. We learned from the previous hospitalizations and from the countless tests performed; both ongoing lab work and various organ tests to determine damage levels. We gained insight and we applied our knowledge – especially Paula. She simply outshined all others in this area. I'm not sure who I'm comparing her with, but she was amazing as a "medical mom."

Every August, Noah was required to visit the Pittsburgh transplant team for a complete and thorough medical examination. The surgeons who performed the surgery in 2004 (there were three superstars) all followed him and the other patients with liver/small-bowel transplants. It was a testimony to the brilliant program the hospital had developed and had offered to the world. Yes, to the entire world and all of the sick children around the globe. The annual follow up was just another method created to adhere to their strict guidelines of closely-monitored care. Not one of their patients was ever allowed to be left behind or be forgotten.

The special part of his annual visit was the strain he would place upon Dr. Squires. Physical pain, no less, in the form of push-ups. Yes, the push-up count continued. There was nothing that could interfere with Noah's brain cells in charge of collecting and preserving such data. Specifically, those cells trained with the mission of monitoring Dr. Squire's ongoing physical torture inflicted by the young devious mind – his star patient.

"Drop and give me twenty-seven, Dr. Squires," Noah confidently demanded, but all the while wearing a goofy grin. That would be twenty-seven intestinal scopes performed to date on our son. The doctor gave his typical weak refusal and delivered his best sales pitch as to why he thought those silly exercises would no longer apply. He was shot down every single time by our fearless son with his third-world dictator-like persistence. Noah was ruthless – in a comical sort of way.

The relationship between the highly trained medical team and our son was pretty amazing to witness. Our trust in their bedside manner and overall quality of care was solid. They treated Noah like a son, a brother, or a nephew. That level of health care just doesn't exist these days in the world of numbers and the bottom dollar running the show. We appreciated every encounter with the transplant team – every step of the way.

Another positive take away from the annual check-up was a photograph with the surgeons. Usually, it was with the physician who would conduct the exam and provide his lab results. Here's the great part – every year Noah would sit or stand next to one of the three surgeons who performed the 2004 transplant. With every passing year, the most trained eye could detect even the slightest changes in Noah's physical attributes; whether his height, or perhaps his facial structure and shape – it was obvious that our son was making gains in his health and growth. Yeah, the best part was witnessing this surging life within Noah and how he continued to take the shape of a man-child with every passing year.

It was like the growth chart proudly displayed on the walls of our children's bedrooms during their toddler years. But in his case, the marks of each new birthday celebrated the ability to remain alive as well as year-over-year growth.

**

As days and weeks had passed, we experienced such intense concern for Noah's health. We realized more and more the best efforts of the local medical team and exceptional efforts from Dr. Nanjundiah was no match for our son's fragile state of chronic illness. Yes, on one hand, we had the incredible life-saving organs and million-dollar surgery that rescued him and on the other, we had a son who without a doubt required daily care and full-time monitoring in order to maintain his state of health. One slip up or one missed detail and he would fall to earth in a fiery tailspin – every time.

You see, it came down to the timeframe of when he was sent to Pittsburgh for medical and transplant evaluation. Months of wasted time were spent by the local medical team, led by his first GI doctor (before Dr. Nanjundiah). His game plan was to see if his extremely small intestine (we'll call it a nub) would actually grow. There was some supporting evidence, supposedly, which was encouraging to us. But it was difficult to see any of these results actually occur. Wait to see it grow, stretch, or lengthen. *Do you want me to tug on it with a wrench doc? 'Cause it ain't movin'!* I thought.

It seemed like a wonderful plan for us hopeful parents at the time. We didn't know anything about small and large intestinal medicine and all of its fantastic intricacies for that matter. So, we heaped our trust into this first GI doctor and followed his guidance.

Well, looking back we could see the flash-flood onset of liver disease had crushed our little boy's health. The decision to wait was poor and birthed many consequences. No, he should have been sent to Children's Hospital in Pittsburgh six months to a year earlier than when he actually was. Our son's transplant surgeons made it very clear to us that this should have been the course of treatment for him. By doing so, he could have not been at death's door and may have been able to receive his organs – perhaps even so much more of a small bowel than what he had actually received. The words echoed and became that "what if" psychosis mantra. Yeah, this type of thinking was unhealthy, but man – if only he would have been listed so much sooner he could have been in a much better place today. Instead, it was so much touch-and-go in his day to day life.

And that's where persistent, loving, strong-minded, ferocious-willed, and stubborn parents come into play. We never gave up with Noah. We forged through pain and suffering with him to keep him alive. Even if for one more day, he was the one who was going to have that one more day…period.

Give up? Nah. Let this overtake him? No way. Take this lying down? Never. We showed up to fight at his side every single day. Are there parents who would have it any other way? Like that famous and wonderful poem called "Footsteps," when Noah couldn't walk anymore, we carried him – and God carried all of us. And likewise, his courage and laughter through it all somehow gave us the drive to continue. And we weren't giving up anytime soon. Uh, like never.

**

Scary is always lurking somewhere close by.

It was busy in the emergency room on a mid-week afternoon. A nurse brought Noah back to the general treatment area. We followed. It was a familiar place there at Lakeview and the ER had not changed since we were last there.

Noah was fighting something that was taking the life out of him. His blood pressure was on the low side and fever was persistent. Again, it was another one of those moments where we've seen this all too often and had a sense that he would receive the immediate care required. But, this time the staff was preoccupied with other urgent patients or just had no idea the patient they had on the floor had such an intense medical history and their ignorance was blinding them – you pick.

"Can you please check his pressures again," Paula asked a passing nurse.

"We'll be right with you," she replied.

Minutes later, that seemed like twenty to me, someone checked on him. Blood pressure reading: ninety-five over seventy. Yeah, pretty low and no relief in sight. With minimal care administered, the nurse said she would let the doctor know his latest readings. We sat there trying to comfort Noah with the usual tactics we were familiar with. More time had passed and he was fatigued.

Finally, a doctor showed up and began the usual line of questioning. We gave him the details and another blood pressure check was made. It was dropping still and no one could understand why – nor was a solution or treatment was offered. We couldn't believe it. We suggested connecting him to fluids immediately to help with his pressures. The doctor agreed and left to get that started.

It was becoming a tremendous load of stress as we waited another ten – fifteen – twenty minutes and still no fluids. He needed help and we were in the very place that could do something – but they wouldn't. I stood up and walked beyond his privacy curtain. I located a group of staff members at a nearby station.

"Can you please help me get my son a doctor now? We've been waiting for someone to help him and his pressures are dropping," I sternly asked. They all had that "deer in the headlights" look on their faces. One of them spoke and said they would have someone come right over.

Another nurse came over and took another blood pressure reading: fifty-five over thirty-eight. Are you kidding me right now?! Noah was becoming lifeless and wouldn't talk. We told the nurse he needed help right now. She said she would get his doctor. And then we waited and waited and waited.

Paula and I looked at each other and had that same look in our eyes. It was the look only years of love and raging pain could forge. The look that told timeless stories of enduring deep hardship and carved out gouging wounds with pain's cold bitterness. We've been there before and it wasn't good.

"Is this how it's going to end?" her words fell alongside pouring tears that streamed from her eyes. She spoke softly and cautiously so Noah couldn't hear her. We fought so hard and so long, but was this it? I can't describe how strange this felt. Unlike the endless days and nights that totaled months while he waited for those organs in that Pittsburgh ICU, we spent less than two hours in this local hospital emergency room without any hope. His life was slipping away right in front of us while the masses of medical staff busily handled their affairs. We're we invisible or blacklisted somehow? We couldn't grasp the despair we suddenly found ourselves living in.

We prayed; we asked our God for His touch. Desperate moments seem to freeze time and all surroundings. Life slows to a crushing pace. Where beating hearts pumping blood can be deafening. We sat at his bedside and told Noah to hang on. He moaned slightly.

Like a flash of lightning, out of the darkness came a familiar face that walked into the main area right in front of us. We had the curtain pulled open to one side as we waited for help. And there he was – Dr. Murtari, one of Noah's physicians who cared for him often on the upper pediatric floor. I stood like someone just hit a grand slam out of the park and rushed at him.

"Dr. Murtari!" we both loudly called to him. He sharply stopped in his tracks and caught our eyes right away.

"Hi there," He was shocked to see us with Noah laying there and immediately rushed to his side. "What's going on?"

We began to brief him on Noah's status and told him we were waiting for someone to help him with some fluids. He moved swiftly and used his stethoscope to listen to Noah's chest while the blood pressure machine was filling his cuff with air. Forty-eight over twenty-eight – the blood pressure was gravely low. You could see the incredible frustration in his face as he called out for a nurse and turned towards the main area. He shouted orders like a commander on the front lines of intense warfare.

Within seconds a nurse rushed to his side and they immediately began to work on our son. They had several large tubes of fluid and Dr. Murtari began to attach one to Noah's IV line. He slowly and methodically pushed the clear fluid of saline mixture into his vascular system. We watched Noah and the doctor timed the manual infusion carefully. The nurse handed him the next large syringe and he exchanged the empty for the fresh one and attached it to his IV – one by one. He pushed fluids into Noah with care. He was focused and determined.

Finally, the pressures increased and provided us with a sense of relief. After a while of Dr. Murtari's procedure, Noah began to stabilize and we knew he was out of danger. We experienced relief and incredible happiness for the doctor's efforts.

About thirty minutes later, the nurse who monitored Noah said he was doing much better. We walked Dr. Murtari out away from our son and down the hall. He couldn't believe how fast Noah declined but knew that if he didn't act immediately he would not have much time. He apologized for the lack of effort and care on behalf of the emergency room staff. It was shocking to him. He told us he was on his way to the fourth floor and had to swing by the ER first.

Only his previous experience with Noah and his known difficult, medical history helped him act appropriately. Whereas a child with no medical issues, unlike our son, would not be in any sudden danger or decline as rapidly.

That was a tough moment for us both. It reminded us how fragile our son was. Noah was a fragile patient regardless of the bucket full of medications, daily hydration infusions, impeccable dressing care we provided (both sanitary and germ-free), bionic organs, Kryptonite immunity treatment, well...you get the point. After all of the strict medical care we as parents provided every hour of every day, it could all collapse in just a few minutes. And that, ladies and gentlemen, yes that was kick-in-the-throat scary.

Our reliance became dependent upon the One who gave life initially. Who else can we run to and who else is worthy of such praise and adoration? The balance was real. We trusted in our Lord with all respect, reverence, and glory given to Him. We also managed to have daily multiple heart tremors and experience intense concern for our precious Noah. After all, we are just flesh and blood. Yeah, his life was so very delicate.

Instantly, with just one episode, a smack-down from a reality check grounded us. Can you see how we became so gracious and thankful for every living minute we were able to gain with him? Life is a huge blessing. Life is a wondrous and fulfilling adventure in this fantastic wonderland.

Sept 7, 2006 6:35pm

Greetings all! The summer has ended and what a memorable one it was for us. Noah had a spectacular summer filled with fun-filled memories and incredible events. It was a blessing to have no major setbacks during the summer as he was very healthy throughout. His level of fitness has greatly improved over last summer and he is able to handle more activities. His only trip to Pittsburgh this summer was for his 2-year post-transplant exam/physical and transplant camp. The doctors say he is doing very well and is on pace to break the all-time milk drinking record (that is with or without Nestle Quick). In fact, he has just passed Paula by 1/4" in his height and has put on a handful of pounds since June. His thighs still look like broomstick handles, so I must put him on a running back training regimen.

Of course, the big news this week is Noah's return to school (7th grade) at a full-time level (first time since October 2002). Yup, five days a week with only minor restrictions for P.E. (no linebacker contact drills or base-jumping). His anticipation for school was only matched by his love for milk and cookies, and so far he loves it! Paula had to go meet with the nurse today because it was a new school and review his medical history. Ha! You got a couple of hours? Anyway, the school is ready for Noah The Great and his special medical needs - we will keep praying for a safe year for him.

Noah will be having a new IV line replaced tomorrow. He currently has a PICC line that is pretty much shot. I mean, it was meant to last a few weeks and he has had it for about 6 months now. Paula and I learned about a different type of IV line/port when she was in Pittsburgh earlier in the year that seems to be popular with the other transplant kids. It must be placed under the skin in his chest area and is accessed with a needle. All of his current supplies and ports are non-needle or some call it "needle-less" or some may call it "non-pokie", so that means more training for mom and dad. Yup, we know quite a bit of stuff. Paula said she should go to school and become an RN with all of the experience she has. I tell you what, she knows a little bit about surgery too. So Noah will have this Mediport placed tomorrow and it will allow him to get wet easier than the current system of water-proofing his arm and re-cleaning then re-taping, on and on, and so forth. It looks like he will have to wait a few more months before the doctors start to reduce his daily IV fluid intake. I think we've made tremendous progress since last summer, don't you?

God Bless,
Roger

The fall season began with school and with great football. Noah was a fan of the game and enjoyed our time cheering on the players. Snacks didn't hurt either. We would watch our team battle on the television screen and then run outside for a quick toss of the pigskin. Luke sprinted around the yard like he was a star running back. The NFL was a perfect diversion for us men in the house, especially for Noah and his medical demands. The women would have no part of it, which was another bonus for us Y-chromosome, meat-eating beings. No dollies around our feet to accidentally trip over or girl talk concerning hair styles or boys. Yeah, the ritual was real and Noah ate it up.

School was a success for him and 7th grade was good to Noah. After missing so much of a normal school schedule over the past four years, it was a blessing to finally see our son return to campus in a regular schedule.

The necessary accommodations were made by the school and he seemed to do very well academically. Of course, he was a bright student and his main obstacle was returning to such a regular pace of both classes and homework. He was up for the challenge, though. Nothing would prevent him from pursuing 7th grade and doing his very best.

The newly installed Mediport-Portacath was also a success. It was placed securely beneath his skin (attached to the underlying muscle) and over his right upper chest area. He was able to lavish in the showering ritual without hesitation or fear of saturating the IV port site (or even a sprinkle of moisture for that matter).

Because, as we all know by now, every single odd that exists in life waited for their number to be called to infiltrate a peaceful day. Yes, the odds were ready to wage war against our son and wreak havoc. They would bring with them a battalion of bacteria (ferocious Gram-negative strains, no doubt) and collapse the empire of his soul. But – not today. No, those same odds were now in his favor and they struggled with this new imbalance caused by his new Mediport. No sickness today, you losers.

Instead, Noah enjoyed the gently flowing spring water while in the shower and soaked up every humid molecule of steam that accumulated on his skin. He was in his glory. No Tegaderm. No plastic taped to his tender and sensitive skin. No IV port wrapped in seventy layers of saran-wrap. Nope. Never again, barring any reason to remove that super-duper device.

We loved that thing! We tried to nominate it for President and we threw parties for it. You see, it was saving our son from so much chaos. Only those who experienced such bliss would fully appreciate this small but precious victory.

Until, each moment we had to connect Noah to those daily – yes, daily – hydration infusions. Oh no! The only way to access this port that rested safely under his skin was to pierce it with a large caliber needle on the end of the line itself. Was it the size of your favorite Big Gulp straw? No, but it sure seemed like it was given the nature of this violent procedure and how sensitive his frail skin was. His eyes opened wide like he was playing guitar hero on the advanced level, with the likes of Edward Van Halen opposing his skills. Eyes open wide! He was focused on that tip of the spear ready to puncture his life and force large volumes of fluid into his chest. Boom! In it went. Like a dagger from the outer blackness yielded by the mighty Thor himself. I was the masked executioner assigned to this duty. *Hey, wait a minute. Why me?* Well, I tried to make it as gentle of a prick as I could. You know, like some tickling beneath the armpit. A gentle stroke of a feather across his ear. No, really. But, in the end, the pain was real – every single time.

Sometimes his eyes would well up with tears and it just killed me to pieces. I mean I felt terrible for doing that. It was the cost of eliminating the central line or pick-line system.

As time went on we tried to make light of it somehow, if Noah was up for it. I would joke with him, of course.

"Hey Noah, let's try to numb the skin with something more than this wimpy cream that we use." We had to apply the skin with numbing cream an hour before the puncture, but the numbness was weak at best. Like I said, wimp cream.

"With what?" he replied with a glimmer of hope in his voice.

"Let's use a shot of surgery-grade Novocain right into the skin and you won't feel a thing son." I couldn't sell it. My words fell flat regardless of my best attempt and false enthusiasm. And with a look of ridiculousness and a bit of disdain, he rolled his eyes and announced sharply,

"Well, that's stupid! The shot will hurt just as much as the needle port. Duh!"

I tried and as weak as my joke was, we usually laughed about it most of the days after that. So, day after day we chose the lame version provided by decade's worth of medical scientific breakthroughs – wimpy numbing cream. Geez.

**

Our 2006 ended with some nice victories and a little momentum. Yes, the Noah-Train ran in full force! He finished off December with a resonating BANG and he was on his way to greatness.

The Pittsburgh doctors were amazed at how well his important numbers remained (liver counts, hemoglobin, etc.) and said they are the best levels they have ever seen in him. That was just amazing to hear since they have been following him since the middle of 2004. Dr. N added that these levels have been the best she has ever seen in over four years. Wow! This was a huge blessing for us.

The best part was how Noah felt like he was improving and was able to do more physically ever since his illness knocked him to the ground in

2002. He handled every single activity PE class demanded of him. We're talking weekly push-ups, endless rowing machine repetitions, and running that dreaded mile. Yeah, mile! I should have started filling out his application for tryouts held by the National Football League.

This comeback kid makes Rocky Balboa look like a runner up to a bubble gum chewing contest. And he continued to impress us with his physical prowess and increased endurance. It was a far cry from when he was bound to that hospital bed.

The doctors even cleared him for little league baseball! With mom and dad a bit nervous Noah was excited to take on this new level of strenuous activity and have the time of his life. Noah must do these things. You know, the deepest desires of normalcy. He must celebrate his new life and live it to the fullest. In some way, he honors his donor that made this all possible, through God's plan for him.

He earned another achievement and this time it was related to his education. Yes, he earned a special achievement award at the junior high school he attended so sparingly! This was quite a feat for a student who really did not attend school for a full-time basis for over four years. Noah continued to rise above and amaze us.

**

Our year seemed to be on track for Noah, to reach new heights in his overall health and well-being. Yet, the not-so-subtle reminders of his uphill battle with short-gut syndrome and other obstacles were ever present. I think my Carepages entries speak volumes, between February and November.

Feb 8, 2007 7:59pm

Well, do you want the good news or bad news first? Ok, the bad news is that Noah was admitted on Monday for what appeared to be severe dehydration and increased output through his ostomy. He was feeling a little "off" throughout the weekend and Monday morning blood lab work confirmed that he needed medical care. At least he was feeling much better by Tuesday and continues to feel well as of tonight. He was scoped and a biopsy was performed of his bowel. As of this evening, a decision was made to send him to Pittsburgh tomorrow sometime via air ambulance. He was already scheduled to return to Pitt this coming Monday for his 6-month check-up. Paula is not looking forward to the tight confines of a medical Learjet.

Now let's rewind just a bit for some of the good news. I think most of you know that Noah made the honor roll this past semester, right? Well, he was also chosen from his school to receive the "Every Student Succeeds" award. This is presented to one child a year based on teacher input and what obstacles were faced to achieve high grades and performance. We are extremely proud of Noah's achievement. I think Harvard should be contacted for application consideration. Or perhaps the University of Pittsburgh's prestigious medical program. Or even stand in for intestinal transplant surgeons that call in sick. Well, you may call it a stretch, but I know he can do great things through our Lord.

More stuff...Noah was signed up for little league baseball after Pittsburgh surgeons cleared him in December. Talk about a Merry Christmas present for Noah - he was excited. His last baseball adventure was back when he was 8 years old. Now that his stamina has increased and muscle tone strengthened, he is ready to tackle the baseball world. I think the Anaheim Angels should be contacted for an application consideration. Anyway, you know the drill...Noah is the best...yada yada yada...He is gonna hit grand slams every time...yada yada yada. Well, after Friday's practice, he had these symptoms that suggested he was dehydrated. Now don't say, "Just give him a little more water." It doesn't work like that for him. This complicated situation involves deeper issues with his bowel transplant and damaged kidneys and stuff in between. Because he is still on 8 hours of IV fluids every day makes it even more urgent to discover why and fix it - not so easy though. I wish it were.

There is a chance he may be removed from baseball. I don't want to see the disappointment in his face if that happens. He has only participated in three practices and he loves it. It's like he never had any illness - ever.

Well, as of this evening he is being slammed with Solumedrol to counter the possibility of intestinal rejection. We don't want Noah there for weeks at a time. If it is serious, then he will be.

I'll keep you posted.

God bless,
Roger

Feb 12, 2007 5:18pm

Whew!! Now that was close! Noah is officially NOT rejecting his organs or anything else at this point (other than wanting to do homework). Paula and Noah flew out of Van Nuys on what Paula called a larger than normal medical Learjet. I guess she is becoming the authority on these planes since she rides them frequently. She said the ride was much more comfortable than the typical air-ambulance they ride on. She was told by the on-board nurse that it would be about a $30,000 plane ride to Pittsburgh. Thank you, Kaiser! Now that comes with a lifetime supply of chocolate, right? So anyway, they arrived around midnight and Noah settled down on the 7th floor (intestinal transplant ward) where he has become quite the celebrity of sorts.

"Here is the kid from California," or "Look out, it's Noah. Let's see what pranks he's got up his sleeve," is what one may hear as Noah makes his grand entrance into the ward. Yeah, you nurses have better stock up on milk (I am serious) and cocoa puffs! So, the doctors performed another biopsy on him and determined that there was no rejection present. Since all other things are ruled out, he may just have a virus in his bowel (maybe a little ringworm or gangrene too– hey now, just kidding). He is doing much better today. In fact, they let Paula take him out on a day pass to see if he could get some frostbite. Oh yeah, it's cold outside.

Noah remains positive (so long as he's holding a nice 8 oz. ice cold carton of milk in his left hand and a moist, dark chocolate brownie in his right). But, he is thoroughly missed and we are eagerly waiting for both he and Paula to come home soon (her birthday is right around the corner). She explained that a special kidney test will be performed on Noah to see how much and what type of Kidney damage exists. One of the surgeons told Paula that Noah may have to require additional IV fluids for the rest of his life. She told him that was unacceptable (I bet she followed her response with a roundhouse kick to his head – in love of course). There is no reason for this dependency when other kids are not on IV fluids. We just need to resolve this dehydration/ kidney dysfunction issue in order for Noah to reach a whole...nutha...level.

Thank you, everyone, for your faithfulness in prayer and devotion to Noah. His fight continues...

God bless,
Roger

Feb 16, 2007 4:46pm

Happy Friday. Well, barring any last-minute testing, Noah and Paula will return this Sunday from the cold (barely double digits during the day) region of Pittsburgh. They are spending these last few days with our very close friends from Calvary Chapel and enjoying each other's company. It certainly is a nice change for Noah being out in the snowy, wintery land. He gets a big kick out of it. I told him he should walk barefoot in the snow for about 45 minutes and see what happens (now come on, I didn't really say that).

Onto the not-so-good news. Noah and Paula met with a highly respected renal doctor about Noah's dehydration issues and how it relates to his kidney dysfunction. After several tests were completed and all doctors were consulted, the following was determined: The root of these issues seems to stem from the fact that he is not absorbing enough sodium to maintain a normal balance. When this occurs (usually through physical activity), his sodium levels decrease to the point where replacing them cannot be achieved through our small "medical center" at home or even by drinking gallons of Gatorade drinks (that include sodium). You see, he can't absorb enough through his small intestine. Yes, I know what you're thinking – he received a transplant of a small bowel (and liver). But...the potential length of the donated organ tissue was 14 feet and the doctors could only put in eight feet due to his physical limitations. That results in a huge loss of potential bowel! We didn't know this either until this week. When Noah went into surgery, the doctors described his insides like war had taken place. This was due to his extreme stage of sickness (it still amazes me that he pulled through based on how he was at the beginning of the operation). Now, the eight feet of bowel can and does wonderful things – how we take its function for granted. It has allowed Noah to have a completely normal diet and it absorbs vitamins and life-sustaining nutrients. It even takes sodium from food and drink, but not enough in his case. In fact, he will be getting traces of increased sodium through his nightly IV runs at home now. We have to keep a very close eye on him as too much sodium can have dangerous side effects.

So, you ask what does this mean for Noah's future. Well, it basically means that he may require IV maintenance fluids for several years or longer which requires an IV central line (or like his current medi-port beneath his skin). Not so bad, huh? Well, you are absolutely correct. It can be a lot worse for him. But, as for us and a very saddened Noah, this was a step backward. The first and second highest life-threatening dangers for these kids are IV infections and dehydration...both of which Noah has. It's deep within a parent's heart to want their children to do what kids do. Not to live in a bubble of fear or restrictions. So please forgive me if I sound a little disappointed here. We do cherish every moment we have with Noah – based on every doctor's expert opinion - he should not have made it this far. Thank God, because He has allowed Noah to live. This means we will continue to see how Noah does in baseball practice as we draw nearer to opening game day in March. If he can sustain a healthy balance of sodium and not dehydrate, then it will be God's grace to see him through to the end of the season. You see, Noah is built to have friendships, operate in a team atmosphere, laugh and converse with people, express himself, and thrive in these areas – even excel! He is truly an amazing person!

God bless,
Roger

Mar 15, 2007 6:34pm

Noah was not feeling right on Tuesday and we had to get him over to the emergency room for an immediate blast of IV fluids. Of course, he had a fever, a terrible headache and was very weak – so on and so forth...you know the drill by now. So I wheeled him past the crowd in the ER waiting room and directly into the waiting doctor's arms. Yeah right. It was a zoo. Usually, Dr. Nanjundiah can use her muscle and get him directly into a room on the pediatric floor, but there was no room available. So, once he was seen and treated by the ER doctors, we made it to a room close to midnight.

The nurses asked Noah why he was back and he replied, "Because I miss you." Yeah right, he misses nothing about the hospital stays once he's back at home. But, he did earn a rather nice "Awe, how sweet he is" gesture – that little monkey. No, better yet – he is a teacher's pet gone bad...how about a nurse's pet instead. Anyway, he was admitted and we are waiting for Dr. N to give her blessing. He may be there a couple of more days at least. The admitting office person walked in and had that shocked look on her face and said, "You guys are back again?" Yup. Noah has officially enrolled in the once a month hospital plan for 2007. Let's see how many different hospital wrist-badges I can collect in a year. Or better yet, let's see how fast I can get my hands on a new hand-held, electronic, entertainment device from my parents for my current state of illness, hopelessness, and weakness. (He kind of plays on the heart-strings a little if you know what I mean). He puts Ralph from 'A Christmas Story' to shame in this category. Red rider, 200-shot, range-model, air rifle my foot. Noah likes the PSP NASA satellite communication, link-system piece of equipment. You know, the kind that can interface with the world's dominant warfare hardware and start WW3.

Anyway, he is doing better today and I will tell him that y'all said hello when I see him after work. I think at this point his baseball career is over. We will have to pull him out as hard as it is to do. In fact, he just took pictures with the team. He will have to cheer for his brother Luke while sitting in the grandstands. Just breaks our hearts.

God bless.
Roger

Mar 16, 2007 5:30pm

Rats!! Noah has pneumonia. It was discovered today in his lower left lung. He is weak and fatigued, but still has that spark in his voice. They also discovered that he has an ear infection, so it makes sense as to why he felt crummy. We will be spending the weekend with him at Kaiser Lakeview and keep him laughing as much as we can. Please keep him in your prayers.

God Bless,
Roger

Mar 25, 2007 12:10pm

Home sweet home. It's nice to have Noah back after almost two weeks in the hospital. He has been sleeping a lot since coming home, but he sure looks good.

One of our goals is to keep him out of the hospital until August when he will be flying to Pittsburgh for his 3-year post-transplant visit and camp. He's missed a bunch of school, so we need to help him get back on track. And of course, there is baseball...I think it has become day by day now. The coach understands his situation and is allowing anything we decide to happen. We figure since he enjoys it and the coach doesn't mind, Noah can show up at practice anytime and play just a couple of innings during a game.

Thank you for your ongoing prayer support. You are truly God's warriors!

God bless,
Roger

Apr 16, 2007 3:01pm

Hello all. As we anticipated last week, Noah was admitted very late last night in the hospital for dehydration. We kept him as good as we could during last week's spring break and he had fun with his buddies. We saw his output continue to increase as last week progressed and we gave him additional IV fluids at home, but there is only so much we can do for this type of problem. There are so many internal issues and biological processes that are not working 100% and the results for the intestinal studies performed last week will be available this week sometime (sorry, I don't think I mentioned those). The discussions between Paula and the Pittsburgh doctors don't seem to produce any answers – at least to our satisfaction about what can be done. We are starting him on Sandostatin to help decrease his output levels, but after that what's next? Well, the unspoken reality is that he may require a second bowel transplant. We know the statistics have shown that a second bowel transplant increases the mortality rate, so our hope is to avoid it if possible.

We also began Noah on a strict diet similar to what he was on during those pre-transplant years. This will help keep his output down as well, but his taste buds are annoyed. The bottom line – Noah hates it. You see, in his mind, he wants to keep getting better and make advances in his health, so for him to drastically limit his sugar and milk intake is a huge bummer. Before, we told him that one day he would have his organs and be able to eat what he wanted. So, in his mind, he is going backward. We remind him that his overall gains to date have been immense and life-changing. The struggles he faces only seem like the end of the world, but he's still experiencing a life of fullness that God has blessed him with. We may be losing the battle, but we will win this war.

So, you may want to sell your milk stock right away as the Ziegler household will no longer be causing the supply to peak. Yup, get rid of that dairy cow you've been keeping in your backyard. Got milk? No, not lately. At least the amount that Noah was used to drinking. You know, milk with his five bowls of cereal, milk and cookies (but without the cookies)...you name it, he's had it. So, aside from his milk withdrawals and non-sugar highs, he is experiencing mental anguish more than anything. Maybe we can substitute that with a chore binge, or a homework blitz, or some kind of a Noah sublime activity.

I've got just the thing for him. How about a 2-day, Disneyland blast-o-fun? Wishland (a non-profit wish-granting organization for kids like Noah) has given Noah and the family 2 days at Disneyland with those amazing special "no line required" passes. Yeah, baby! To the front of every line please. Excuse me, I have a short-gut kid coming through...here's the pass to cut in front of you and hundreds of others – BAM!! Hey, Noah deserves it. Well, we selected the dates over a month ago and we picked this Thursday and Friday. Now the goal is to get him discharged by Wednesday. You see the bigger picture here? Noah needs some "me-time" in order to get past this "where's the milk?" depression he's going through. This should keep him happy until the next phase of bliss comes his way. Like camping, or playing on-stage with P.O.D.

Please keep him in your prayers.

Thank you.
Roger

Apr 19, 2007 12:59pm

It's Thursday...and Noah is still in the hospital. The earlier reports of a discharge today have been changed due to his ongoing output struggles. He will remain until sometime next week. Disneyland will have to wait for a couple of weeks. He did manage to meet another 13-year-old patient (being treated for Crohn's Disease) and they immediately hit it off. It was Xbox one minute, playroom the next. Together they ruled the hallways and kept the nurses on their toes. Of course, Noah brings the best out of everyone. His new friend has a hard time eating due to his condition, but when they are together in their glory, there is food and fun O' plenty. Noah told Paula that his friend has been eating pretty well for the past couple of days. Yeah, leave it to Noah to figure a way to call down directly to food services and request various things like chocolate cake, Pizza Hut pizza, and other delightful num nums. All with a few keystrokes on his room telephone – that little schemer.

I guess the doctor is letting him have a few sweets and a little milk to test this new drug efficiency. It's helping decrease the output, but we are in no way there yet. Unfortunately for Noah, his friend was discharged yesterday. They exchanged info and his buddy called Noah from the elevator to see if the number worked. Noah said, "Of course it works. I wouldn't give you a bad number." Noah said his friend will be moving to Texas soon. Another long-distance buddy to stay in touch with.

Yesterday was difficult in that more discussions were made with Pittsburgh doctors about Noah's condition. If there is not a dramatic change and a complete turnaround, then how do we continue to keep admitting Noah to the hospital every month for these episodes? The doctors all agree that Noah can't keep living like this and they are doing what they can for him to prevent a second transplant. There were tears and telephone calls made for prayers across the country.

After work, I drove home to pick up Luke and we went to visit Noah. Luke has known nothing else his whole life but Noah in the hospital. Without a blink of an eye, Luke greeted Noah, threw off his shoes and climbed into bed with his big brother. It was a very precious sight. Of course, the best part was when Noah picked up the phone and ordered chocolate cake for them both. You should have seen the look on Luke's face. It was better than a MasterCard commercial.

God bless,
Roger

May 3, 2007 5:21pm

Well, where do I begin today? Noah was discharged Friday evening (after 11 hours of deliberation) as the doctors, nurses, pharmacists, and U.S. Military couldn't get Noah's paperwork and release orders written accurately. Needless to say, I was very frustrated Saturday morning having incorrect vials, no syringes, and no IV pump, but I will leave that story for another day. Basically, Noah was given about four new meds to start at home and his medicine schedule was revamped. The goal was simple: to keep his watery-output as low as possible (hopefully around 1-2 liters a day) and make the consistency like peanut butter. The result: his output was 4 or 5 liters a day through the weekend and into yesterday. Oh, he went to Disneyland alright on Monday – it would have taken Seal Team One to curtail that plan or perhaps Mars suddenly crashing into our orbit.

The family day was great and everyone had a blast. The weather was perfect, the laughs were plenty, and the lines were non-existent (thanks to a "Guest Assistance Pass"). They should call that a "Noah's Transplant - Celebrate Life - Cut in Front of Line Pass." Of course, it fell on Brooke's birthday (144 months old) so she secretly thought it was partially for her. Ok, I will give her that. A big thanks to Wishland for their generous gift for Noah and for our whole family!

Now, onto further business. Last night Noah's output reached the 5.5-liter mark and it was as watery as a Mississippi swamp (Noah would have giggled from that one). Combined with his side cramps, flushed face, and decreased blood pressure, we immediately started him on a bolus of fluid and called the doctor. A couple of hours later, we were in the hospital room making his surroundings comfy. He was bummed with the thought of returning only having been in as early as last week. Also, with school nearing its end, there is nothing he wants more than to be in class.

The latest change is having the Sandostatin infuse over 12 hours rather than the daily 3 doses we were doing at home. We'll see. I don't see any reason why we can't rule out Noah being airlifted to Pittsburgh either, because the doctors there are able to control every aspect of his care and make timely changes accordingly. We just need to find Noah's internal faucet controls and turn them down. Yeah right, I wish. Maybe if everyone writes a letter to Noah stating your wishes that he stop growing it will bring back a normal hormonal balance. Yeah right. He loves being taller than mom now. I told him he just needs to add small particles of quick dry cement to his diet. Of course, he giggled. When does he not?

I will keep you posted.

God bless.
Roger

May 4, 2007 4:59pm

Ok, you must be sitting down for this! I called Noah this morning and he answered with a kick in his giddy-up,

"Hello?" I said.

"Hi, dad! Want to hear the good news?!" he replied. Now, I am one for receiving good news these days. Yes, I will have the good news platter with happiness on the side, and a slice of joy pie, please. Oh yes, that will be to go. Now that we have that straightened out, allow me to continue. Noah told me that he is going home today. Excuse me?! I must have dialed the wrong room or something. I asked him how he did that (after all, the little schemer is known for convincing many a nurse to get what he wants). Noah said that the change in his Sandostatin has helped decrease his output. He didn't have much more detailed info so I called the doctor at the pediatric ward. He explained how Noah's output was down to 2.5 liters yesterday with a 10-hour continuous drip of the med. Now that's what I call results! All you prayer warriors out there – this is for you!!

Dr. Van Winkle went on to say that they will administer the 10-hour dose and have him discharged tonight after dinner. He also said he is looking for a special pump for home infusion. Well, you better look good doctor because we already went through this last Friday. Hopefully, the correct portable pump can be delivered to our home by the medical equipment team in time for his morning dose. That would be a neat trick. I spoke to Noah's GI doctor and she is demanding to get him a portable device. What the hospital doctor wants to do is send Noah home with an IV pole/ pump. No way, that ain't gonna fly. You might as well chain Noah to his bed and feed him bread and water if you're gonna do that. No, it must be portable. So that is where we are as of this afternoon.

Will this portable pump/infusion throughout the day allow him to remain in school you ask? I don't know as of yet. It does mean that he will be on a pump for 20 hours a day, but that beats being hospitalized. The real question is: can he perform double flips on his skateboard while wearing the said device? I don't know. How many licks does it really take to get to the center of a Tootsie Roll lollipop?

So, there is a strong chance we will get him home today. The great news is that the output today is even lower than it was yesterday. Yessss!

God bless,
Roger

May 8, 2007 1:48pm

Yikes!! It has been quite an ending to this past weekend. We began with Sunday night charting Noah's ostomy output and intake for Dr. Nanjundiah. You see, Noah had a headache and his blood pressure was dropping – dehydration. His output was elevated and it seemed as though what Kaiser was doing for him (in terms of the new 10-hour infusion of Sandostatin) was not working. So, at approximately midnight, I drove him to the emergency room. Of course, we had already infused about a liter of saline over the previous few hours at home which helped tremendously. At 2:00 AM he was wheeled up to a room (the same one he was discharged from Friday) and I already knew that he would be transported to Pittsburgh sometime Monday. Dr. Nanjundiah and I agreed when we spoke late Sunday evening that it was necessary to get him there to be under the care of Children's Hospital.

The ambulance arrived yesterday to pick up Noah and drove him over to Chino Airport. Paula and Noah were scheduled to arrive in Pittsburgh at 4:00 AM via air ambulance. I received a call early this morning to inform me that they arrived safely and Noah was already scheduled for various scopes and tests this week. The doctors aggressively began with a 24-hour Sandostatin infusion and will try subcutaneous doses if necessary. The doctors assured Paula that Noah will not be discharged until this matter is resolved. Needless to say, we are at peace with his care as of now.

Paula told me that a friend who works at the hospital is now assigned to the intestinal/liver transplant floor. Frank is a child life specialist supervisor who we met when Noah was in the ICU prior to his transplant. He wears a big smile and has a huge heart for Noah. He helps families and especially kids get through some of these difficult times by scheduling outdoor events with music, crafts, and other activities. He also can get goodies like notebook computers and coordinate the likes of Big Ben Roethlisberger visits. So, naturally, Noah was very excited to see Frank on the 7th floor and discuss the possibility of getting some Pirate game tickets or just hang out. Noah proudly wore his Steeler jersey and Pitt Panther (University of Pittsburgh) cap last night. That helps create good mojo with the nursing staff and doctors there. We will take all the good we can right now.

I will keep you posted.

God bless,
Roger

May 10, 2007 4:23pm

Here's the skinny: Noah is improving day by day. I think his output has been as low as 3 liters, so we are moving in the right direction – or at least his poop is. Sorry, I had to throw that in there. His 24-hour infusion is doing something good and they are trying him on the same drug via subcutaneous injections today. They say this works well in some cases. Hey, I'm all for it as long as Noah can tolerate it. The doctors also tested and found Noah positive for C DIFF, which is an intestinal virus that causes extreme and nasty diarrhea (hence, the 5 liters of watery output and related disasters). So, the docs are dialing into what can slow this train down. He was quarantined yesterday, but mom is back in the room today telling him to brush his teeth and change his clothes.

The big picture looks a bit different now and we are hearing more and more about this being a normal pattern for Noah. You see, he has what they are calling a "resection bowel transplant" instead of a normal one. Resection meaning that Noah had received only about 8 feet or so of small intestine rather than a full 14 feet or more. We learned that Pittsburgh's transplant center is no longer doing these resections because of the high watery output these kids are faced with afterward (thanks for the advance warning, explicit details, and complete training to handle this type of post-transplant care for our beloved Noah). I didn't get that memo in 2004, did you?

Well, we have what we have and are doing the best with what hand Noah was dealt. They recognize that this may be the best scenario for Noah and that's fine - up to a point. If the best they can do is slow this down to 2 liters and Noah has a bad day (because he loves to tip-toe on the edge of volcanoes from time to time), then any slight dehydration episode can set this off again. He's back and forth to the hospital then one day it will catch up with him and his blood pressure drops dangerously low – we've seen this before and it's scary. Then we are looking at the possibility of a second bowel transplant. We will be gathering up more data about this in the near future. What we are hearing so far (now this is very early in these discussions) is that Children's Hospital of Pittsburgh has performed 11 of these 2nd bowel transplants recently. Of the 11, one patient did not make it, and the other 10 are doing well. How well, you say? That is one of the many questions I ask.

Initially, the patient's responses have been favorable and some have said that the second time around is better than the first. Well, for Noah, it will definitely be better compared to his condition the first time. It was by the grace of God that he made it out of that 15-hour surgery. I nominate Noah as the all-time Fear Factor Champion. He looked fear in the eye and snarled like Rocky Balboa; he chewed up fear and spit it out like the cowardly Lion AFTER he received his courage; he took the bull by the horns and dropped kicked that fear and turned it into a porterhouse steak dinner. Do you get my point? His grand prize is – a lifetime supply of chocolate crunchy-puff-crispies cereal and ice cold milk.

So this is where we find ourselves today. Please keep praying for Noah that he would continue to have peace and that they would come home soon.

God bless,
Roger

May 15, 2007 4:09pm

It's been a hard day and it's only halfway through. Noah is now having constant nausea around the clock. The doctors have slowed his small bowel's normal movements in an effort to help absorption, but the tradeoff is stomach pain and nausea; very similar to having an intestinal virus. Well, he is at times curled up on his bed when the Zofran (anti-nausea med) wears off and as a result, he is eating less. The output has decreased since he was admitted a week ago, but it still requires management. As the team rounded on the patients this morning, Paula asked Dr. Sindhi about what's ahead for Noah – both now and later. It was difficult to hear Paula cry as she spoke the words over the phone. The doctors will push the maximum amounts of both meds (Sandostatin and Paregoric) into Noah today, tomorrow and see how he does with it. One of the methods used is having two injections daily with a very thick liquid that causes a stiff pain that is difficult for Noah to tolerate. Paula asked them to scale it back to once a day.

So here we are. The leading intestinal transplant center in the world is not sure how Noah will respond over the next several weeks. The bowel may recover and begin to work normally or it may not. There is no conclusive test, evidence, or report that can give them a clear projection of how, when, or why. Remember, this is relatively new to the medical world. Dr. Sindhi added that some of the short length bowel transplants (such as Noah's) are very successful and some have complications – in some instances, some have not made it this far. As a result, they have decided not to do the short length transplants. In some cases, the need for a second bowel transplant is necessary (due to rejection or other situations). Dr. Sindhi advised Paula that we should place Noah on the transplant waiting list and see if his bowel recovers as we wait for a second intestine. It may be that we have to turn down offers for a new organ if Noah does better in the near future. All of this is unknown. He told Paula that he will meet with the head of the transplant dept. and with the committee to discuss Noah's case. My mind raced back to when he was waiting for his organs in 2004 and how it was such a desperate time for us.

Noah was floored. He walked back to his bed and began to sob. Words sometimes don't help at those moments; only a gentle loving hug from a mom who climbed into his bed to comfort him. I'm telling you, this road is not easy. To see what your child must endure at times is unreal. The load must be extreme for Noah. I hurt for my son and so does Paula. My heart aches to see him endure this. And what kills me the most is that I can't be there for him and embrace him or be there for Paula to lean on. But...God's grace is sufficient.

I'll keep you posted.

God bless.
Roger

May 22, 2007 2:08pm

Hello all. Sorry for not writing anything sooner. My heart is being tugged in many different ways as we continue to see how Noah's care develops. All in all, God is the One who sustains and continues to be the common thread woven in the fabric of our lives.

At the end of last week, Noah's output levels worsened. His diet directly influenced how his output levels reacted and the doctors arranged a dietician to meet with Paula and Noah. They reviewed some key elements in his medical history and formulated an eating plan that made sense. It consisted of eating smaller meals (almost like snacks) about 8 times a day. This would give the bowel a break from trying to overwork in processing and digesting the food he consumed. At the same time, sugary foods and dairy products were reduced dramatically. Another key element was to eat a meal and then wait 20 minutes before drinking a liquid. Once he followed this eating plan we noticed a huge decrease in output levels, but a huge increase in Noah's anger. He's been told to do this, then do that, then stop eating this, then eat this that way, but without that this many times a day - so on and so forth. It would make the strictest Weight Watcher pupil disgusted. He has declared countless times he will do what he wants and eat whatever he desires. Basically, he is over and done with this mess. I don't blame him one bit.

But, the reality of without some discipline in eating properly and taking his meds successfully (which by the way have been increased to taking pills every couple of hours and with meals as well), he will delay his return home and ultimately affect his health. Well, we honestly believe this road for Noah will not be getting any easier, based on countless discussions with specialists. I guess it's mostly based on how Noah is responding to the best-of-the-best medical team's care. There is no way the care back home will come close to what he's received in Pittsburgh. No disrespect to anyone, it's just a fact. We are preparing for the worst and hoping for the best. As a result, Noah may be hospitalized frequently over the next many months for dehydration.

As far as the second transplant goes, they are trying to delay this as much as possible and hope for Noah's bowel to recover immediately. A second transplant is a final option because there is not a third or more transplant if after the second one fails. Period. End of story. So why chance it? What if he gets new organs and he rejects them to the point they must remove them? Then his days are numbered (well, all of our days are numbered, but you know what I mean). So, keep on cheering for the little engine that could, to get over that hill. His short piece of the intestine has done some great things so far, like helping Noah to grow and get stronger. We know it can do more for him. Just keep cheering for him and praying for the situation. There is joy in the morning and we will taste it.

Noah was supposed to get discharged yesterday, but that never happened. If he gets out tomorrow, there is a slim chance he will get released from care and come home by the weekend. As of now, June 1 or 2 looks more realistic. He is negative by a liter or two today (which means very dehydrated) and must remain on the floor. Bummed. Yeah, he was bummed. Sometimes he works through disappointment as a hot knife slides through butter. Today he seems like he is doing well. Oh, he did have school today in the hospital. What's next, drum lessons from Wuv (P.O.D.) in his room? Hmmm.

Waiting. Today is what it is. We hope for tomorrow and through God, we hold on to His promises. Today – some disappointment. But that's ok. That's ok because Noah is alive and we can be together for now. Tomorrow – there will be joy in the morning.

God bless,
Roger

May 29, 2007 4:00pm

Happy Tuesday! Wow, it's nice to say that word happy. Happiness comes and goes, but true joy from God lasts a lifetime. So, I can say happy Tuesday today because Noah's doing quite well these past few days since being released to the hotel last Wednesday.

Let me recap this past weekend: He has been to Ohiopyle State Park – an hour or so from Pittsburgh and is a wonderful place to enjoy trees galore, trails, and whitewater rafting. Tim and Jan picked up Noah and Paula and made a day of it. Of course, Noah slipped down the man-made slides and into the fierce, raging river. Tim was the official lifeguard and caught Noah before he escaped into the dreary, heart-stopping rapids. Paula said that Noah had a blast! It was just what he needed.

They also spent Memorial Day with Tom and Bernadette. Noah said he enjoyed the very best ribs and he played games on Joey's and Alina's Wii system. I think he has his heart set on it now. Tonight, they are going to Kennywood. It's like Knott's Berry Farm, but on a smaller scale. Pastor Kevin, his wife Krista, and Darla will be their hosts. Between all of these great times, Noah has been keeping up (with the help of super mom) with his wacky medicine schedule and zany eating pattern to keep his output down to much better levels. (FYI, you won't ever see the words "wacky" or "zany" in a medical journal describing jejunostomy motility). Anyway, we are waiting for Thursday when Noah will meet with the doctors at clinic and see about being set free. If so, we can have the world's greatest mom and the world's finest star-patient home as early as Friday around 8:00 PM. I think that would be fantastic! The word of the day is – fantastic.

Noah and Paula have been blessed by the incredible self-less support by our dearest friends in Pittsburgh. They love by doing, by showing and by demonstrating...they are the hands and feet of what is being manifested through everyone's prayers here back home. You see, your prayers do so much! When you can't be there to visit Noah, someone else is. Or when you want to take Noah outside of his circumstances and place him into a glorious wonderland where the river runs wild and you just can't get there, someone else is. That, my friends, is the power and beauty of serving Christ. The body of believers globally is united in one common desire to help others. Thank you all from the bottom of my heart! I have nothing to give but my appreciation to ALL who serve us in this time of need.

God bless,
Roger

Jun 1, 2007 1:27pm

Hello all. Paula and Noah met with the doctor yesterday and it turns out that they will not be coming home for a while longer. It may be a couple of weeks more or a month - we don't know. The concern is Noah's body continues to remain at the edge of dehydration, so one bad day will put him back in the hospital. Because he has to get immediate fluids infused at high doses to hydrate, more stress is put on his already compromised kidneys. Also, his blood pressure is a concern when his body dehydrates – it gets low very quickly. All in all, they don't want to send him home until he demonstrates a consistent level of very low stool output. Some days it climbs to over 3 liters or more and some days it is down to the 2 liters. I don't blame them for their concern for my son's health. After all, they are the same team of doctors who have kept him alive.

Noah was very upset about the news. It took a few hours before he would talk with me over the phone. And Paula, well, she is hanging on by the grace of God. I don't know what else to say – we are all very disappointed.

God bless,
Roger

Jun 7, 2007 3:53pm

THIS JUST IN...Sources from inside Children's Hospital of Pittsburgh tell us that a 13-year old patient was officially released from care this afternoon and will be flying to his sunny California home along with his mother as early as tomorrow. The boy was admitted on May 8 after being airlifted from a hospital on the west coast. His condition was not good at the time, but he has steadily improved with the expertise and careful strategy of the transplant team in Pittsburgh. The father of the patient was quoted as saying, "God has brought our son through these difficult times and we are very blessed." The patient's siblings were interviewed as well and they were visibly happy with the news. The younger brother and youngest sibling said, "Yo dude, that is so cool! I can't wait to get my brother back so we can ride skateboards and play Xbox. Maybe my dad can get us airsoft guns so we can shoot the dog...I mean paper targets."

The sources say there were cheers and a little pandemonium from within the confines of the transplant clinic when the news was released. Confetti and multi-colored ribbons were seen throughout the office and there were flashing lights on large banners that read "Hooray for Noah." He is going home! Hooray!

One source indicated that a surgeon was seen jumping up and kicking his heels repeatedly as he cheered, "Boom! Here comes the Boom! Ready or not here comes the boy from the south!" (P.O.D. song).

Let's keep smiling. If you only could see my face!

God bless,
Roger

Jun 26, 2007 1:40pm

Summer is here! Can you feel the heat? It's definitely time to mosey on down to the beach and dip those toes in the shark-infested waters. Noah can't wait to get in with his boogie board and hit the surf running. Now that he has the Mediport IV, he can remove the needle from his chest (which looks like something out of a Sci-Fi movie) and have a waterproof injection site. Not bad huh? Yeah. That is great news for us because those bacteria critters love to build colonies in those IV lines if given the right circumstances.

So here we are at the end of June and Noah is doing very well. He's followed his modified eating plan to perfection and taking his meds as prescribed. We're very proud of him. Now the goal is to keep him out of the hospital through the summer so that he can be good for transplant camp on Aug. 3 (only a little over 5 weeks away). Wee hoo! This year it will be a Pirate theme. Arrrgggh. I guess Noah has no choice but to dress like Captain Jack Sparrow. He's now grown to an amazing 5'-2" stature and towers above Paula. That little bowel that could is making it over that mountain. Three cheers for the short-gut: Hooray, hooray, hooray!

Noah will be spending his time off of school riding his skateboard, having a few buds over, maybe some late afternoon beach action (you know, when it cools off), fighting with Luke, picking on Shelby, and telling on Brooke. Paula will try to keep harmony and maintain order during the day. Noah loves to read and his cousin McKenna loaned him a couple of those Left Behind books. When he's done, maybe a trip to Barnes & Noble will tame the savage beast. I think Noah will pass on the tattoos and piercings this summer. Maybe a light and refreshing smoothie will suffice. I think he also has his heart set on seeing the new Transformers movie in July. All in all, it is expected to be a kinder and gentler summer for him. No burning rays from the angry sun. No dehydration causing heat spells brought on by lack of fluids. No more hospital bed sores and absent-minded, cruel, mad-scientist doctors. No way. These are not on our wish list this summer. So when you turn the page of your calendar to July, just think of Noah embracing the bliss of an endless summer night. A kiss of dawn on his cheek as he rises to the mellow sounds of... Ok, I know it's getting a bit corny.

God Bless,
Roger

Nov 28, 2007 6:47pm

Thanksgiving was great and Noah enjoyed the spread of large fowl bliss - twice! You know, both grandma's houses in a single day. Noah had his share of great food and good times with his cousins. After all, it probably was our last one here. He didn't hesitate to display his Guitar Hero skills to his cousins.

Noah has been gaining weight and height steadily. I still remind him who the boss is when he tries to blast me into a wall or something with little or no warning, sort of like they do in hockey. Notice how I stated "tries." A simple Aikido move is all it takes to make him slip past me into a wall of bricks or a swarm of killer bees or something. Ok, maybe not really killer bees, just the gentle tickling bees you see in this part of the country in the winter (wimp bees no less). Anyway, Noah is making friends at his school and performing at a high level as far as his schoolwork is concerned. You should have seen his hair last week. Man, it was at least four inches long. He looked like Edward Scissorhands when it was fully spiked up. We recently drove him to Mt. Zion barber shop this weekend for a cut at his request. Scott really hooks him up with a sweet cut.

So, after all of this positive news, I have to end this on a slightly bummed note. Noah decided to catch a cold and sore throat this weekend (one of those wimpy ones you see). But, because he is Noah, and because we can't control his crazy high output levels at home when he is sick, he will be admitted tonight at the hospital. He'll be at Kaiser Lakeview for as long as it is necessary to keep him from dehydrating. It will be a record this year for the longest time between hospital stays – almost six months. Let us pray that it doesn't become what he came down with this time last year and took several months to completely bounce back from.

But, you see, Noah likes to bounce back. That's what he does best – bounce. He is in the bouncing business. Tigger has nothing on Noah. Let us synchronize our watches now and see how fast he can be discharged. We'll see what pranks he pulls on the doctors this time. I should bring him some fake blood and have him start choking and spit it out when the doctor runs in. Oh my, that's so wrong. I shouldn't do that. Ok, maybe a Santa Claus figurine that you can place on the table that has a sign that reads: "Shake my hand," and have a swarm of gentle, tickling bees attack from his sack of toys. Wimp bees, no less.

God Bless,
Roger

The Decision

Paula and I had long discussions over Noah's current state of health and over his short-term future. The countless hospitalizations that seemed never-ending, sudden, and many times unexpected all in various locations of Los Angeles and Orange County, California were never an easy part of life or were short drives. One too many air ambulance flights from our home to Pittsburgh, PA where he received the urgent medical care, was concerning each and every time. Even those necessary check-ups for small bowel scopes, thorough medical testing, and annual clinics (although he was able to have those scheduled along with the transplant camp weekends) made life difficult.

We experienced hardship through our medical carrier in a variety of issues that were also concerning. One instance was after we switched from his previous GI doctor to the exemplary GI doctor (Doctor Nanjundiah) and received excellent care from her for a few years, we learned that the Director of pediatric care in Los Angeles was trying to transfer Noah to his office for care. Really? So that he can now take credit for all of the magnificent care he received from Dr. Nanjundiah and make our star patient his crown jewel – being the miracle transplanted child? We fought that ridiculous notion and didn't allow the switch to occur.

It just blew our minds the complete nonsense of insurance carriers and all of their aggravating political schemes we experienced firsthand. I should have reminded them that one of their physicians should have transferred Noah months sooner to Pittsburgh Children's Hospital for his transplant and perhaps we had a legal matter based on all of the information we learned by the Pittsburgh team? The best thing that happened to our family through this massive medical provider was our blessing of a doctor and her intense desire to protect Noah's life and ensure his future.

It didn't take long to decide on the most obvious plan to keep Noah alive and provide him with the greatest opportunity to live beyond his life-saving transplant. We drew a line in the concrete and said, "We are moving to Pittsburgh." With no monetary resources available to fund such a bold move and medical bills/expenses piling on (even though I paid for two medical insurance plans for our son – one through my job and the other separately), it was a no-brainer. We must do what was necessary to keep him alive. What parent wouldn't?

The plan included our exodus from Westminster and relocate temporarily to West Covina. It was about an hour drive north and inland, east of Los Angeles. We would move in with Paula's mother and begin our countdown to the move to Pittsburgh – sometime in the summer of 2008. This move would allow for the time necessary to look for work and find a place to call home in Pennsylvania.

We were familiar with our future home because of the long stays Paula and Noah had during the 2004 transplant and from the other multiple times they flew there for medical treatment. We already had a church family and a small support group of dedicated friends who were there for Noah, Paula, and for our family during those extremely difficult crisis days and months. Our lasting impression of these loving few ensured we had a built-in network, a team, willing to help. Yeah, we only had to find a home and a job.

The thought of moving to this part of the country was exciting to Noah. He could visualize starting over and build new relationships in another school. It was natural for him and he mastered these skills – his ability to be charming, witty, and very friendly. He always shared his enthusiastic mentality with others.

He liked the idea of having four seasons and experiencing a different way of life. Unlike the one and only sunny season we experienced. Day in and day out, the sunshine was consistent. We knew we would miss the glorious display of heat and sunrays, but the trade-off was worth the sacrifice – except for the icy roads during the winter months. Yikes!

Our conversations began to center around fall and winter clothing, which were usually reserved and tucked away in our closets for those cold days. You know, those chilly fifty-six degree weather moments that would send a bone-chill sharply down our spine. Needless to say, we were not equipped physically and emotionally for the environmental changes we would encounter between November and April, back east. The kids would begin to shiver just thinking about it and we would end up making rounds of steamy, hot chocolate to soothe the conversation of certain frostbite. Yeah, we were pretty dramatic.

"Noah, do you remember that time we were in Pittsburgh during February and we enjoyed ice cream?" I asked.

"Oh, yeah," he replied with his eyes growing double their size. "We were freezing outside walking from Baskin Robbins to our car at night."

"Yup. Didn't we get in the car where mom waited for us blasting the heat in oven-like conditions?" I laughed as I told the story. "And here we were freezing outside and licking delicious ice cream, but when we got in the car it started to melt like crazy!"

He smiled and chuckled abruptly. It was a great sight because his small boney shoulders would quickly shake up and down in unison with his laughter. Laughter was priceless. It was his medicine.

We laughed together because that was insane and we knew it. But, those are the moments we reflected on and held onto. When so much of his life was stacked with illness and lifelong medications, those memories of licking freshly scooped, ice cream cones while shaking in the freezing evening temperature made everything alright. This became our preparation for our life within a new environment.

The others knew the cold lifestyle would require an adjustment. After all, Brooke, Luke, and Shelby were frigid when it was a balmy sixty-two at night. Well, maybe not Luke. No, he is built differently than his siblings. I think he received a special set of chromosomes from the Viking Norsemen and somehow had Eskimo blood running through his tender young veins. He was the one who sported shorts and a t-shirt as the others piled animal pelts on their backs. We knew he would be the one least likely to have any issues with the Pittsburgh winters. Lead the way, Luke.

We felt like we were locking arms together and nothing would be able to separate us – not like before. As our ship rocked unsteadily, lost in a troubled and angry sea, we had each other to depend on. Our children could lean on each other and rest in our comfort, knowing we would fight together through this storm. It meant something to fight and battle together. Like a few cords tightly wound together make a rope of strength, so was the bond we made. I stood with my wife and children during these hardest of times and we held each other when trouble struck our home.

It reminded me of the touching song written and performed by Journey decades ago, called "Mother, Father." The song paints a vivid picture of a family suffering through hardship and moves the heart with a powerful melody. The lyrics are undeniably moving and pierce right into the soul.

"She sits alone, an empty stare
A mother's face she wears.
Where did she go wrong?
The fight is gone
Lord help this broken home.

Through bitter tears
And wounded years, those ties
Of blood were strong.
So much to say, those yesterdays
So now don't you turn away.

Hey, mother, father, sister
Hey, come back, tryin', believin'
Hey, mother, father, dreamer
Don't you know that I'm alive for you?

I'm your seventh son.

And when lightning strikes the family
Have faith, believe."

Yes, we knew what those words meant – they were personal. We breathed them in and exhaled them out, time and time again. We wore empty stares and had a broken home in our separation. Our bitter tears and wounded years spoke volumes of distress and pain. We lived them firsthand and without fail held onto faith in our God to see us through. Because lightning strikes were frequent and constant, but our hope was unshakable.

ROGER R. ZIEGLER

19
A FUTURE AND A HOPE

Jeremiah 29:11

THE MORNING CHILL WAS NO MATCH for my hot cup of coffee. It didn't matter that it was July 31, a typical blistering-hot day in Southern California. Our air-conditioned environment felt cool. No, that coffee hit the spot and began to circulate my neurons, brain matter, and set my mind in motion. And we needed all of the motion we could muster. It was the official moving day.

2008 never felt this awkward. Maybe it was because my sweet wife and kids were nowhere to be found. Perhaps it was the awkward sensation of having them with boots on the ground over 2,500 miles away. I remembered their embraces – each one – when I dropped them off at the Los Angeles International Airport a few days earlier. They all wore nervous expressions as they were officially ready to embark upon the journey into their historic future. But, not Noah. He was relaxed and poised to make his mark on the new town. Plane trips were nothing for him. Nah. When you have several air-ambulance trips across the country under your belt, a passenger airliner seemed like just another day in the park.

He was packed with his medical rolling suitcase that had everything he needed…for the rest of his life. There would be no turning back.

I said my goodbyes and they began their long walk through security and ultimately to the terminal. I was happy for them because they didn't have to endure the three-day drive across the United States, but instead only a five-hour, one-way flight to Pittsburgh, Pennsylvania.

Paula and Noah were able to secure this flight as it coincided with his annual clinic appointment. It was paid for by the insurance company including the Residence Inn week-long accommodations (they extended the time to include the weekend Camp Chihopi trip). We just had to pay for Shelby, Brooke, and Luke's one-way ticket. That worked out nicely.

And there I was, hopeful and ready. I sipped my coffee and stared at the clock. It was 5:35 in the morning. I heard my dad walk through the living room toward me. He needed some of the same intense coffee beverage to kick start his day as well. He had accepted the challenge of being my designated minivan driver (my mother gladly accepted if he could not help) and I was the lucky one to drive the enormous, twenty-six-foot beast named Penske Truck. My co-pilots were Spike, Noah's pup, and Bunny, our family...well...bunny.

"Good morning, dad." I used some of the enthusiasm provided by my cup of Joe. "It's gonna be a nice day for driving."

"Good morning, Rog," he replied as he grabbed a mug. "Looking forward to it."

It was almost time to head out of West Covina, CA and make our trek through the desert on our first leg – day one. We mapped out about eleven hours each day of driving and had our spots picked out for the two overnight stays. With destination: Pittsburgh in our sights, we began our mission.

Now, I always imagined this trip to be slightly different than what reality would bring. You know, a minor variation here and there. It kind of looked something like our family getting to fly out together (with a respectable professional moving company handling our things on the ground). I could see us in the passenger area of a huge airliner. You know, the one that the Pittsburgh Steelers use to fly the team to and from steel town.

Yeah, there was our family surrounded by the team and staff enjoying the best exotic foods the NFL could supply. We all wore black and gold apparel (because we had to embrace our new team, right?). I envisioned myself deep in conversation with the head coach. I tried to show my communication skills in hopes that a long term employment contract would be drafted up and signed before our descent into PA (hey, this is my dream, okay?). Of course, we would have the team's massage therapist working out the stress of Paula's shoulders while she lay comfortably in a pillow-like, soft polished leather recliner holding a "Mocha locha rock ka ka" drink in her hand. (Again, my dream.) And each of the kids playing with the team's pony and sipping back their favorite hand-scooped milkshakes. (A pony...really?!)

Finally, there was Noah. Yeah, he had the first-string offense huddled around him as he drew up masterful plays for each one to execute. He kept staring down Big Ben, the quarterback and tried to convince him that his current style of play could use improvement. He kept asking for root beer float refills and seemed pleased with the P.O.D. music selections that played in the background. I knew he was in a state of bliss when the team carried him up on their shoulders and paraded him around the very large airplane, shouting and cheering his name: "When I say *Noah*, you say *love him*. Noah – *love him*!"

It was a nice thought. As I turned the key to the ignition and started the truck's engine in the early dawn, the roar of the diesel machine reminded me of my mission: to boldly go where no Ziegler has gone before. I glanced at Spike and Bunny to be sure they were in position, then I put that beast into drive.

The mammoth truck began to move forward and I inched slowly from the driveway and onto the street. I made sure pops was behind me in our minivan as we moved through the sleepy residential streets. As we entered the massive freeway and hit the open road, I paid little attention to the thick traffic on the opposing side that headed towards Los Angeles. We had a smooth drive ahead with little or no vehicles sharing the road.

I had my cell phone at the ready just in case I needed to communicate with my dad who remained a safe distance behind. There was a small water supply and snacks on the large bench seat as well. It wasn't long as we made our way into the Inland Empire and onto the interstate highway I-15 en route to the desert plains.

My mind began to wander as I kept a steady eye on the driving conditions. I thought about leaving our home of California behind and how long it would be before we were able to return and visit everyone we knew. Transplanting from one area to another seemed doable on paper, but once the moving truck was actually set in motion, the reality began to sink in. And I had three days ahead to think of such things.

We must have been on the road for two hours and moved at a comfortable pace. And then life happened…again. My cell phone rang. It was my dad.

"Hey, Rog. I'm not sure what's wrong, but the van is driving very rough." He said with a concerned tone. "Oh no, the engine just died!"

I could see him in the rearview mirror as my minivan slowly came to a crawl on the shoulder and out of the roadway completely. I quickly slowed my truck and stopped on the shoulder, but I was quite a distance further down the highway. I put the truck in reverse and crept backward until I was closer to the stalled vehicle. I climbed out and felt the intense heat bearing down on the desert valley, even in the early morning hours.

I left the truck engine running with the air conditioner on low for the pets and walked over to the passenger side of my minivan. This was really happening. Big time. And this was not part of our plan, of course, but life had this way of toying with our family and laughing hysterically at us as we were stricken with our crazy circumstances. I couldn't laugh back. No, I couldn't see anything except slight despair thinking of how to resolve this situation. This was only the very first handful of hours of about thirty-five total we had to drive, over the next three days – across the vast country.

We called AAA Auto Club and arranged for a tow to the nearest town. After we waited for about an hour in the truck, air conditioning blowing, our tow had arrived. So, now I gained a real-life co-pilot and we followed our roadside service vehicle (and our minivan secured on the flatbed) to the closest Toyota dealership over twenty miles away.

An hour later, we found ourselves contemplating our next move while we sat in a local diner over lunch. The vehicle was at the dealership service shop being diagnosed. It wasn't too long when I received the call from the service manager who explained to me that the issue was a water pump failure that caused some damage to the heads. No, not a simple or inexpensive repair by no means. Especially for a family who was smack in the middle of fighting chronic illness and the financial burdens that accompany years of ongoing issues. They wanted a little over two-thousand dollars to repair. They could have said two-hundred thousand dollars because either amount was equally a stretch for us.

I was disappointed because I didn't have the money to pay for the costly repairs. My dad didn't either. He had just transitioned into full-time ministry as a chaplain for a San Diego prison and had no way to help financially. So, we sat there discussing our less than few options. Then, we prayed.

We decided to leave the car there at the dealership and continue the journey in the Penske moving truck. The good news was the manager at the dealership understood our unique situation and they kept it in their center until a breakthrough occurred. Eventually, our minivan was repaired when my mother and stepfather, Lionel, gladly paid for it. The huge blessing grew when they both drove it across the country and delivered it to our home in Pittsburgh. God continued to blow my mind. The huge expression of love from my mother and stepfather was purely amazing!

Our journey resumed the next day after we spent the night in that fateful town. We shook the desert dust off our feet and hit the open road. Our large vessel sailed over the asphalt like we had no worry in the world. No, it was time to finish what we started and arrive safely to our new home.

I couldn't erase their faces from my mind. Noah, Luke, Brooke, Shelby, and of course Paula. They drove me. They were my inspiration. They were my "WHY". And it was a powerful motivation indeed.

The next three days went pretty smoothly. Hours of endless driving was so much easier with a partner as opposed to the previous long distance drive I made in 2005 by myself. Our conversation was sprinkled with many topics and we enjoyed having each other during those few days. I still think having our family move with the Steelers would have been a little more enjoyable in some ways. Although having time with pops was pretty cool.

Of course, the open road made for tiresome and drawn out periods of time. Sometimes I glanced over and noticed my co-pilot taking a break from the mundane, long distance ride. Nap time crept up suddenly between stops for him, like a Ninja stalking his unsuspected prey. It made me chuckle when I noticed with my peripheral vision his head slowly buckle to his chest. He later described me as a machine because I didn't allow him to spell me. Nope. I gripped that large wheel and felt the urge to push through the driving duty myself. I was highly motivated to get there and start our new chapter…and for Noah to live.

In those moments of extra quiet time, except for the steady hum of the Penske beast, I reflected upon many things. I sorted through a library of events that shaped us as a family.

Those that stood out from the rest were moments that resembled incredible pain or tribulation as well as those that were blissful Hallmark-type memories. I couldn't help but remember how it all started for Noah. He entered this world with the odds stacked against him – stacked. And we were there alongside him cheering and loving him through the ordeal when he was just an infant.

I thought of his first month of life, being hospitalized in the NICU due to his undetected gastroschisis and urgent surgical procedure. It was a tremendous time of appreciation for his and for our lives. Oh, how these traumatic events helped to shape us and awaken us to life!

I caught my mind wandering and replayed those images of him at his milestone eleventh birthday party. We celebrated his special day at Children's Hospital of Pittsburgh when he waited and waited for that life-saving transplant. Little did we know that he was only one day away from a spectacular finish and end his grueling summer of suffering.

I reflected on his adolescent years when he began to challenge us years later. Like the time when he, as a frustrated teenage boy, stormed out of the home and sped off on his skateboard. An act of defiance and our first taste of such rebellion at this level. I pursued after him in our minivan shortly after I arrived from work and caught up to him a few blocks down the street. The angst in his eyes was fierce. It was a taste of his disdain for his difficult life, which led him to an eventual self-labeled misfit status. The bitterness slowly grew and began to capture a portion of his heart. No, he didn't ask for this life – it was not a chosen one.

I firmly asked him to get inside our van. He ignored me and continued to try and get away. When I stood in front of him, he paused knowing I was not going to back down. The traffic on the main street behind us moved slowly and I could feel the stares from every driver. I must have looked like some freak trying to lure this teenage boy or attempt to take him against his will. I figured the police would show up at any minute. Then, one of the cars that was passing by had slowed and stopped next to us.

"You alright, son?" the driver's voice was filled with concern and her glances in my direction were judgmental.

"Yeah, I'm fine," Noah replied. "He's my dad."

Her expression instantly changed as she realized what the true story was.

"Then maybe you ought to listen to him," she replied. I glanced at her and nodded my head in agreement. It was a few seconds after that he submitted and climbed into the passenger seat. It was a very tense moment and I knew he was at the age where confrontations would become more difficult to manage. I remember thinking to myself, *this was a tough day.* With all of the trauma he has endured with his illness, I could only imagine the battle that raged inside of him. And yet he would keep it to himself most days.

The bondage was not always an obvious one, except to those around him in his inner circle who witnessed the IV pole that chained him to his circumstances. It was the physical reminder that his life was held captive to a devious illness. Yes, devious. Chronic illness is a living and breathing organism. It plans and executes against its victims; plots and lies in wait for precisely the right moment to strike. And strike it does.

But, Noah was always a champion. He stared this beast and stood toe to toe with it. We reminded him that our God was bigger than any of his circumstances, including the chronic illness bully. He was brave and courageous. He used his sharp wit and humor to slay his dragon at every opportunity he could. He locked arms with his friends and created a unity with them that would transcend defeat. Because when you have buds, well, you have an army who will fight alongside you.

I could see his warm and inviting smile throughout his childhood years. It was his signature characteristic, his greatest strength. Like Superman has the ability to fly and soar, our Noah wielded his smile like a terrific superhuman attribute. And superhuman it was. It reminded me how God can take our natural and add His super to make incredible things happen. All to His glory.

Yes, he was our champion day in and day out. He ran that ongoing marathon and he chased, pursued and reached for the finish line. It was elusive and the path was windy, be he kept a steady pace when his body wouldn't go anymore. He was the epitome of someone having a will to survive.

I believe God used this time on the road as a therapeutic means and for me to turn the page of the chapter we left behind. It was a process for me to digest all of those incredible details surrounding my son's intense health and how it affected each member of our family. Because his story is also our story. His life is also our life in a sense. We shared this journey with him and we bore deep scars as we fought right beside him. The collateral damage was all too real.

We completed the driving challenge and arrived safely in Pittsburgh four days after our California departure. It was a huge sense of relief. The best part of arriving at our destination was getting to hug and to hold my family. To see them with my eyes and discuss our next chapter with them; to live each day we were blessed with and begin a whole new course ahead.

We said goodbye to my father and hoped to see him and other family members very soon. He flew back to San Diego the very next day. The loneliness was bitter and foreign as we only had each other in this new town we now called our home. We would learn to depend on each other deeper as the years unfolded.

Noah and the others began settling in our rental house. It was just what we needed at the time. A little Tudor-style home in the middle of thick woods rested in a nice, little hollow. It was peaceful and brought a soothing calm to our days. We really enjoyed the acre of property that overlooked the foliage landscape that surrounded us. The owners, The Gerbe's, were tremendous folks that allowed us to rent their home sight unseen.

We filled our home with our belongings and started anew. We built new hopes and dreams. We also encountered the medical nightmares we faced years before and learned there are certain things in life you simply cannot run away from. No, we were not running from anything, but we were sprinting towards something else. A chance for Noah to live.

**

It takes guts to do something you've never done before in order to get something you've never had…but it's worth it.

I cannot say enough about how our lives have been affected by our son's chronic illness. It would take volumes and hours upon hours to share it accurately.

Life is a marathon, right? And sometimes we attempt to reduce it to a dash or a sprint, but then life happens and suddenly reminds us of the long haul required. Then those unexpected circumstances spring out from behind the corner and demolish those wonderful plans we have created.

And that is the beauty right there…right there. When life bashes us with circumstances, turmoil, and disappointments we are faced with a choice. Either allow those murky thoughts of despair to infiltrate our minds, our hearts and be held captive to them or we can duck, juke and simply keep moving forward – even when setbacks strike. Our plans should be flexible and our course should be unaffected, but able to be adjusted if necessary, keeping the ultimate destination in mind.

We had a new physical address, but those usual suspects (Noah's medical issues) somehow knew what we were up to. They had followed us across this country in our magnificent plan of evading the enemy and they camped out in our yard, so to speak. But, we had our secret weapon now in hand: Noah's transplant doctors and the expertise of Pittsburgh Children's Hospital right on our doorstep (figuratively speaking of course). And it was such a blessing to know that we were only a twenty-five-minute drive away from treatment. No more air ambulance trips. No more long distance transports in emergency mode. No more monkeys jumping on the bed.

Autumn in the 'Burgh.
Oct 23, 2008 8:46am

Hello all. I can't express to you how busy we have been during this past couple of months. As we continue to adapt to our new surroundings in Wexford (just north of Pittsburgh), new and exciting adventures wait at every turn.

It's fall around these parts in a very big way. Noah absolutely loves the colorful display of autumn. It's like living in a painted mural of fall bliss. Since he is a native of Southern California, he is often outdoors with just minimal clothing. Of course, his sisters don't help as they continue to wear sandals to school when the early morning temps hover around the 30's and 40's. Please. Luke seems to be the only sensible one on his way to school with a nice warm coat and beanie. After all, this cold is nothing. Wait until we see the daily highs in the teens and below.

Noah has grown some more. We are now eye to eye and his legs are much longer than mine. I think he's gonna be taller than his pops. Isn't that great!? Yeah, his internal pipes are working well and his spiky hair is helping in some way I'm sure. The docs like his recent progress so much that they decreased his daily infusion rate of IV fluids by a half a liter. He responded very well, so they decreased it again last week. He is now down to half of his 2 ½ liters he was getting for a very long time. Our prayer is that he is completely off of hydration fluids one day. That would be sensational.

Noah has been enjoying the wildlife that surrounds our home. To the left, we have deer. To the right, we have turkeys and deer. Straight ahead, we have chipmunks and deer. Behind us, we have groundhogs, birds of many kind and deer. I know there are raccoons that wander around as well as some deer. Noah often pulls out his book of birds that grandpa sent for his learning pleasure. He loves reading about the Cardinals and Lillyback Sucklemanders. Alright, I made that last one up. He thinks it's great when he can open his book and see that specific bird fly around his home (one of those simple pleasures we take for granted). He gets a kick when that pesky woodpecker starts up on the side of the house. Tap-tap-tap-tap...

Noah's class was asked to write a poem about themselves. He proudly showed me his draft when I arrived home from work. He had a big grin, glowing face, big eyes and all. It was touching and he said that it brought tears to his teacher when she read it. I will post that below.

As I close, please understand how thankful we are for everyone's prayers and support through this most difficult move across the country. One of our goals is to help other transplant families in this area in some way or another. If nothing else, we can be a shoulder to lean on during the most difficult times. After all, we have certainly been there ourselves.

God Bless,
Roger

Now, for your reading pleasure, Noah's poem:

I am a 15-year-old student, but much more.
I work hard, fighting for my life daily, hourly.
Trying to get through life.
Trying not to be so different.
Changing from the inside out.
It's a miracle I'm still here, alive.
My disability, it started when I was young.
It gave me many problems, still to this day.
Having multiple surgeries, each time getting me a
Little bit better.
But only one changed my life forever.
A transplant to be specific.
I was only 11 when this happened,
But now I'm better.
Again, still fighting.
Trying, 'til the end.

We could see that Noah was comfortable here in Western Pennsylvania. I know he missed his friends back west, his family (especially his cousins), and the swaying palm trees that lined those sunny beaches, but he was making his best effort to enjoy the process. He knew it was for the better and he wanted to enjoy this ride as much as possible.

He continued to utilize his craft of humor and kept a strong upbeat attitude concerning his illness. Like I said, those usual suspects came knocking at his front door – uninvited, of course.

He wasted no time becoming sick. We started the New Year, 2009, with more of the same obstacles.

Noah trying to escape from the hospital
Jan 14, 2009 12:37pm

Hello all. Just a quick post to let you know Noah was admitted at Children's Hospital Sunday evening for symptoms related to his cold. Unfortunately, with his history of dehydration during illness, he has been kept under close watch and was given extra fluids. The blood pressure numbers have been wacky. He was down to only 1 liter of his daily maintenance fluids (from 2.5 liters) when this hit. Now they are trying to manage his fluid levels by giving him extra doses. He feels ok, maybe a headache or two, but nothing serious. I spoke with him a couple of hours ago (late morning) and I asked him if he urinated this morning (this is one of those questions most folks don't ask their kids, but very common for Noah's parents). He said no.

"What?! When was the last time Noah?"

He said, "I dunno."

"What?!" I quickly answered. Hello? McFly? "You don't remember when?"

After clarifying his answer, it was determined that he went late last night. So, that was over 10+ hours ago. Not good. Nope. He might as well click his heels together and say - there's no place like home because he's going to be there for a while.

Please keep him in prayer. What has happened in the past, in these scenarios, is that he develops these twists in his bowel - which leads to other complications (including ridiculous behavior). I will keep you updated.

God Bless,

Roger

Noah trying to escape - pt. 2
Jan 14, 2009 1:13pm

Alright. I just heard that Noah has C DIFF. Yup. That nasty virus that attacks his bowel. It's kind of like that character on SpongeBob - Plankton - always trying to steal the secret to the crabby patty. Anyway, the C DIFF virus is not Noah's friend at all. He will be on Flagyl now and remain in the hospital at least until this weekend. Rats!

God Bless,
Roger

Noah trying to escape pt. 3
Jan 15, 2009 12:43pm

Hello all. Noah's feeling horrible. His bowel has twisted causing nausea and discomfort. Paula is with him all day trying to do what she can for him. He received anti-nausea medicine throughout the night and they had to delay a CT scan because he cannot drink any contrast. In fact, he is NPO (nothing oral at all) so he is hungry and has nausea bouts - not a good combination.

They continue to infuse him with lots of extra fluids. We'll see how he feels tonight.

God Bless,
Roger

Noah escapes.
Jan 20, 2009 1:06pm

Hello all. Sorry for the late posting, but I was ill over the weekend.

Noah is home. He was discharged yesterday afternoon with a little of his own persuasive skills. Paula called me yesterday from the hospital with the news (I was home with a stomach-flu bug and quarantined in my room). She said his hydration levels were normal, but he still put out 3 liters from all of the massive IV fluids given to him. The doctors felt he was well enough to be sent home and continue to work with his fluid management. Also, his liver numbers were elevated and have been creeping up since last week. Initially, this suggested that perhaps he was rejecting his liver, but could also be a false reading due to his illness and from all of the meds used over the last week. Noah will be brought back this week for an ultrasound exam at a minimum and go from there. We are praying that they see enough with that less invasive test and prevent the need to take a liver tissue sample – which is extremely painful.

I greeted him from the top of the stairs as he made himself comfortable in the living room downstairs. He saw the wood logs by the fireplace and thought a warm, glowing fire would hit the spot. So he did his thing. He looked very tired and exhausted. He was up all hours with the strict medicine schedule the nurses had to enforce. Now he is home resting. His fluids were increased to 12 hours again, but we will see how fast he can decrease moving forward.

Paula said she walked in Noah's hospital room on Sunday afternoon and noticed a pizza box. Hmmm, she thought. She asked the manipulative 15-year-old boy what the pizza box was for. His answer was simple and direct: "Lunch." You have to understand something here, the 7th floor North (where they keep the intestine/liver patients) do not allow these same patients (who happen to be children) to order food delivery. Now, if I wanted to place an order and meet the restaurant staff at the front desk, no problem.

So, Noah and his little buddy (also a patient) talked about how nice it would be to have cafeteria food for lunch that day. There's nothing like a hot meal cooked to order from the cafeteria. Noah told his buddy that he didn't have any money, but if they could somehow get some cash, he would gladly escort his friend (who is a few years younger) to the cafeteria. "After all," Noah said, "I am old enough to take you." Okay, whatever. Tell me that Noah wasn't feeding his buddy a line just to get out of isolation. Oh yeah, he was in isolation the whole time, due to his C DIFF virus. I can see his little mind churning this one around. His buddy said that he would get some money and return to Noah's room (his pal was not kept in isolation and he was free to roam the floor). So Noah waited until his friend returned.

After a short wait, there appeared his little buddy at Noah's door with a big smile. "Look what I have Noah," his friend said as he showed Noah fifteen US dollars. Real money! He went on to explain that he walked around to all of the nurses on the floor and asked for a donation to feed their two bellies. I cracked up when Paula continued with the story.

Noah and his quick little mind began to think...and think...and BINGO! "I know. We can order pizza delivery since we have 15 bucks," he told his buddy. "We don't even have to leave our rooms." His Lucille Ball-like mind was a furious machine. So, to make a long story longer, the nurses agreed to their little plan since it was Steeler Sunday (AFC Championship game). Can you believe that? I mean, really.

Paula cracked up at Noah's brilliant tale. I just had to share it with you. After she regained her composure, she noticed something by the sink near his bed. She walked over and grabbed a Chinese food menu and turned to Noah. "What is this?"

"Dinner," Noah said with a big grin.

God Bless,
Roger

His brilliant ideas and skillful execution were on point. You put Noah along with these other transplant colleagues in a room (or on the same hospital floor for that matter) and these are the interesting results.

You've got to give him incredible credit. After all, it was his way of fighting through these insane moments of crisis mode. When he was not fighting back overwhelming pain or some other debilitating illness, he was always creating a way for the endless hours to be spent having fun, laughing, or getting something great to eat – usually all three at once, of course.

These transplant kids push back against the odds. They want to survive and do so with a passion. They understand each other when the world does not truly understand the complexity and gravity of their medical situations. No, they were heard by each other. That's why the transplant camps were so wonderful...and so successful.

Through the uncomfortable, Noah remained calm – mostly. Through the inconvenience, he outlasted the falling dominos. As the rainfall continued to douse his head, he held onto that very large umbrella with both hands tightly.

**

Closure. That's what we had. It was closure from the past crisis mode incidents that plagued Noah and our family in Southern California. Closure from that part of the past that we chose to leave behind...leave behind, huh. To move forward forever, but knowing full well these experiences we left behind would also manifest themselves in our days ahead, on new ground.

But that's alright, you see. We knew this opportunity was one of life and one born from hope, with this new Pennsylvania address. Now we could begin to advance and move forward as a family. My pastor always taught us during my teenage years, that where God leads He also provides. He certainly has led us here, into the beginnings of our future and with all of those obvious uncertainties that come with a new town, we knew God would positively provide for our needs. And He did.

I cannot say we did not have more hardships, because we sure had a bucketful. Especially in Noah's life after the move. I could count them all with my fingers and toes...and...well, yours as well. There were tears, pain, disappointments, and so much more. Numerous liver rejections (number of episodes into the teens) and other struggles ensued. Some were in different shapes and sizes than what he had experienced before. We loved him through them all and stood by his side. Through every single one.

I could probably write a complete story of how the next several years unraveled. I suppose that it could be written and told by Noah himself one day.

We also encountered more heroes while in Pittsburgh. The names of those who helped us and supported us unselfishly in many ways are written on a *Hall of Valor* located somewhere special, I'm certain. God inspired those hearts and moved them with compassion to accompany our family during some tough days. They stood in that gap and fought toe to toe with us. They valiantly shed many tears with us as they embraced our pain and our conflict. They locked arms with us and we held our ground together. It was amazing! And we were so blessed. Overwhelmingly, blessed!

**

We hoped for two special days in Noah's life. The first was to see him start his first day at a job. You know, as a teenager that event is special and is something to look forward to. Well, in our son's case that would mean he would reach the magical age of sixteen years old. Do the math: at least five years post-transplant! A significant milestone in his overall health to say the least.

Yes, to reach that hopeful day of watching him put on that uniform and join the workforce would be huge; we dreamed for that day. And so, with tears in her eyes and a huge lump in my throat, there we were – transplant parents – in the parking lot of McDonald's of his first day. With Noah perched in the back seat, we made sure he had his name tag, his uniform cap, his uniform shirt, his special non-slip shoes, his ostomy bag (was not leaking), he took his most recent medications, blood pressure was within normal range, no rejection present, and certainly no dehydration symptoms were on board. You see, this was a very big day for us. I thought perhaps the local television news stations should be filming this auspicious occasion. But they were nowhere to be seen. Cloaking device engaged? Possibly. Or maybe they didn't have the correct address.

Noah rolled his eyes as we went through the important checklist and he shook his leg in anticipation.

"I've gotta go now," his words carried a bit of sarcasm and nervousness.

The rear door gave in to his special powers and he climbed out of the family vehicle like he was invading the beaches of Normandy. We strategically parked in such a way so that our line of sight placed him in our view as he scurried into the restaurant and through the lobby area. We must have blocked the path to the drive-through lane, but I didn't care. Nothing could break my concentration as I stared intently at his every move towards the front counter and approach the waiting store manager. Yeah, we were creepers alright. Wouldn't you do the same?

And then, like a passing shooting star overhead, he was gone. He disappeared into the wild blue yonder of McDonald's Land. Ready to learn the finer points in customer service and food science 101. We remained in our car, all blubbery and such. It was priceless. I looked around for a Channel 11 news van as I engaged the transmission into drive and slowly moved forward. They must have shown up at the wrong restaurant because if they knew Noah's story as we did they would have been there. No matter. We captured that one in our hearts and in our minds. We added that to the collection of precious and magnificent memories of our son.

The second moment was just as amazing. No, in fact, it superseded his first day at work. For years we prayed and longed for that early summer day when we would hear his name spoken during his high school graduation ceremony. On June 6, 2012, that day became reality.

The late afternoon was partially cloudy and a bit warm. We were unsettled in our seats about midway up in the grandstands and we had a perfect view of the ceremony. It was difficult to contain our enthusiasm.

The crisp new football stadium, home of the Rams, was on full display for all to see and touch. The field was transformed into a formal graduation event with all of the wonderful trimmings. Hundreds of seniors were seated off to one side of the center stage area. The numerous rows of chairs were perfectly aligned in an enormous rectangle. The air was electric and our veins were charged with intense emotion. This was the day we had long awaited for.

The ceremony began with the Pledge of Allegiance and several moving speeches followed. Then, it was that special moment of the day. As we focused on Noah from our seats over seventy-five yards away, like a sniper in a reconnaissance mission, we watched him stand with his entire row of classmates. They all turned, faced to their right and began the final walk towards the aisle. Then, each name was announced over the PA system. We were thrilled! As he drew closer to the beginning of the center aisle we stood to our feet. And with thunderous applause, his name filled the open air stadium and the words rose above the rafters: "Noah Paul Ziegler," pronounced with clarity and accuracy.

We cheered as if he threw the winning touchdown in the Super Bowl. We clapped until our hands ached and we stood proudly as he walked forward to accept his diploma from the Principal. He reached out his left hand to accept his document, shook hands with his right, then immediately turned towards the crowd and raised both arms in victory to the sky! It felt like my throat swallowed a brick as my emotion overcame my weakened senses. It was a beautiful moment of triumph for Noah and for our family. It felt like several minutes had passed in our few seconds of celebration.

Noah walked in a confident stride down the rest of the aisle. His smile seemed like it was surgically implanted and would probably take a nuclear submarine's power to partially remove it. Without losing his stride, he turned to the student body seated to his left and he raised his hands high – one hand holding his precious diploma and the other making the sign of love (thumb, index and pinky fingers raised). It was his declaration on his terms. As if he were saying to the world and to his peers: *I did it! I made it this far! I survived!*

No one and nothing could take that moment away from him. Not liver rejection, not dehydration, not a gram-positive bacterial infection, not a twist in his gut, not a deathly reaction to the wrong blood type infusion, not a five-hour air-ambulance ride, not short-gut syndrome, and not even gastroschisis. Nothing.

Yes, he did it. By the grace of our loving God and by His mercy on his life, Noah was victorious. Most of the hundreds of other parents and students really had no idea as to the depths of his story, his suffering. But we did. And we held on to that fact tightly because it made this victory taste sweeter. Where there is darkness, the light shines brighter.

When the ceremony had ended, we made our way down those tall grandstand steps and onto the field. We found our son and we embraced his tall, thin frame like no other time before. He was filled with complete joy and he was overwhelmed with a sense of finality. This time he was not in the hospital or sick in his bed. This time he was upright and elated. Each one of his siblings hugged him and congratulated the graduate. He was now able to take on the world with this chapter now safely behind him. He always talked about the future; he always looked ahead. And the future was now.

I imagined this moment playing out many times and for many years. I can tell you those moments did not compare at all to the actual day. Those moments were mere glimpses compared to the actual brilliant achievement and poignant display of courage. Yes, courage. It took guts to walk the life my son was given day after day. And sometimes through the staggering defeat of chronic illness, he longed for the sweetest victory. Death stood nearby waiting to capture our son with its fierce clutches. But, God...yes, God saved him and up until this day there was nothing that could take his life away from us – no, nothing.

Paula and I hugged our 5'-9 ½" young man, all grown up. We smiled for many pictures and we held our son tightly. We were witnesses to this testimony of grace. What a tremendous day it was. The grassy field all around was a deeper shade of green and the air was just a little bit sweeter than what was typical for June. Our facial expressions told the story entirely and convinced the whole world of how proud we were. It was the greatest moment in recent history. A tremendous day indeed.

**

And then the adolescent chapters of his life came to a close. Just like that, he entered the brave new world of adulthood, in all of its splendor and its glory. Our son now held the reins to his future. Like all high school graduates, waves of nervous and anxious thoughts pressed into his mind. He stood at the doorway to a blank canvas that was labeled:

Your next steps of life begin here. Pick your brush and apply the color. It was certainly a big task.

For Noah, there were two paths that coexisted simultaneously. The first was an open door to chase a dream; to become the person who would explore life and launch into his purpose. He knew the only one who had the power to hold him back was himself.

The second was this chronic illness battle that would ensue for as far as the eye could see. A battle not only reserved for the two-thirds of his life awake but a twenty-four-hour strategic fight against the odds. And they were stacked against him in specific areas.

His purpose – this would be the most powerful ally moving forward. It would become the wind in his sails, the quick in his step, and the beat in his heart. When illness bangs on his door, he could resist with his sharp wit and humor combined with his incredible will to survive and harness the power of his purpose to push forward. God has an incredible plan for his life. The key is to learn what it is, understand that it is waiting for him and then step into it boldly.

We were front seat passengers on this crisis-mode, rollercoaster illness Noah lived and we still are to this day. The extreme g-force twists and sudden heart-stopping turns have taken our emotional breath away. Sometimes our motto of "prepare for the worst, but hope for the best" echoed in our hearts to the point we were ready to engage in the fight before the battle cry ensued. Ready to meet the worst head on – that's who we were. Yes, always up to the challenge and never out of the fight – that's who we became. In fact, you could say we were the special forces of transplant parent life. We said, with any of our children, we would go to the ends of the earth if that's what was necessary to give them the best chance to survive.

And like that seasoned distance runner who endures mile after mile through the calm of the desert without hesitation, Noah made his trek through the desert-like conditions of life. These harsh elements beat upon his head, against his heart, and within his mind, but he put one foot in front of the other like clockwork – consistently. Noah set his mind forward when he faced all of his chronic illness distractions, even amidst tearful pain; he stayed in the fight and endured. Sometimes, the fight was hour by hour. Sometimes, it was minute by minute. This fighter is our son; Noah – our patchwork kid.

**

His future is bright, but it has come at a high cost. The precious life of a donor and the endless grief felt by the family…yes, a severe price was paid. The loving parents didn't leave behind a few words written about their precious child, carefully selected to appear on a stone monument. No, it was a dear life and the delicate fabric of life-sustaining tissue that was carefully woven into our son. We are eternally grateful.

Noah – to carry on and to take others by the hand, is your future. To share the very hope you have allowed to breathe from within is your path. To give the very love that has saved you is your calling. Because people are hurting.

Hardship is everywhere. The rain will most certainly fall in our lives. From the greatest achievers to the most humble servants, to those who cry profusely to the ones who laugh hilariously – everyone is a victim of the rainfall. It has no favorites and holds no one in higher regard than others. But, it falls generously on some and partially on others.

And sometimes the stormy days in our lives are ongoing and seem to never end. During those moments when disaster strikes, just continue to know there is hope – amazing, powerful, and unending. Take your eyes off of the crashing waves and take hold of hope. Reach out to God and take His hand. He will lead you through your storm.

And when lightning strikes the family…have faith, believe.

PATCHWORK KID

Graduation day. 2012.

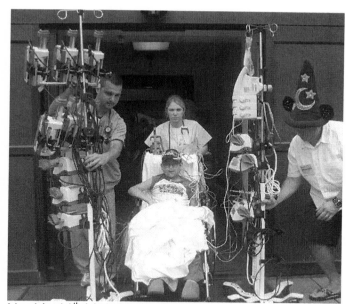

Noah's 11th birthday party. The day before his transplant.

ICU days. 2004.

Post-transplant, October 2004. Noah making treats.

Dr. Nanjundiah.   Dr. Squires (push up victim).

Dr. Soltys.   Dr. Sindhi.

Dr. Mazariegos.

Our family in 2013.

ABOUT THE AUTHOR

Roger R. Ziegler finds his inspiration within the struggles of life, where hope shines brighter than fear. He is a former youth leader at his church and finds solace in seeking after God. With the vision of touching hearts and lives through his story, a fantastic purpose emerged: a deep desire to encourage others. You can read more of his work and learn about his upcoming books by visiting **FantasticPurpose.com**.

Roger and his wife, Paula, live in Pittsburgh, Pennsylvania. They have raised four wonderful children and are blessed with one extraordinary grandson.

Sadly, a year after the release of *Patchwork Kid*, Noah passed away from aggressive, mutli-organ failure. He was 25 years old. The Ziegler family continues to honor his life and bring glory to their Lord, Jesus Christ, by sharing their powerful testimony.

52031364R00163

Made in the USA
Middletown, DE
06 July 2019